Inspirations Unbidden

Inspirations Unbidden

THE "TERRIBLE SONNETS" OF GERARD MANLEY HOPKINS

DANIEL A. HARRIS

UNIVERSITY OF CALIFORNIA PRESS · BERKELEY · LOS ANGELES · LONDON

University of California Press
Berkeley and Los Angeles, California
University of California Press, Ltd.
London, England
© 1982 by
The Regents of the University of California

Library of Congress Cataloging in Publication Data

Harris, Daniel A., 1942–
    Inspirations unbidden, the "terrible sonnets"

    Includes index.
    1. Hopkins, Gerard Manley, 1844–1889—Criticism
and interpretation.   2. Sonnets, English—History
and criticism.   I. Title.
PR4803.H44Z6467   821'.8   81-11497
ISBN 0-520-04539-4   AACR2

Printed in the United States of America
1   2   3   4   5   6   7   8   9

For Ruth

"Wit learnes in thee
perfection to expresse."

CONTENTS

ACKNOWLEDGMENTS

It is a pleasure for me to thank Richard J. Schoeck, James R. Kincaid, J. Hillis Miller, and Thomas M. Greene for their generous and wise assistance. They read an earlier version of the present book and gave me much valuable criticism; the faults and limitations that remain are my own.

My thanks to the John Simon Guggenheim Memorial Foundation for providing me the leisure to put this book into final form.

For permission to publish the manuscripts of Hopkins's "terrible sonnets," I am indebted to the Society of Jesus (English Province); for permission to reproduce photographs of the manuscripts, I wish to thank the Bodleian Library, Oxford University.

New Brunswick, New Jersey
St. Cecilia's Day, 1981

A NOTE ON THE TEXTS

All citations from the "terrible sonnets" are taken from my transcriptions of the manuscripts as given in Appendix A; all citations from Hopkins's other poetry are from *The Poems of Gerard Manley Hopkins*, 4th ed., revised and enlarged, ed. W. H. Gardner and N. H. MacKenzie (London: Oxford University Press, 1967), abbreviated as *Poems*.

In addition, the following abbreviations are used in references:

Sermons   *The Sermons and Devotional Writings of Gerard Manley Hopkins*, ed. Christopher Devlin (London: Oxford University Press, 1959)

Journals   *The Journals and Papers of Gerard Manley Hopkins*, ed. Humphry House and completed by Graham Storey, 2nd ed. (1959; rpt. London: Oxford University Press, 1966)

For a list of sigla used in transcriptions of Hopkins's manuscripts, see Appendix A, p. 147.

PREFACE

Hopkins's "terrible sonnets" of 1885, the bitter fruit of his pained years in Dublin, culminate his sporadic career as a poet. These six sonnets have attracted more attention than any of his other works except *The Wreck of the Deutschland* (1875 – 1876) and "The Windhover" (1877). In all their brevity, they command a respect accorded greatness that can scarcely be claimed of any comparably small group of poems in Victorian or modern British literature. It must therefore seem odd, if not perverse, to write of them, as I have done throughout this book, as failures. An explanation is in order.

By "failure" I do not intend a critical or aesthetic judgment about their ultimate poetic worth. Instead, I use the word in a comparative sense to suggest the differences—in imaginative temperament and religious vision—between the "terrible sonnets" and Hopkins's earlier poetry: these poems "fail" to embody the methods he had previously employed, the aims he had formulated. If this were all, however, a more neutral term might well have sufficed to describe these achievements of his late career. Yet Hopkins himself considered the poems failures, albeit of a subtle kind; and it is to his own perceptions that I adhere in using the word.

Hopkins saw in these poems the fragmentation of his capacity to represent his Christian vision adequately; he took their radical shift in imaginative procedure, as measured against his earlier work, to be the mark of his decline. As he wrote frankly to his lifelong friend Robert Bridges, the poems came to him "like inspirations unbidden and against my will." Hopkins's oxymoronic simile, loaded with nuance, is not only a religious confession but the implied statement of an aesthetic position. Although he derived his phrase from Shelley ("To a Skylark," stanza 8), he here winced at Shelley's delight in the spontaneity of "hymns unbidden." By "unbidden," Hopkins meant "unwanted." The six sonnets did not manifest that penetrating delineation, that inscaping of Christ in nature which had formerly been his joy; nor did they serve a communal function by implicitly ministering to an imagined congregation. The poems verged towards nightmare: they revealed a deformed image of his own humankind and a violation of Christ's body; they failed to enact the gradual attainment of colloquy with God which he had previously made the basis of his poetic structures. Certainly the "terrible sonnets" were a new kind of poetry, and Hopkins was uncomfortable with their heterodoxy. In the phrase "against my will," he judged himself by the strictest standards of

Christian volition and acknowledged that he had been compelled by instincts merely natural into writing the "wrong" kind of poetry. He recognized that he could no longer generate the sole kind of poetry he cared to produce or felt justified in producing: poems in praise of God. He would later admit to Bridges that in his "lagging lines" Bridges would "miss / The roll, the rise, the carol, the creation" which had informed his earlier work. Private torment was no fit subject for poems, and particularly not for a man who honored obedience as much as Hopkins did.

Hopkins's attitude, however, was more complex than this. Although he construed the poems as failures in the terms just stated, he also named them "inspirations"—even if not divinely prompted. What the very occasion of *having* inspirations must have meant to a man who wrote Bridges of "that coffin of weakness and dejection in which I live" can only be surmised. He must have had some sense of their poetic merit, whatever their spiritual worth; for he subjected them neither to neglect nor to burning (as he had most of the poetry written prior to his conversion) but to extensive revision. And he had the courage to revise with an eye for literary excellence, not conformity with religious convention. If one or two muddled images mar the poems (notably in "Patience"), they are the minute but significant indications that the spiritual crisis which prompted the poems left its mark upon his craftsmanship. But there is precious little here that evinces any diminution in power of conception, diversity in technical skill, or emotional range in delineating the soul's operations. Indeed, the "terrible sonnets" show a sudden and darkly brilliant heightening in Hopkins's scope and linguistic incisiveness. It is an irony in his tragic life that the "inspirations unbidden" he could not entirely accept have generally achieved a fame far greater than the poems of which he approved. For the religious and aesthetic failures Hopkins saw mirrored *in* the poems—their deviations from his former designs—never became a failure *of* the poetry itself.

This book attempts to understand the peculiar greatness that the "terrible sonnets" exhibit. Despite some thirty years of commentary, the poems have hardly begun to show their proper lineaments. Partly because their religious agony is rendered with such stark power—but also because the evidence of the manuscripts has been misread—they have seemingly defied aesthetic consideration. With the exception of Elisabeth Schneider in *The Dragon in the Gate: Studies in the Poetry of G. M. Hopkins* (1968), critics have rarely probed Hopkins's style in these poems; yet their imagery and structure are distinctive. Next, the relation between the "terrible sonnets" and Hopkins's earlier poetry has not been explored, though differences have vaguely been felt to obtain. This analysis examines those differences, indeed discontinuities, not by showing Hopkins's evolution from the Oxford poetry to the last work but, dispensing with teleology, by taking the characteristics of the 1885 poetry as a perspective from which to consider the earlier output. Finally, while Hopkins's general position in English literary history—as a neo-Romantic whose debts to Wordsworth, Coleridge, and Keats were deeper and more persistent than those to Tennyson—is gradually being realized, the place of poems so startling as the "terrible sonnets" in the development of nineteenth-century poetry has yet to be ascertained. The present essay engages the first two of these matters directly while suggesting modes of approaching the third.

My concern with the imagery and structure of these poems, and with the change in Hopkins's imagination, has led me to a very bleak view of the "terrible sonnets" as a whole: there is a hideous despair at the center of these poems, an experience of chaos scarcely duplicated elsewhere. I would not, however, want my interpretations to be taken as constituting a partial biography of Hopkins's last years. Nor would I be thought to doubt what he wrote in 1888:

> I was a Christian from birth or baptism, later I was converted to the Catholic faith, and am enlisted 20 years in the Society of Jesus. I am now 44. I do not waver in my allegiance, I never have since my conversion to the Church.[1]

[1] Gerard Manley Hopkins, *The Sermons and Devotional Writings of Gerard Manley Hopkins*, ed. Christopher Devlin (London: Oxford University Press, 1959), p. 261 (hereafter cited as *Sermons*).

I
"THE BEST OR WORST WORD LAST": PROBLEMS IN THE MANUSCRIPTS OF THE POEMS

St Ignatius speaks of the angel *discharging his mission*, it being question of action leading up to, as now my action leads from, the Incarnation. The Incarnation was for my salvation and that of the world: the work goes on in a great system and machinery which even drags me on with the collar round my neck though I could and do neglect my duty in it.

GERARD MANLEY HOPKINS,
Sermons (1888)

THE "terrible sonnets"—"Carrion Comfort," "No Worst, There is None," "To Seem the Stranger," "I Wake and Feel," "Patience," and "My Own Heart"[1]—are unique in Hopkins's canon; it is both rare and provocative to find so abrupt an alteration as these poems represent. While they obviously share much with Hopkins's work of the previous decade, they can also be distinguished from it on specific, and meaningful, grounds. The contrast is so sharp that, once the necessity of comparison is recognized, it involves a reconsideration of his entire production; and the points of distinction themselves have a pertinence not only to Hopkins's individual maturation but to the definition of central problems in Victorian literature.

In the "terrible sonnets," images from nature all but disappear, the general structure of the natural metaphors that remain differs radically from that in Hopkins's earlier poetry, and the dominant imagery is that of distorted and animalized sensory functions. These major changes in poetic method and focus entail nothing less than Hopkins's unwilled submission to solipsism and its possible consequence, the void in self-conception that gapes when exterior reality dissolves, becomes the perceiving mind's plaything, and is then recognized as being only a private or narcissistic fiction. As such, they show the paralysis of true perception against which Ruskin, Hopkins's mentor, repeatedly cautioned; one remembers that Arnold's Empedocles, acknowledging his inability to control his solipsistic projection of his own self-image upon the world (II.301–322), commits suicide rather than suffer a further corruption of his vision. Indeed, the shift from Hopkins's earlier work, as decisive as the similar shift from self-expansion to phantasmal emptiness in Tennyson's "The Palace of Art," virtually epitomizes the nemesis of Victorian sensibility, the threat of vacancy that attends any quest for identity based on subjective idealism: the appropriating ego is suddenly rendered fragile by its own machinations to transform the world, in Coleridge's phrasing, into an "Echo or mirror . . . of itself" ("Frost at Midnight," line 22). The shift thus illustrates the

[1] Gerard Manley Hopkins, *The Poems of Gerard Manley Hopkins*, 4th ed., revised and enlarged, ed. W. H. Gardner and N. H. MacKenzie (London: Oxford University Press, 1967), pp. 99–103 (hereafter cited as *Poems*). I have accepted the dating of Hopkins's poems as given in this edition. All citations from the "terrible sonnets" are taken from Hopkins's final drafts of the poems. See Appendix A.

grave anxiety the age experienced in seeking a sound basis for epistemology in the face of a metaphysics exploded by Lockean empiricism and a Biblical authority devastated by the Higher Criticism. For Hopkins, with a philosophical training and a Jesuit's discipline in argumentation, had founded his poetics upon what should have been the firmest ground of all, the historicity and dogma of Christ's Incarnation, and yet endured the crumbling of Christian hermeneutics.

Simultaneously and concomitantly, the "terrible sonnets" deviate sharply from the patterns of meditation that Hopkins had derived largely from St. Ignatius Loyola's *Spiritual Exercises* and that he had previously meshed with the sonnet to create his primary poetic form. Sometimes verging on a self-parody of the *imitatio Christi*, all the poems detail his speaker's failure to achieve the climactic and redemptive colloquy with Christ which, he knew, Ignatius and others had stipulated should conclude each meditative exercise. Some of them omit the colloquy altogether; others wrench it into strange and unlikely shapes. Such a failure occurs not because the speaker is impure or lacking in desire, but because Christ is presumed absent. The speaker's excruciating consciousness of Christ's disappearance correlates directly both with the solipsistic images from nature and with the altered—indeed, truncated—structure of the poems: Christ, previously the divine validation of exterior reality, vanishes from the natural world at the same time that His absence undermines the poetic form. One has in the "terrible sonnets," therefore, a unique opportunity to study the connections between theology and technique.

Neither Hopkins's pain nor the convergence between the private turmoil of a devout Catholic and the vexed sensibilities of a largely Protestant culture can be adequately understood without an examination of these special imagistic and formal properties that distinguish the "terrible sonnets" from Hopkins's earlier work. That these particular alterations occur in conjunction has a bearing on literary history as well. In the decade of 1875–1884, Hopkins made the last great systematic effort before Dylan Thomas to construct and render within his poetry a sacramental vision of nature. He is the only one among his major contemporaries in poetry to have done so; and his crisis differs from theirs accordingly. However anomalous in its belatedness, that effort was essentially Romantic in cast, both in its "natural supernaturalism" (to use Abrams's phrase) and in its stress upon direct perceptual encounter. But whereas Wordsworth saw in the natural world merely the shadowy "types and symbols of Eternity" (*The Prelude*, 6.639), Hopkins was rigorously literalist in his vision. Through the medium of Ruskin, he attempted, with precision and care for objectivity, to "see into the life of things" and to find there the Christ who could make those "beauteous forms" speak in answer, enter into colloquy with him.[2] At the same time, while Hopkins plainly accepted the Romantic convention of a meditation on nature, he sought to reshape it through classical meditative methods. To speak exclusively, and doubtless too crudely, in the terms of literary periods, he gave to the theme of Christ's Incarnation a Romantic treatment and imagery within the rhetorical structure evolved in the Renaissance by St. Ignatius and his followers. The total imaginative form— abetted by the compression of the sonnet, which freed Hopkins from the discursiveness of "Tintern Abbey" or "This Lime-Tree Bower My Prison"—was one in which Catholic and Romantic impulses towards colloquy could swiftly merge in the instantaneous illumination of the poem's closure.[3] The fusion which Hopkins thus accomplished was remarkable if brief, constituting a phase *sui generis* in the development of the meditative poem. The breakdown of that synthesis comes in the "terrible sonnets" with Hopkins's spiritual crisis. Beginning with his shattering doubts about the supernatural vitality within nature, it continues, formally, in his failures to achieve colloquy; it is part of the history of Romanticism.

Critical commentary has, however, blurred the distinctive features of the "terrible sonnets" and thus the areas of literary relations into which they lead. The reason for this imbalance in attention is important. The criticism has focused chiefly on discovering a theological design that can be claimed to control the poems; it has regarded them as a sequence, and has then concentrated on showing the spiritual or psychological evolution of Hopkins's speaker within it. But to explain why it should have been this particular preoccupation that has driven out other legitimate critical concerns, and why the matter of sequence should have assumed such a prominence, is to raise questions that cannot be satisfactorily answered by analyzing the religious qualities of the poems themselves. The questions, followed through, end with the most fundamental of issues in interpretation: the nature of the manuscripts of the "terrible son-

[2] Wordsworth, "Lines Composed a Few Miles above Tintern Abbey," lines 49, 22. For a sound discussion of Hopkins's indebtedness to Wordsworth and Coleridge, as well as his deviations from them (through Ruskin's influence), see Patricia M. Ball, *The Science of Aspects: The Changing Role of Fact in the Work of Coleridge, Ruskin and Hopkins* (London: Athlone Press, at the University of London, 1971), pp. 105–14.

[3] Because of Hopkins's strict meditative discipline in this mode, his productions may be considered the only true successors of the work of Southwell, Donne, and Herbert. Compare Louis L. Martz, *The Poetry of Meditation: A Study in English Religious Literature of the Seventeenth Century*, rev. ed. (New Haven, Conn.: Yale University Press, 1962), pp. 321–30. See also the elaborate effort to make Coleridge's "This Lime-Tree Bower My Prison" conform with Richard Baxter's *The Saints' Everlasting Rest* in Reeve Parker, *Coleridge's Meditative Art* (Ithaca, N.Y.: Cornell University Press, 1975), pp. 26–52.

nets," the first appearance of the poems in print, and the state of the received text. It is to these manuscripts, now in the Bodleian Library (Bodl. MS. Eng. poet. d.150, ff. 31, 35) and here reproduced in Appendix A, that I now turn.

Folio 31 (figs. 3 and 4, Appendix A) contains a final draft of "No Worst" and a nearly complete revision of "Carrion Comfort," the two poems Hopkins mentioned to Bridges in his letter of 17 May 1885.[4] The material on this page is as follows:

(1) [*recto*] "Carrion Comfort," line 11, final version (for earlier drafts of this poem, see folio 29, figs. 1 and 2, Appendix A);

(2) "Tom's Garland," lines 1–10, early version;

(3) "Carrion Comfort," line 12, final version;

(4) "No Worst," lines 1–2, earlier versions; lines 1–7, final version, with revisions;

(5) [*verso*] "No Worst," lines 8–14, final version, with revisions;

(6) "Carrion Comfort," lines 1–10, final version, with revisions.

The draft of "No Worst" shows several tries at the first quatrain, all of them quite similar, and important alterations in the diction of lines 10 and 13. By comparison, the draft of "Carrion Comfort" is essentially a distillation of the earlier drafts. While "No Worst" thus appears to be the later poem, the manuscript nevertheless offers no conclusive evidence for the order of composition; Hopkins seems to have worked at perfecting both poems simultaneously.

Folio 35 (figs. 6 and 7) gives the poems to which Hopkins referred in writing to Bridges on 1 September 1885;[5] all but the first are among the "terrible sonnets." The page, neatly penned in Hopkins's delicate hand, is an unmistakably fair copy of the following poems:

(1) [*recto*] "Ash-Boughs," in curtal-sonnet form (see folio 33, fig. 5, for the complete sonnet);

(2) "To Seem the Stranger," virtually clear of revisions in the octave but enormously altered in the sestet, so much so that the "original" version of the final tercet does not survive;

(3) "I Wake and Feel," lines 1–8, with occasional revisions;

(4) [*verso*] "I Wake and Feel," lines 9–14, with occasional revisions and significant changes in lines 11, 12, and 14;

(5) "Patience," with occasional revisions;

(6) "My Own Heart," with occasional revisions and significant changes in

---

[4] Gerard Manley Hopkins, *The Letters of Gerard Manley Hopkins to Robert Bridges*, ed. Claude Colleer Abbott (1935; rpt. London: Oxford University Press, 1970), p. 219. See *Poems*, p. 287, for further details.

[5] Hopkins, *Letters to Bridges*, p. 221.

lines 5, 6, and 9 (folio 33, originally attached to folio 35, gives the probably later version of lines 13–14).

The thorough revision of the sestet of "To Seem the Stranger" makes it plain that this was the last of the "terrible sonnets" to be completed. By comparison with the revisions of "No Worst," these are far more extensive, for they alter both the tone and the general direction of the poem. This is the most dramatically informative evidence conveyed by folio 35, and it is central to an understanding of the poems as a group.

Hopkins's "terrible sonnets" provide an unusually instructive example of the manner in which an editor's procedure can influence the subsequent history of literary interpretation. In the present case, it involves not only the critical perception of Hopkins's development (spiritual as well as stylistic) but also our sense of his relation to the literary and religious history of Victorian culture. Bridges, Hopkins's literary executor, decided to publish the "terrible sonnets" given on folio 35 in the order in which Hopkins transcribed them; the "terrible sonnets" of folio 31, presumably written a bit earlier, he separated from those of folio 35. Subsequent editors, while grouping all six poems together, have followed Bridges's lead in accepting the manifest order of poems on folio 35. Now Bridges obviously did not intend his 1918 edition to appear as a work of scholarship, though assuredly it demanded much; he was concerned to gain public acceptance for Hopkins, not to risk making him inaccessible. But the nature of his commentary on this manuscript of the "terrible sonnets" left its mark. Without actually inviting critics to see the poems as a designed sequence in which a governing theology of redemption might be discerned, it nevertheless permitted them to do so without much trouble. While Bridges frankly acknowledged that he had "no certain nor single identification of date" for the poems of folio 35,[6] he gave very little information about folio 35 itself. He did not state that the manuscript provides no evidence for the order in which the poems were composed prior to the making of the fair copy. He did not indicate that the draft of "To Seem the Stranger" gives palpable proof of at least two major stages of composition—the first of which *may have* occurred earliest in the composition of all these poems, the second of which almost certainly occurred last. And he did not consequently suggest that the order of the poems' transcription is wholly suspect as the basis for any interpretation— first, because the order of transcription carries no presumption concerning the order of composition; second, because "To Seem the Stranger," while placed

[6] Gerard Manley Hopkins, *Poems of Gerard Manley Hopkins*, ed. Robert Bridges (London: Humphrey Milford, for Oxford University Press, 1918), p. 119. Bridges's notes to the "terrible sonnets" may conveniently be found in the Gardner and MacKenzie edition, *Poems*, pp. 287–88.

first, was finished last. It may properly be argued that it was not Bridges's business to offer such a commentary on the ambiguities of folio 35; but it is certain that, had he provided a fuller description of the manuscript, both the number and kind of interpretations, prevalent for decades, that have been based on the poems' supposed sequence would have been reduced.

For it is the nature of folio 35, together with a lack of editorial commentary, that has, by its manifest order of transcription, seemingly substantiated the many sequential interpretations of the "terrible sonnets." Most of these postulate Hopkins's gradual progression from the exile and desolation of "To Seem the Stranger" to his renewed vision of God's beatific presence in the final tercet of "My Own Heart." Critics, however, have either not consulted the manuscript, or, when they have studied it, have misunderstood both the difficulties and the implicit directions for interpretation that these final drafts pose. To state the matter briefly: they have confused Hopkins's suspect order of transcription with the supposed order of composition, have taken the artifact of folio 35 as conveying genetic information; they have regarded the order of transcription as being equivalent to a progressive literary sequence with a definable beginning, middle, and end; and, finally, compounding these questionable procedures, they have freely superimposed upon the poems a doctrinaire Christian narrative or spiritual autobiography whose teleology is fulfilled by God's extension of consolation and Hopkins's intact survival of extreme trial. That this autobiography supposedly corresponds with the actual chronological development of Hopkins's crisis has been another staple of the criticism. Where critics have actually perceived *some* of the ambiguities in the manuscript—for example, the unknown genetic relation among the poems of folio 35—they have invented their own plots or sequences in order to arrive at roughly the same comforting interpretation; in constructing these sequences, they have in some cases (despite the difference in date between folios 31 and 35) intermixed the two sets of poems.

But the manuscript allows no such manipulations. On internal evidence alone, folio 35 confounds all attempts to equate the order of transcription with the order of composition. For "To Seem the Stranger"—as the drastic and brutal revisions of its sestet make plain—is both the first poem transcribed and the last poem to be finished. Obviously, the forbidding and unredeemed bleakness of this poem makes crucial the determination of its relative position in the group, particularly if one is trying to construct a "sequence"; yet it is exactly the ambiguous status of "To Seem the Stranger"—ambiguous on the page itself—that can never be resolved and must thus be accepted as such. Although half of the "original" sestet does not survive, and although the poem's genetic relation to the other poems of folio 35 cannot be known, it appears that Hopkins, in the very act of transcribing what he assumed would be the fair copy of "To Seem the Stranger," was again overwhelmed by those gnashings of despair which "My Own Heart"—had it truly been designed to conclude a sequence—was supposed to have ameliorated. As he wrote out the octave, he could not keep an impersonal distance from its stark delineations of isolation, separation from Christ, utterly blocked powers of communication. One does not say that Hopkins, in struggling through a new sestet, surrendered to his sorrow at the expense of his original poetic intent; rather, he discovered a deeper, more tragic vision of his own condition. The final version self-reflexively implies, in its reference to the "baffling ban" against his own language, the forestalling of the "original" sestet during the process of transcription; and it closes by evoking his own unwilled muteness both more heroically and more poignantly than anywhere else in the "terrible sonnets." The whole business of creating these poems, whatever the other facts of composition may be, ends, on the page of transcription, not with the "lovely mile" illuminated by God's "smile" in "My Own Heart" but with the speaker's "lonely began" in this sestet. The manuscript thus offers no support to those who assume that "To Seem the Stranger" was in its final state an early or middle poem in the "terrible sonnets." The accepted critical position that there exists an observable and verifiable chronological correspondence between the poems and Hopkins's biography is proved untenable; for the same poem represents two chronologically distinct states of mind, and one of these cannot be known.

The major revisions of "To Seem the Stranger," moreover, combined with other evidence, discredit interpretive efforts to construct from folio 35 a literary sequence that can claim any more validity than that conferred by desire— unless, of course, the critic is prepared, as no commentator or editor has yet been, to position "To Seem the Stranger" at the end of the series. Had Hopkins intended the poems to constitute a sequence, he would hardly have headed folio 35 with "Ash-Boughs," a poem which, although its last lines certainly foreshadow the "terrible sonnets," has touches of delighted ebullience reminiscent of the earlier poetry.[7] Hopkins himself plainly regarded the poems

[7] Folio 31, with its radical juxtaposition of drafts for "Tom's Garland" with those of "Carrion Comfort" and "No Worst," shows a similar vacillation in mood. See Norman H. MacKenzie, *Hopkins* (Edinburgh and London: Oliver and Boyd, 1968), pp. 94–95. See also *Poems*, pp. xlvii–xlviii, where, however, Mackenzie incorrectly remarks that "Carrion Comfort" and "No Worst," in *"their only known autograph drafts,* follow on the same sheet of paper an unfinished version of 'Tom's Garland'" (p. xlvii; italics mine); "Carrion Comfort" exists in separate drafts on folio 29.

not as a developmental sequence but as a group whose unity derived primarily from a common emotive pressure: "I shall shortly have some sonnets to send you, five or more. Four ["Three," cancelled] of these came like inspirations unbidden and against my will."[8] Nor, in initially writing "Three" rather than "Four"—i.e., in rescuing one of the poems from the category of "inspirations unbidden"—did he necessarily view either "My Own Heart" or "Patience" as much of a beneficent recoil from the Job-like temptation to blaspheme against God that he courted so perilously in "No Worst" and "To Seem the Stranger." In the end, all four poems erupted—despite his devout labors to suppress by act of will his remonstrations against divine chastisement—from the same source: that condition of black and jaded lassitude, all nature's beauty having withered, in which he knew himself a "straining eunuch," not God's (*Sermons*, p. 262), a priest barred from knowing the Incarnation in his own life.

That Hopkins nevertheless transcribed the "terrible sonnets" of folio 35 in a certain order cannot be denied. While he hardly shared Yeats's predilection for designing sequences of poems or arranging volumes, his order has a meaning; it is rather more complicated and perhaps unintentionally self-revelatory than commentators, positing a simple progression from despair to consolation, have supposed. A poet may either map out a sequence before composition (Auden's *Horae Canonicae*), discover it in the process of writing (Tennyson's *In Memoriam*), or create a sequence from partly or wholly completed work (Wordsworth's final version of "Memorials of a Tour in Scotland," Yeats's "A Woman Young and Old"). Each of these procedures, especially in Romantic and post-Romantic literature, entails a different conception and strategy of self-presentation. Hopkins, though he began with no intention of constructing a literary sequence, plainly molded his poems into a series after he had completed his work. He chose this particular series not so much to demonstrate the operation of orthodox Christian patterns of recovery but to persuade a distinct audience that the patterns were valid. Although Hopkins once defended his own ambivalent refusal to publish by claiming that "a poet is a public in himself,"[9] the series seems consciously or unconsciously tailored to anticipate the responses of the only actual audience Hopkins could expect for these poems: Bridges. But however valued a friend Bridges may have been, he fundamentally disapproved of Hopkins's ascetic submission to Roman Catholicism; the undercurrent of antagonism so unmistakable in the surviving correspondence saddened Hopkins perpetually. Bridges disliked Jesuits as a class; he had little tolerance for religious ritual; from Hopkins's perspective, he misunderstood

[8] Hopkins, *Letters to Bridges*, p. 221 and n. 1.
[9] Ibid., p. 59.

the "mystery," the "incomprehensible certainty" of the Incarnation; and, understanding too well Hopkins's need for a genuine reading public, he often expostulated with him to rebel against his excessively scrupulous interpretation of Jesuit discipline and thus to let his genius breathe.[10] To Bridges, Hopkins had wasted his exquisite charm and aesthetic sensibility; in his prefatory poem to the 1918 edition, Bridges bridled as he praised: "God's terror held" Hopkins's "sainted sense trammel'd in ghostly pain," his "rare ill-broker'd talent in disdain." Bridges was also a man whom Hopkins had once, naively, hoped to convert and whose spiritual welfare he continued to urge in his letters: "You understand of course," Hopkins wrote him, "that I desire to see you a Catholic or, if not that, a Christian or, if not that, at least a believer in the true God (for you told me something of your views about the deity, which were not as they should be)."[11] And Bridges, even as he worked loyally to insure his friend's posthumous fame, objected to "the exaggerated Marianism" of some poems and, in others, to Hopkins's "efforts to force emotion into theological or sectarian channels."[12] It is thus unthinkable that Hopkins, knowing Bridges's lack of sympathy, if not outright animosity, for the Church, would send him a "series" that closed in despair—a series, that is, which implicitly corroborated all of Bridges's objections and acknowledged that it was Bridges, and not Hopkins, who had rightly chosen his vocation. The order of the series was perhaps Hopkins's mask against Bridges's disapproval and against his own recognition of an interior agony which, if it sometimes abated, also seemed endless. With the unexpected, astonishing revisions of "To Seem the Stranger," however, the mask fell, leaving any intelligible notion of a self-protective series in shambles.

It is not simply because critics have disregarded the manuscript evidence that they have been able to see the mask Hopkins wanted Bridges to see—a triumphant exhibition of God's grace—rather than the abyss Hopkins saw. Catholic and non-Catholic commentators alike have persistently hesitated to acknowledge the phenomenon of an impeccably devout Jesuit priest who gives witness to God's brutality ("Carrion Comfort"), courts nihilism and suicide ("No Worst"), puns with ferocious sarcasm on the idea of Christian "comfort" ("No Worst," "My Own Heart"), and insinuates through ambiguous syntax

[10] Ibid., pp. 40, 148, 186–87, 196. See also Elisabeth W. Schneider, *The Dragon in the Gate: Studies in the Poetry of G. M. Hopkins* (Berkeley and Los Angeles: University of California Press, 1968), pp. 128, 142. For a full account of the relationship between Hopkins and Bridges, see Jean-Georges Ritz, *Robert Bridges and Gerard Hopkins, 1863–1889: A Literary Friendship* (London: Oxford University Press, 1960).

[11] Hopkins, *Letters to Bridges*, p. 60.

[12] Hopkins, *Poems*, ed. Bridges, p. 96.

that his own disaster is "worse" than that of "the lost" ("I Wake and Feel").
Throughout 1885 Hopkins was terrified of an encroaching derangement, a re-
currence of the melancholia he had experienced before his conversion in 1866:
"I think that my fits of sadness, though they do not affect my judgment, re-
semble madness"; "soon I am afraid I shall be ground down to a state like this
last spring's and summer's, when my spirits were so crushed that madness
seemed to be making approaches." [13] But commentators, with few exceptions,
have justified Hopkins's torment by placing it within the narrative context of a
providential teleology of suffering and have claimed that Hopkins's disintegra-
tion brought him closer to the perfection of spirit he so avidly craved, the
"higher cross" he so morbidly and sincerely desired (*Sermons*, p. 254). The first
of these positions gives evidence of the dread that these poems prompt; the
second can be neither proved nor disproved. Critics have quickly enlisted St.
Thomas à Kempis and St. John of the Cross (not to mention St. Ignatius) to
show that Hopkins's arid misery corresponds with recognizable and traditional
Catholic modes of purgation and illumination. The central mythic pattern to
which they all implicitly refer is the death and resurrection of the Lord whom
the poet repeatedly lamented he could not find. Wolfe's judgment of this sup-
posedly victorious spiritual autobiography typifies many: "The sonnets repre-
sent successive stages in the poet's progress towards a resolution" in his crisis
of identity. "As the redeemed he finally establishes a relationship with God
[by] surrendering his mortal selfhood to the immortal selfhood of God." [14]
Lahey, Hopkins's influential first biographer, writes that Hopkins was "on the
bleak heights of spiritual night with his God. All writers on mysticism—St.
Theresa, St. John of the Cross, Poulain, Maumigny, &c.—have told us that
this severe trial is the greatest and most cherished *gift* from One Who has
accepted literally His servant's oblation" (Lahey's italics). [15] Downes notes a
seemingly undeniable "parallel between what Hopkins expresses in his sonnets

[13] Hopkins, *Letters to Bridges*, pp. 216, 222; see also *Sermons*, p. 262.
[14] Patricia A. Wolfe, "The Paradox of Self: A Study of Hopkins' Spiritual Conflict in the 'Terri-
ble' Sonnets," *Victorian Poetry* 6 (1968): 85. See also Alan Heuser, *The Shaping Vision of Gerard
Manley Hopkins* (London: Oxford University Press, 1958), p. 91; and W. H. Gardner, *Gerard
Manley Hopkins: A Study of Poetic Idiosyncrasy in Relation to Poetic Tradition*, 2 vols. (1949; rpt.
London: Oxford University Press, 1966), 2:339, 345, 360. Gardner, overlooking Hopkins's ten-
dency toward self-parody and regarding his speaker as an *"alter Christus,"* views both "Patience"
and "My Own Heart" as a partial "easement" from the desolation of the earlier "terrible sonnets,"
a despair he thinks Hopkins finally conquered in "That Nature Is a Heraclitean Fire and of the
Comfort of the Resurrection" (1888).
[15] G. F. Lahey, *Gerard Manley Hopkins* (London: Humphrey Milford, for Oxford University
Press, 1930), p. 142. Lahey continues, "The celebrated 'terrible' sonnets are only terrible in the
same way that the beauty of Jesus Christ is terrible" (*ibid.*).

and what St. John describes in the Chapter entitled, 'The Dark Night'," and asserts that the poems "dramatize Hopkins's artistic reflections of his attempt to use Ignatius's Rules in order to raise himself out of his own desolation into a state of spiritual consolation"; "even the bitterest moments of the 'terrible' sonnets are unmarked by anything like despair." [16] Cotter, while rightly criticizing those who annul "the authenticity of Hopkins's grief and anxiety" by seeking "ready remedies in St. John of the Cross and 'the dark night of the soul'," nevertheless concludes his own discussion of "My Own Heart" by affirming Hopkins's "slow ascent upward from his *Inferno* to the dawn of Easter Day." [17]

Cotter's caution should be taken seriously, and not only because such "sequential" readings have in the main impeded a study of the poetry. The *Ascent of Mount Carmel* and the *Dark Night of the Soul* cannot be easily enlisted to explain the "terrible sonnets." St. John's program for spiritual illumination, founded like that of à Kempis on the *imitatio Christi*, is rigorously sequential; [18] as such, it cannot be adjusted to the problems in sequence raised by Hopkins's manuscripts to the poems. Even if that manuscript's evidence is disregarded, pitfalls remain. To explain the "terrible sonnets" through St. John's writings is automatically to consider Hopkins a mystic who sought "to attain to the state of perfection" in "Divine union with God"; [19] the view is both generally disputed and extremely difficult to prove. No evidence exists that Hopkins thought his sufferings a necessary phase in his progression towards final communion. During his distress he never mentioned St. John (whom he may well have found inimical because St. John so roundly condemns the use of

---

[16] David A. Downes, *Gerard Manley Hopkins: A Study of His Ignatian Spirit* (New York: Bookman Associates, 1959), pp. 131, 136, 146. See also William T. Noon, *Poetry and Prayer* (New Brunswick, N.J.: Rutgers University Press, 1967), p. 111.

[17] James Finn Cotter, *Inscape: The Christology and Poetry of Gerard Manley Hopkins* (Pittsburgh, Pa.: University of Pittsburgh Press, 1972), pp. 221, 230. John Pick, *Gerard Manley Hopkins: Priest and Poet*, 2nd ed. (New York: Oxford University Press, 1966), pp. 129–32, was the first to take serious exception to the "Dark Night" theory of Hopkins's "terrible sonnets"; see also John Robinson, *In Extremity: A Study of Gerard Manley Hopkins* (Cambridge: Cambridge University Press, 1978), pp. 142–43. These cautions have not been readily accepted in Hopkins criticism, even by those who make them; MacKenzie, for example, while stating that "to the priest himself his experiences did not seem to correspond to any familiar ordeal on the road to sanctity," nevertheless proceeds to remark of Hopkins's contemporaneous Retreat Notes that "The terrible experience of self-loathing and hopelessness which his meditation notes reveal show how close he had come to the blinding light of Heaven, though he seemed to himself to be groping in utter darkness" (*Hopkins*, pp. 88, 92).

[18] For the pattern of the *imitatio*, see St. John of the Cross, *Ascent of Mount Carmel*, trans. and ed. E. Allison Peers (New York: Doubleday, 1958), pp. 106–7; for the stress upon sequence, see, e.g., ibid., pp. 20, 98 ff.

[19] Ibid., pp. 20, 22.

imagination in the meditative exercise); St. Theresa appears only once (*Sermons*, p. 138). Doubtless Hopkins experienced arid emptiness, anxious desolation, knew the horror of self-knowledge and the pain of abandonment by God, and one may grant a general correspondence between these emotions and certain passages in the *Dark Night*. But there are no grounds, on such a tenuous basis, for invoking the whole of St. John's design for the soul's sequential purification, particularly since (to take but two examples) the passivity enjoined in the *Dark Night* cannot be reconciled with either the violence of "Carrion Comfort" or the firm self-instructions of "My Own Heart." Behind these difficulties, however, is a far more fundamental issue: the justification, or lack of it, for suffering. St. John's program is ultimately directed by God, who "leads into the dark night those whom He desires to purify."[20] All trials are thus benevolently and purposively controlled, St. John reiterates,[21] *even if* the sufferer does not recognize God's guidance behind his torment. The absence of a sign from God is itself a sign of His watchful Presence and care; the contemplative, if he does not understand this sign, has simply shown his imperfection. St. John thus proposes a conventional teleology of suffering that, founded as it is upon an authoritarian escape-clause (the paradox of the absent sign), cannot be answered. The upshot of such a position, as a perspective from which to view the "terrible sonnets," is that the suffering of Hopkins's speaker must necessarily be purposive, even though he may not know it, and that God is really present when Hopkins's speaker cries that He is not. The "dark night" interpretation of the "terrible sonnets" thus cancels—first by purposive sequence, next by paradox—both the experiences and the linguistic characteristics manifested by the poems; it has been attractive because its inviolable consolation is safe, not because it is true.

It is a testimony to the threat these poems pose to their readers that even those commentators who have seen the fallacies of using the order of folio 35 as a basis for interpretation have nevertheless embraced, in their freedom from the merely artifactual progression of the manuscripts, the same critical mythology of a triumphantly resurrective design in the poems. The variety of their orderings resembles that created by the rearrangers of Shakespeare's sonnets who, knowing that the 1609 text was pirated and thereby sensing a "possible corruption," have felt free to design their own orders.[22] Pick, for exam-

[20]St. John of the Cross, *Dark Night of the Soul*, trans. and ed. E. Allison Peers (New York: Doubleday, 1959), p. 44.

[21]Ibid., pp. 66, 74, 85, 100.

[22]See, e.g., Brents Stirling, *The Shakespeare Sonnet Order: Poems and Groups* (Berkeley and Los Angeles: University of California Press, 1968), p. 28.

ple, meshes the poems of folios 31 and 35; he begins with "To Seem the Stranger" and "I Wake and Feel" (from folio 35), continues with "No Worst" and "Carrion Comfort" (from folio 31), and concludes with "My Own Heart" and "Patience" (from folio 35). Although he seeks to avoid emphasizing a spiritual progression, he still imagines a regenerative sequence: in the end, Hopkins "*comes to see* that the soul must attain the virtues of patience among its trials and desolations" (italics mine).[23] Mariani characterizes his own version of the sonnet sequence with deceptive aplomb:

> *To seem the stranger, I wake and feel the fell of dark,* and *No worst, there is none:* each descends deeper into the emptiness within. Then there is the beginning of the upswing in *Carrion Comfort,* which continues in *Patience, hard thing,* and *My own heart.* Of course the sonnets can be read in and for themselves, but the series provides an added dimension which follows too closely the classical descent and ascent of the Ignatian Exercises to be fortuitous.[24]

Mariani's insertion of the poems from folio 31 into the middle of his sequence makes the design entirely his.

Only Hillis Miller, in his phenomenological study of Hopkins, has approached the "terrible sonnets" without relying on a supposed or imagined sequence. It is thus not surprising that, in rejecting a governing concept of sequentiality, Miller should have had the heterodox temerity to state that "Hopkins has, beyond all his contemporaries, the most shattering experience of the disappearance of God."[25] The only hyperbole in this interpretation results from Miller's forgetting Ruskin's great crisis in Turin (1858), an upheaval of faith that rendered him agnostic or atheist for twenty years. Although Miller decided on his perspective and conducted his study without consulting Hopkins's manuscripts, the evidence of the manuscripts clearly corroborates his treatment of the poems as synchronous entities, indeed permits no other. The present essay takes that evidence as the precondition of critical analysis and dispenses with the safety of any sequential narrative that might predetermine the contours of interpretation. It regards the poems as a mere group, in a contiguous but not patterned assemblage, one whose aspects must

[23] Pick, *Hopkins,* p. 148.
[24] Paul L. Mariani, *A Commentary on the Complete Poems of Gerard Manley Hopkins* (Ithaca, N.Y.: Cornell University Press, 1970), p. 212. Mariani takes his order for the poems from Jean-Georges Ritz, *Le Poète Gérard Manley Hopkins, S.J.: L'homme et l'oeuvre* (Paris: Didier, 1963), p. 250.
[25] J. Hillis Miller, *The Disappearance of God: Five Nineteenth-Century Writers* (1963; rpt. New York: Schocken Books, 1965), pp. 352–53.

be elucidated from within. At the same time, as a nearly self-contained world whose constituents appear in such marked definition, the group differs so demonstrably from Hopkins's earlier work—in crucial matters of natural metaphor, Ignatian structure, and, by extension, theology—that its own poetic "behaviour" (to use one of Hopkins's preferred terms) in itself provides readers with the appropriate means of judgment. If the delineation of Hopkins's crisis thus gains a new accuracy and scope, the problems presented by folio 35—problems not likely to be entirely solved—will have served their purpose.

II
NATURE AND THE
HUMAN BODY:
ALTERED IMAGES

We, life's pride and cared-for crown,

Have lost that cheer and charm of earth's past prime:
Our make and making break, are breaking, down
To man's last dust, drain fast towards man's first slime.

GERARD MANLEY HOPKINS,
The Sea and the Skylark (1877)

TO Seem the Stranger," the most bar-
ren of the "terrible sonnets," contains no images from nature at all. "I Wake
and Feel" evokes the natural world only through a pun ("fell": animal pelt).
These facts suggest a central poetic truth about the world of these sonnets:
nature has virtually disappeared from Hopkins's ken. In contrast to the density
of natural images in his preceding work, only seven images from nature appear
in the "terrible sonnets."[1] Three of these, however, have their source or ana-
logue (appropriately) in Job: the whirlwind in "No Worst"; the tempest and
the chaff and grain in "Carrion Comfort." They are, indeed, so traditionally
Biblical that their very conventionality demonstrates the failure, in the entire
group, of what Ruskin called the "penetrative imagination,"[2] the faculty
through which the ideal artist "plunges into the very central fiery heart" of
phenomena.[3] Hopkins's loss of capacity, learned from Ruskin, to "catch" the
inscapes of nature is equally evident in the remaining four images: the moun-
tains in "No Worst," the ivied tower and the beehive in "Patience," and the
dappled sky in "My Own Heart." As I shall presently explain, these images
exhibit a structure of metaphor wholly at variance from that of the earlier work.
At best, they are decorations; they instance, too, Hopkins's solipsistic and un-
controlled self-projection upon things. In no case, though Ruskin had urged it
as the suitable end of a properly Christian poetic language, do they reveal the
powerful capability that "affirms from within" the phenomena themselves.[4]

This radical cautery of images embodying God's manifested structure and
beauty—and the altered form of those few natural images that remain—is the
clearest possible index that Hopkins's universe has suffered a cataclysmic frag-
mentation, a crisis whose bereft aftermath seems a large-scale enactment of
Shakespeare's "Bare ruin'd choirs, where late the sweet birds sang." To define
the *absence* of a particular poetic feature as constituting a peculiar characteristic
of a certain body of poetry, and to show the values implied by that absence, is a

[1] Compare Susan A. Hallgarth, "A Study of Hopkins' Use of Nature," *Victorian Poetry* 5 (1967):
90–91. Hallgarth unaccountably finds only two nature images in the "terrible sonnets"; she sees
them used only to describe the "violent means God can use in his plan for salvation."
[2] John Ruskin, *The Complete Works of John Ruskin*, 39 vols., ed. E. T. Cook and Alexander Wed-
derburn (London: George Allen, 1903–1912), 4:227–28, 249–53.
[3] Ibid., 250.
[4] Ibid., 251.

difficult enterprise. Some backtracking in argumentation will be necessary. For it is possible, from the vantage-point of 1885, to discern earlier intimations of the crisis: in the themes of the transitional poems just prior to the "terrible sonnets," in the mordant aspects of Hopkins's sensibility, and in the gradual encroachment of pathetic fallacy upon his style.

Although Hopkins's abandonment of nature as his chief figurative mode for visionary expression notably has no precedent in his work, it is heralded thematically by the dissolution of nature's presumed coherences in several transitional poems: "Ribblesdale" (1882), "The Leaden Echo and the Golden Echo" (1882), "Spelt from Sibyl's Leaves" (1884–1885), and "Ash-Boughs" (1885), the poem which heads folio 35. In "Ribblesdale" the speaker addresses an unthinking earth which has ceased to be the cipher of God's fecundity. Although the world still displays the Hopkinsian emphasis on absolute existence, it "canst but only be": its identity, seemingly without function, is now a limitation. Significantly anticipating the stress on dysfunctional language in the "terrible sonnets," this earth has "no tongue to plead," and thus cannot answer the speaker's apostrophe. In turn, the speaker's lament represents the surfacing of a new need, one Hopkins would not earlier have countenanced: the need to anthropomorphize nature in order to obscure, and thus ameliorate, the upsetting division between self and nature that he was then discovering. The God of "Ribblesdale," moreover, like the mechanist God of the deists, has absconded, left the world to its own devices: its miserable alternatives are "rack or wrong." Hopkins, so much the Incarnationist in his earlier poetry, has here admitted what he had refused to acknowledge: the sin in nature, Adam's withered rose. His previous conviction, nearly heterodox, that nature remained immune from human corruption (e.g., "God's Grandeur" [1877]) has vanished.

This disillusioned vision of the natural world so permeates "The Leaden Echo and the Golden Echo" that, in its undercurrent of nihilism, the golden echo as well as the base echo is repeatedly described through negative terms. Earthly beauty now connotes no more than "tombs and worms and tumbling to decay"; no longer does it have a valued function in leading humankind (as in "To What Serves Mortal Beauty" [1885]) through a graduated scale of perception that ends in recognition of "God's better beauty, grace," for the disjunction between natural and divine realms has become absolute. As in "Ribblesdale," Hopkins has again rejected his former immanentalism and turned his attention to "beauty-in-the-ghost," a wholly transcendental conceptualization that dissolves the previous fusion of Creator and creation. In the apocalyptic rhapsody "Spelt from Sibyl's Leaves," the earth is consumed by a death-wish that may reflect Hopkins's own: "Evening strains to be tíme's vást,' womb-of-all, home-of-all, hearse-of-all night." Anticipating the atomized world of the "terrible sonnets," earth has become "unbound; her dapple is at an end, as- / tray or aswarm, all throughther, in throngs." And the bitter speaker joins in urging that dissolution: "lét life wind / Off hér once skéined stained véined variety." The jubilation that he had previously gained from the empirical observation of God's majesty in nature has disappeared; as coming darkness bars his visual faculties, the speaker knows only self-laceration: "thoughts against thoughts in groans grind" in a solipsistic vacuum much like the claustrophobic self-enclosure of the "terrible sonnets."[5]

In "Ash-Boughs," for all the liveliness and tender vivacity with which the speaker first sees the motions of the trees, he must finally recognize the melancholy sign of death within his emblem: "then they [the ash-trees] are old Earth groping towards that steep / Heaven once Earth childed by." Spring in its sexual abundance acts as foil to the pathetic barrenness of "old Earth," who craves the return of fruitful pregnancy yet knows her seed-time finished. Earth and Heaven, once identical in Hopkins's ambiguous syntax, are now antithetical; that Earth is "old" suggests the ravages of sin that, theologically, prevent reunion. The Old Testament imagery of broken marriage anticipates "To Seem the Stranger"; and because the poem thus closes in such desolation, the earlier image of the trees as they "nestle at heaven most high" must seem nearly an illusion. As in "Ribblesdale," the speaker ultimately perceives in an anthropomorphic mode, subsumes individuated observations to personification. In turn, the personified figure is no longer a cipher of God's immanent power but rather of His absence; in herself, Earth—like the speaker of "My Own Heart" —can only make "groping" gestures towards the distant Presence who once informed her.

The thematic importance of these poems for the "terrible sonnets" is not, as Miller has said, that their speaker "ceases to participate in the on-going vitality of nature."[6] Rather, in the years immediately prior to the "terrible sonnets," Hopkins began to suspect that his earlier vision of nature's vitality had been a falsehood. For he now saw earth becoming a confused and incoherent chaos, nearly emptied of God, and so wracked by human sin that its beauty was contaminated. Such disillusionment led Hopkins, in the "terrible sonnets," to jettison his natural images abruptly and almost entirely.

[5] Paul L. Mariani, A Commentary on the Complete Poems of Gerard Manley Hopkins (Ithaca, N.Y.: Cornell University Press, 1970), rightly argues that the poem is "first of all an Ignatian meditation on the state of hell" (p. 199). Equally striking is the Manichaeanism of the sestet: God's unitary creation has fallen into division.

[6] J. Hillis Miller, The Disappearance of God: Five Nineteenth-Century Writers (1963; rpt. New York: Schocken Books, 1965), p. 353.

The shift in imaginative temperament and method has not been satisfactorily explained. Hallgarth remarks that in the late poetry "Hopkins is concerned with his own relation to God so that nature is used very little."[7] But the causal argument is faulty. Natural images had previously been Hopkins's chief means of defining his service to God: in poems like "God's Grandeur" and "Pied Beauty" (1877) he had explored his priestly vocation by celebrating Creation; he had "used" the cosmic geographies of *The Wreck of the Deutschland* to examine the complexities of his own conversion and salvation. More to the point, perhaps, is that the kind of relation Hopkins had with God in his last poetic phase was different from that of his middle period, and it is possible that it was his altered perception of nature which changed his approach to God (and not the reverse). Furthermore, while Hallgarth perceives the new antithesis between God and nature in Hopkins's work, it passes without comment. The element of judgmental apocalypse in "Spelt from Sibyl's Leaves," for example, is doubtless partly responsible both for the antithesis and for the darkened presentation of nature; but why the apocalyptic vision itself—embraced so joyously at the end of *The Wreck*—should have turned so grimly pessimistic is a question still unanswered. Downes argues that Hopkins, obedient to St. Ignatius's "counsel about the proper use of things," deliberately sacrificed the baroque richness of his earlier style, including the images from nature, in order to imitate Christ.[8] If so, the ascetic impulse remained partly unfulfilled, for Hopkins certainly did attempt, in "Patience" and "My Own Heart," to inscape aspects of nature in his former manner, though not with the same success. One questions, too, Downes's stress on pure volition in Hopkins's adherence to St. Ignatius, and not only because the "terrible sonnets" deviate significantly from the Ignatian pattern in their structuring. Downes's interpretation views style exclusively through the lens of theology; it leaves little room to question whether alterations in the actual quality and intensity of Hopkins's imaginative perceptions may not have affected the change in his poetic methods and material.

Nor have biographical comments proved entirely adequate. Hopkins, of course, was not happy as professor of Greek at the Royal University: he hated Dublin, was exhausted by the burden of grading examinations, and doubtless

---

[7] Hallgarth, "A Study of Hopkins' Use of Nature," p. 81.

[8] David Anthony Downes, "Beatific Landscapes in Hopkins" (part 2), *Hopkins Quarterly* 1 (1975): 189. There is, of course, a long tradition in Jesuit commentary on St. Ignatius's *Spiritual Exercises*, beginning with Juan Alonso de Polanco (a close associate of St. Ignatius's immediate followers), which actually endorses a mystical "application of the senses" and, in doing so, gives free rein to religious sensuality; Downes's assumption that Hopkins chose to interpret St. Ignatius ascetically in order to perform a poetic *imitatio Christi* is not necessarily warranted.

felt the strain of being an English Catholic in Ireland; his eyesight was failing, his health was poor, he did not take sufficient holidays, and the melancholia that had nagged him before his conversion returned to haunt him.[9] But to argue that "Many of Hopkins' Irish poems were a reaction to circumstances plainly uncongenial" and derive "from something external to the man"[10] is to adopt a kind of environmental determinism that views the desert wastes of the "terrible sonnets" without reference to the inner patterns of the imagination which may resist such outward pressures. More helpfully, Devlin has observed that after Hopkins's ordination (1877), "his interest shifted increasingly from the presence of God's design or inscape (that is, Christ) in inanimate nature to the working out of that design—by stress and instress—in the minds and wills of men" (Sermons, p. 109). Although partly corroborated by the poems of ministry such as "Felix Randal" (1880), this interpretation does not account for the shift in metaphoric foundations from the middle to the late poetry, and it does not explain the change in the type of natural imagery found in the late nature poems themselves. One may grant, too, the stunted involvement in the natural world that resulted, almost inevitably, from Hopkins's ministries in the gloomy urban centers of Manchester, Liverpool, and Glasgow, not to mention his duties in Dublin. But it is curious to note that Hopkins, although partly cut off from contact with the natural world, never took refuge in memory: the emotion of recollected natural beauty—whether in "Tintern Abbey" (lines 22–30) or in Yeats's "The Lake Isle of Innisfree" (written, as it were, "on the roadway, or on the pavements grey")—seems not to have struck Hopkins as a feasible palliative for his urban confinement. It was not, then, Hopkins's living conditions or the demands of his vocation that caused the falling off, but rather something which involved his actual perception of nature. Devlin points out that "by 1884 Hopkins had failed in his major ambition, which . . . was an attempt to show the Grace of Christ working in the universe to form it into one body with many members" and that the "shock of this failure" to make his Scotist philosophy of radical individuation cohere "made it impossible for him to continue any creative work on a large scale."[11] Devlin's conclusion is both just and useful, for it points to a profound inner change in Hopkins's psychic disposition and in his perceptual capacities: "He had failed to extrovert his insight"; he became, to himself, a failed "mediator between

[9]John Pick, Gerard Manley Hopkins: Priest and Poet, 2nd ed. (New York: Oxford University Press, 1966), pp. 111–12.
[10]John Robinson, In Extremity: A Study of Gerard Manley Hopkins (Cambridge: Cambridge University Press, 1978), p. 133.
[11]Christopher Devlin, "Time's Eunuch," The Month, n.s., 1 (1949): 309, 306.

finite and Infinite." [12] In his imagination as well as in his theology, Hopkins became increasingly conscious of a fissure between the mundane and the divine. On the one hand, an object's form or shape was no longer identical with Christ. On the other hand, being unable to see the Invisible within the visible, he could no longer, as perceiver, enter into reciprocal relations with the phenomenon itself and thus could not mediate between the (vanished) Infinite and the finite world of poetic embodiment. The changed aspect of natural images in the transitional poems and their virtual disappearance in the "terrible sonnets" reflect the breakdown of Hopkins's immanental vision.

This, at least, was the situation during Hopkins's critical years in Dublin. But it is well to remember, before proceeding, that his crisis of perception had secular and aesthetic dimensions before it became a specifically religious matter in the "terrible sonnets." Neither Hopkins's perception nor his consequent organization of minute particulars into parallel and analogous forms was ever the function of mere seeing in a strictly physiological or phenomenological fashion. These empirical capacities depended, well before he read Scotus in 1872, upon his prior intuition, however vague metaphysically, of a coherence within nature; and his feeling of unity was itself a necessary evidence of his own sanity and psychic wholeness. But that prior disposition of mind, as scattered comments in his journals make plain, was sometimes quite fragile, easily blocked or upset. For the conditions requisite to his inscaping of the design in nature included more than his conceptual ability, for example, to fuse space and time in momentary vision by aligning the proper physical perspective with the right "time to study" particular phenomena (*Journals*, p. 205). [13] He required meditative solitude for concentration, for the intensity that catalyzed the analytic imagination to "penetrate" and then establish relations between things: "with a companion the eye and the ear are for the most part shut and instress cannot come" (*Journals*, p. 228). He needed to forestall the possibility that sudden changes in his moods might threaten his goal of an integrated perception. Thus, in an entry as early as 1871, he noted that his own terror of death nearly disrupted his vision:

[12] Ibid., pp. 310, 311. See also Howard W. Fulweiler, *Letters from the Darkling Plain: Language and the Grounds of Knowledge in the Poetry of Arnold and Hopkins* (Columbia, Mo.: University of Missouri Press, 1972), pp. 140–44; and Harold L. Weatherby, *The Keen Delight: The Christian Poet in the Modern World* (Athens, Ga.: University of Georgia Press, 1975), pp. 97–98, who shows, through an analysis of Hopkins's Scotism, the philosophical difficulties in his position that led to the crisis.

[13] Gerard Manley Hopkins, *The Journals and Papers of Gerard Manley Hopkins*, ed. Humphry House, completed by Graham Storey (1959; rpt. London: Oxford University Press, 1966), p. 205 (hereafter cited as *Journals*).

> The Horned Violet is a pretty thing, gracefully lashed. Even in withering the flower ran through beautiful inscapes by the screwing up of the petals into straight little barrels or tubes. It is not that inscape does not govern the behaviour of things in slack and decay as one can see even in the pining of the skin in the old and even in a skeleton but that horror prepossesses the mind, but in this case there was nothing in itself to shew even whether the flower were shutting or opening. [*Journals*, p. 211]

Note how, in the second sentence, the presence of death interferes not only with the realization of beauty, but with the assumption that beauty exists. In the third sentence, Hopkins plainly implies that "horror"—hardly a component of the Burkean sublime—can throw perception into chaos. The last clause frankly expresses relief that the "slack and decay" were sufficiently veiled to allow the penetrative imagination to function; it is also, quite noticeably, an effort to counteract the destructive movement of time by asserting (pretending?) the Paterian stasis of the moment. The entire passage shows Hopkins uncomfortably conscious of his own problems in perception—in particular, the connection between emotion and vision.

Yet more significant is an 1873 entry that demonstrates the intimate causal effect of psychic disposition on the perception of the exterior world: "In fact being unwell I was quite downcast: nature in all her parcels and faculties gaped and fell apart, *fatiscebat*, like a clod cleaving and holding only by strings of root" (*Journals*, p. 236). The passage concludes, ominously, "But this must often be." Here Hopkins acknowledges that the blockage of coherent perception through psychic distress was frequent; simultaneously he indicates the kinds of unsettling experiences that he must often have suppressed in writing his journals. Akin to such poems as Coleridge's "Frost at Midnight" or Wordsworth's "Elegiac Stanzas Suggested by a Picture of Peele Castle," the passage examines the effects of changed mood (itself the consequence of bodily discomfort) upon the perception of aesthetic design. Hopkins's sense of failing to establish or maintain a proper relation between self and nature—here, his untoward transformation of nature into mere personified image of his depression—galled him; he may well have given up using images from nature partly because he realized, with characteristic honesty, that he could no longer do them justice. The passage itself, moreover, in all its extremism, embodies a version of apocalypse; and his depression nullifies his inscaping, earlier in the day, of a sunset. But this germ of the later apocalyptic writings is not theological, either in its vocabulary or in its imagistic associations; it serves as caution that, in the later poetry, theology and psychic imbalance are often intertwined and cannot be easily unravelled.

By the time he wrote "Inversnaid" (1881), he was obviously straining to perceive the independent structures in nature with the neat purity and seeming disinterest that had formerly been his gift. His desperate effort to keep the world from "cleaving"—indeed, from vanishing altogether—is marked here by an obsessive sound-patterning and by a nearly hysterical (and largely atypical) concentration on elaborating a single image without recourse to analogy. In the concluding line, the pun on "wilderness" (long ī necessitated by the use of "wildness" in lines 14–15) cries out for a dynamic action in nature that has sufficient power to magnetize his distraught mind to the exterior world: the subliminal image of the *wilde dēor* [14] illustrates by contrast his own tamed and jaded state. These passages from the journals and transitional poems are grim preludes to Hopkins's later gloom, "that coffin of weakness and dejection in which I live." [15]

Hopkins's crisis of perception took a form so definable, and so Victorian in its essential contours, that Ruskin would have recognized it immediately. [16] It was that confusion of proper modes of seeing which Ruskin analyzed as the "pathetic fallacy." The fallacy is caused, Ruskin states, "by an excited state of the feelings" in which the perceiver falsely attributes to the things of nature his own emotions and, in indulging such a proud, usurpative egotism, distorts "the signature of God upon his works." [17] Thus "blaspheming the work of God," the perceiver "refuses to look at the real facts round about him, in order that he may adore at leisure the shadow of himself." [18] Ruskin regards the use of pathetic fallacy as exactly opposite to that of the "penetrative imagination,"

[14] I am indebted for this observation to Professor Donald C. Baker, formerly in the Department of English, University of Colorado at Boulder.

[15] Gerard Manley Hopkins, *The Letters of Gerard Manley Hopkins to Robert Bridges*, ed. Claude Colleer Abbott (1935; rpt. London: Oxford University Press, 1970), pp. 214–15.

[16] See Alison G. Sulloway, *Gerard Manley Hopkins and the Victorian Temper* (London: Routledge & Kegan Paul, 1972), chap. 2, for an excellent analysis of Ruskin's influence on the early stages of Hopkins's career; Sulloway does not, however, study the importance of Ruskin in Hopkins's later development.

[17] Ruskin, *Works*, 5: 205; 4: 75. For a seminal discussion of the pathetic fallacy in critical theory and practice throughout Romantic and Victorian literature, see Josephine Miles, *Pathetic Fallacy in the Nineteenth Century: A Study of a Changing Relation Between Object and Emotion* (1942; rpt. New York: Octagon Books, 1965). Among the more valuable of recent discussions of Ruskin's understanding of pathetic fallacy is George P. Landow's in *The Aesthetic and Critical Theories of John Ruskin* (Princeton, N.J.: Princeton University Press, 1971), pp. 378–86. See also Patricia M. Ball, *The Science of Aspects: The Changing Role of Fact in the Work of Coleridge, Ruskin and Hopkins* (London: Athlone Press, at the University of London, 1971), pp. 59–80.

[18] Ruskin, *Works*, 10: 221; 5: 53–54.

the "highest" of imaginative modes, one which "sees the heart and inner na-
ture . . . of outer detail" and "affirms from within"; the greatest type of artist
is "the man who perceives rightly in spite of his feelings." [19] This foster-
student of a Blakean "visionary realism" also understands the value of Cole-
ridgean receptivity in the act of apprehension: "All the great men *see* what they
paint before they paint it,—see it in a perfectly passive manner." [20] Proper
seeing entails the discipline of self-suppression, the extension of empathy, and
the love of humility without which no Christian art is possible: "the whole
virtue of it depends on his being able to quit his own personality, and enter
successively into the hearts and thoughts of each person; and in all this he is
still passive: in gathering the truth he is passive, not determining what the
truth to be gathered shall be." [21] By contrast, Ruskin associates "pathetic writ-
ing" with morbidity, irrationality, loss of "entire command" of self, pride, and
a "hardness of heart" that aligns its practitioners with the idolatrous who deny
God's authority. [22] Hopkins, as Sulloway has demonstrated at length, accepted
both in theory and in practice the distinctions of his mentor. He virtually
quoted Ruskin as he gently criticized Egyptian and Assyrian art because its
cultural "eye had not been trained to look severely at things apart from their
associations, *innocently* or *purely* as painters say." [23] Like his Oxford essay "On
the Origin of Beauty" (1865), his drawings show Ruskin's fascinated respect
for the interior form of things; he believed with Ruskin that God's plenitude,
as well as His redemptive plan, could only be seen when the perceiver sub-
mitted himself to the precisely accurate analysis of His manifestations; and, in
"The Windhover" (1877), he knew that his speaker's "heart . . . / Stirred for a
bird" exactly because it was, with the Ruskinian passivity and self-control that
foster attentiveness, "in hiding."

The crucial, and tragic, difference between Hopkins as he succumbed to
pathetic fallacy and the egotists upon whom Ruskin heaped his vitriolic scorn
for using pathetic fallacy indifferently and "in cool blood" [24] is this: Hopkins
was miserably conscious of falling prey to a perceptual mode he had constantly
sought to avoid. As he saw his imaginative failure to maintain a pure percep-
tion of the natural world in spite of his troubled disposition, he knew himself a
Christian turned solipsist against his will, knew that his increasing subjec-

[19] Ibid., 4: 228, 253, 251; 5: 209.
[20] W. B. Yeats, "Blake's Illustrations to Dante," in *Essays and Introductions* (New York: Mac-
millan Co., 1961), p. 121; Ruskin, *Works*, 5: 114.
[21] Ruskin, *Works*, 5: 125.
[22] Ibid., 5: 335, 210, 215.
[23] Sulloway, *Hopkins*, p. 67, and chap. 2, passim; see *Journals*, p. 77.
[24] Ruskin, *Works*, 5: 211.

tivity radically compromised the humility he so valued, and understood that
the original solipsist was Satan. The stages of his perceptual decline are clearly
detailed, in method as well as content, in "Spring and Fall" (1880). As with
the simile of the "great stormfowl" in "Henry Purcell" (1879) or the splen-
didly alluring evocation of the "Towery city" in "Duns Scotus's Oxford"
(1879), which is given to illustrate what Scotus himself saw and understood,
the images of nature here have a reduced and subordinate function: once per-
ceived directly for their own worth, they now define aspects of the human
character and imagination. The "grieving" Margaret begins (lines 1–4) with
an innocent freshness of perception in which her cares and affections, spring-
ing from a disinterested Ruskinian empathy rather than from the appropriat-
ing ego, generate a reciprocity of feeling; she understands the mutuality, but
also the distinct separateness, of the deaths in nature and in humankind. But,
as in Wordsworth's "Ode: Intimations of Immortality," "Shades of the prison-
house" will soon enclose her (lines 5–9) as ego-structure develops and an
awareness of the immensities of human sorrow coldly curtails the apparent
wastage of affection upon the nonhuman world. Finally, the speaker speculates
(lines 10–15), Margaret will fall into pathetic fallacy and solipsism, see in the
deaths of nature the "blight" of her own mortality without simultaneously rec-
ognizing the central distinction that nature renews itself in perpetual cycle.
The poem's ultimate solipsism, however, is the speaker's: as its apostrophic
form indicates, the difference between the speaker's voice and the mind of
Margaret is so negligible as to make his own commentary a self-reflection.
Although not without a melancholy self-knowledge in doing so, the speaker
projects upon Margaret the successive stages of his own imaginative decline:
ironically reversing Wordsworth's treatment of his sister in "Tintern Abbey,"
the speaker makes Margaret not a figure of perpetual vitality but the inheritor
of his own world of death. The pathos of "Spring and Fall" derives from his
hapless enactment, poetically, of the same corruption in vision to which he
claims Margaret predestined.[25]

The same intrusion of pathetic fallacy marks the sestet of "Ribblesdale."
Passive, speechless Earth receives its "eye, tongue, or heart" from "dear and
dogged man," and effectually becomes humanized. If such a personification
engendered a praising of God, the speaker's equation would not be disconcert-
ing; but humankind in its egocentric "selfbent," forcing earth to assume an-
thropomorphic form, also compels it to express human sorrow ("this bids

[25] Wendell Stacy Johnson, in *Gerard Manley Hopkins: The Poet as Victorian* (Ithaca, N.Y.: Cornell
University Press, 1968), pp. 117–19, has also noted the relation between this poem and Words-
worth's "Ode: Intimations of Immortality"; but his commentary considers neither the poem's ex-
amination of pathetic fallacy nor the speaker's own solipsism.

wear/Earth brows of such care, care and dear concern"). While the speaker is perturbed by this metamorphosis (it is the chief factor dividing octave from sestet), it is hardly clear that he dissociates himself from such a solipsistic and fallen mode of perception.[26] A similar process occurs in the last lines of "Ash-Boughs": pathetic fallacy, begun by the equation between branches and fingers, continues in the abrupt switch from plural to singular—"then they [the trees] are old Earth"—and the transformation immediately shrouds the entire poem in sad desperation. Ruskin, inconsistently, might well have condoned these passages: "Now so long as we see that the *feeling* is true, we pardon, or are even pleased by, the confessed fallacy of sight which it induces."[27] But Hopkins, whether or not he saw that Ruskin's pre-Romantic appeal to psychological truth and aesthetic pleasure constituted a central flaw in the moral design of his argument, was more scrupulous. He saw himself failing to maintain that disinterested vision in which the eye sees *"innocently* or *purely,"* without extraneous association or projective usurpation. It is no mere coincidence, furthermore, that the signs of pathetic fallacy first appear in Hopkins's poetry at exactly the time when his theology darkened. As the transitional poems attest, his consciousness of the scope and effects of original sin intensified; increasingly he recognized the reflections of that sin—"blight," "selfbent," "old Earth"—in a natural world that, now contaminated, mirrored humankind's wild careening towards doom. Pathetic fallacy as an act of linguistic appropriation was the mirror of human pride; it was thus, in some sense, the disastrous, but logical and morally apt, consequence in poetic method of an ethical understanding that now subsumed all experience to the dogma of final judgment. If the natural world now imaged the state of the human soul, there could be no reciprocal communication between them, only an overshadowing of the one by the other: for interchange had depended, in Hopkins's view, upon the distinct individuality of each participant. As he understood that the natural world, which had embodied divine beauty, was now made ugly by hu-

[26] Mariani, *Commentary*, pp. 183–85, skirts the problem of pathetic fallacy that this poem raises; Geoffrey H. Hartman, in *The Unmediated Vision: An Interpretation of Wordsworth, Hopkins, Rilke, and Valéry* (1954; rpt. New York: Harcourt, Brace & World, 1966), pp. 57–58, rightly observes that "Hopkins has broken with the age-old belief that nature is the language of God," but he places so much emphasis on Earth's pure uninterpreted being that he blinks humankind's misuse of the resultant phenomenological experience. Robert Boyle, in *Metaphor in Hopkins* (Chapel Hill, N.C.: University of North Carolina Press, 1960), pp. 168–70, tacitly acknowledges the pathetic fallacy but discounts it as he pursues his theological reading of the poem: "the earth can frown because she is a mother" (p. 169); "Hopkins builds a rich and complex metaphorical structure which, well founded in physical reality, soars safely to spiritual heights" (p. 170). The foundation in physical reality, however, actually comes from Hopkins's own (prose) description of Ribblesdale (p. 169).

[27] Ruskin, *Works*, 5: 210.

man sin, he could not rashly compartmentalize his moral sense and thus continue to study aesthetically a beauty he knew to be fallen. In Hopkins, for the first time since his youthful (and patently superimposed) reconciliation of sensual delight and asceticism in "The Habit of Perfection" (1866), aesthetic perception and moral vision were now manifestly at odds.

Hopkins cannot but have been appalled to observe the present change from his earlier work. Both *The Wreck of the Deutschland* (stanza 5) and the sestet of "Hurrahing in Harvest" (1877) provide a quick review of the roots of his former perceptual habits in the Wordsworthian and Coleridgean commitment to reciprocity, of which the Ruskinian injunction against pathetic fallacy is an extension:

> I kiss my hand
>   To the stars, lovely-asunder
> Starlight, wafting him [Christ] out of it; and
>   Glow, glory in thunder;
> Kiss my hand to the dappled-with-damson west:
> Since, tho' he is under the world's spendour and wonder,
>   His mystery must be instressed, stressed;
> For I greet him the days I meet him, and bless when I understand.

> These things, these things were here and but the beholder
> Wanting; which two when they once meet,
> The heart rears wings bold and bolder
> And hurls for him [Christ], O half hurls earth for him off under his feet.

These passages are late Victorian and explicitly Christian versions both of Coleridge's admonition in "Dejection: An Ode," "O Lady! we receive but what we give" (line 47) and of his more sustained statement of reciprocity in "This Lime-Tree Bower My Prison":

> Henceforth I shall know
> That Nature ne'er deserts the wise and pure;
> No plot so narrow, be but Nature there,
> No waste so vacant, but may well employ
> Each faculty of sense, and keep the heart
> Awake to Love and Beauty!

> (lines 59–64)

As in Coleridge, the stanza from *The Wreck* moves deliberately from sensory apprehension to the emotional recognition of abstraction, the progression in each case depending upon the speaker's implied metaphysical faith in constant reciprocation by his object of perception.[28] If Hopkins's kiss is a more active gesture than Ruskin's celebration of passive perception would seemingly approve, it is nevertheless, in context, a submission of the loving self to the "lovely-asunder / Starlight"; the body's activity renders the intensity of devout concentration that plays so significant a role in Ruskinian passivity. This act of the "penetrative imagination"—an expiration of breath which imitates God's "arch and original Breath" (stanza 25)—results in the essential seeing of Christ behind His angelic appearances. Notably, the giving of self permits the speaker, in reward, to take on the identity of both light and thunder, the naturalized attributes of his Lord. The speaker's transformation is very nearly his imitative transfiguration, a graced elevation that answers his recognition of Christ's immanence in creation and his internalizing of the "mystery." In the analysis of that experience which closes the stanza, the rhyme of "greet" and "meet" encapsulates the reciprocating energies, divine and human, that intermesh in creating such a moment of mutual recognition.[29] The entire occasion exactly reverses the egocentric possessiveness of vision marred by pathetic fallacy and personification.

Hopkins's conception of "greeting" may recall Coleridge's acts of empathetic imagination in achieving an invisible "meeting" with his friend Lamb in "This Lime-Tree Bower My Prison." But it also has a distinctly Keatsian cast, both in its cordial warmth of feeling and in its delicacy of approach to the phenomenon greeted. Because of Keats's specific interest in creating animate relationships with the nonhuman world, his influence upon Hopkins in this matter may well have been stronger than Coleridge's. Keats had written to Benjamin Bailey (13 March 1818):

Ethereal thing[s] may at least be thus real, divided under three heads—Things real—things semireal—and no things—Things

[28] See Bell Gale Chevigny, "Instress and Devotion in the Poetry of Gerard Manley Hopkins," *Victorian Studies* 9 (1965): 145, who deals with Hopkins's debt to Romantic theories of reciprocity in a somewhat different fashion: as in Coleridge and Wordsworth, "The quest for climactic meetings of energies or wills is for Hopkins a recurrent passion and a major theme in his aspirations." Chevigny also cites Coleridge's "Dejection: An Ode," along with Wordsworth's dictum in "Tintern Abbey" that the world is what the eye and ear "half create, / And what perceive" (pp. 143–44). Chevigny's is one of the very few essays to treat Hopkins's origins in terms of High Romantic rather than early Victorian thought. On the matter of "climactic meetings," however, compare Ball, *The Science of Aspects*, p. 105.

[29] See Sulloway, *Hopkins*: "In a single stanza Hopkins has moved from particular objects of praise—stars, clouds—to the principles of creation behind them, and then to a frank acknowledgment of *his* duty and joy as an artist . . ." (p. 79).

real—such as existences of Sun Moon & Stars and passages of
Shakspeare—Things semireal such as Love, the Clouds &c which
require a greeting of the Spirit to make them wholly exist—and
Nothings which are made Great and dignified by an ardent pur-
suit—[30]

The tact in that "greeting of the Spirit"—as opposed to the more strenuous
imaginative "ardour" required to make "Nothings" substantial—emerges
clearly in "Hurrahing in Harvest." The ability to realize the theophany within
"things," to "greet" the semireal or vaguely apprehended truth and thus make
it manifest, is predicated on a Keatsian act of recognition and a Ruskinian
empathy of perception; for the phenomena of nature will always offer encour-
agement to "keep the heart / Awake to Love and Beauty." "Semireal" "silk-sack
clouds"—as in Keats's image—assume their true identity when their shapes
are seen to be analogous to those of the "azurous hung hills" which are Christ's
"shoulder." The perceiver, significantly, is named "the beholder," a term con-
noting not only perception but the disposition to humble awe. And properly
so: Hopkins's analogy for what the perceiver beholds, in the second quatrain,
is the taking of Communion; it indicates both the divine gift which the cre-
ated world is, as the object of human sight, and the act of purifying obedience
that perception entails. The subject *sees*, as Ruskin says, the object, and with-
out any distortion consequent upon pathetic fallacy. The result of such recep-
tivity is a recognition of Christ's Incarnation in things. Subject and object
"meet": they do not fuse, but enter into a dynamic amalgamation in which
both assume their truest identities. As the object is animated, the perceiver
virtually affirms its identity "from within" (to use Ruskin's phrase) and, in so
doing, shares his own nature with it: the whole experience of reciprocity, while
remaining earthly, is suffused with mystical excitation.

Hopkins understood that the presence of pathetic fallacy in his work meant
that he had lost his sacramental vision of the world. In "To what Serves Mortal
Beauty," he attempted to recover the elation that his earlier representations of
ecstasy had conferred by repeating his old vocabulary: "Merely *meet*" beauty, he
urged himself. But by that time he was disillusioned enough to follow that
injunction with another: "then leave, let that alone." Nor did his loss seem
reversible. Coleridge, who understood—sometimes inconsistently—the dan-
gers as well as the affective *largesse* of pathetic fallacy, had warned in "The
Nightingale" against the breakdown in proper modes of perception, and thus
in the proper conceiving of the world, that pathetic fallacy entailed:

[30] John Keats, *The Letters of John Keats*, ed. Hyder Edward Rollins, 2 vols. (Cambridge, Mass.:
Harvard University Press, 1958), 1: 242–43.

And hark! the Nightingale begins its song,
'Most musical, most melancholy' bird!
A melancholy bird? Oh! idle thought!
In Nature there is nothing melancholy.
But some night-wandering man whose heart was pierced
With the remembrance of a grievous wrong,
Or slow distemper, or neglected love,
(And so, poor wretch! filled all things with himself,
And made all gentle sounds tell back the tale
Of his own sorrow) he, and such as he,
First named these notes a melancholy strain.[31]

(lines 12–22)

Browning had reiterated Coleridge's caution of "distemper," madness, and a self-negating egotism. In "Porphyria's Lover" he had shown, through the speaker's self-reflexive evocation of the tumultuous opening landscape, that the solipsism in such a pathetic fallacy—here rendering a self-exculpation from crime—was a characteristic of his monologist's insanity. But Hopkins's subsequent career reveals how little power he actually had to heed these familiar admonitions and thus halt an imaginative process he considered corrupt. The claustrophobic self-enclosure of the "terrible sonnets" is the extension of a world permeated, in the transitional poems, by pathetic fallacy. The ironic puns on "see" and "saw" in "I Wake and Feel" measure the blockage of outward sight, the lost possibility of taking Communion through perception. In the externally soundless world of "Patience," as in Coleridge's "Frost at Midnight," the presumed possibility of verbal reciprocation between self and nature ends: "We hear our hearts grate on themselves," much as Coleridge's speaker finds nothing but "Echo or mirror" of himself.

Hopkins's failure to remain a poet who, as Ruskin demanded, "perceives

[31] See also Coleridge's attack on personification—to which pathetic fallacy is commonly subsumed by rhetoricians—as "part of an exploded mythology" (Samuel Taylor Coleridge, *Biographia Literaria*, ed J. Shawcross, 2 vols [1907; rpt. London: Oxford University Press, 1973], 2: 58). His "Work Without Hope," upon which Hopkins modeled his late "Thou Art Indeed Just," points the dangers of projective animation precisely: the speaker regards himself as less alive than the personified tropes of Winter and Spring he envisages. Significantly, however, Coleridge, in his note to the passage from "The Nightingale" cited above, retreated from criticizing Milton's phrase directly: "This passage in Milton possesses an excellence far superior to that of mere description; it is spoken in the character of the melancholy Man, and has therefore a *dramatic* propriety" (Samuel Taylor Coleridge, *Poetical Works*, ed. Ernest Hartley Coleridge [1912; rpt. London: Oxford University Press, 1969], p. 262, n. 2; Coleridge's italics). Coleridge's retreat would have been readily understood by readers of Priestley, Beattie, Blair, and other commentators on personification. His opposition to pathetic fallacy thus coexists—yet seemingly without conflict—with a contrary principle, enunciated in "On Poesy or Art": "[Art] is, therefore, the power of humanizing nature,

rightly in spite of his feelings" illustrates the difficulties attending Victorian efforts to escape the element of subjectivizing egotism in the Romantic sublime. Simultaneously, his dilemma dovetails precisely with his spiritual crisis as a Catholic. Whatever fragmentations in his perception of a coherent universe may have been induced by anxieties of temperament, it is doubtful that Hopkins, who had possessed so firm a sense of the concrete autonomy of natural phenomena, could ever have succumbed to pathetic fallacy unless he had felt a vacuum in external reality, an emptiness where there had previously been fullness and objectively defined shape. As Coleridge indicates in calling "neglected love" one of the motives for pathetic fallacy ("The Nightingale"), pathetic fallacy—the urge to "[fill] all things with [oneself]"—is not always occasioned by mere pride; it is also a compensatory psychological strategy designed to fill, by inflating the self, a void produced by the intuition of an unresponding world.

The vacuum Hopkins intuited was created by his dread recognition that Christ had departed the mundane world. Leaving the world to be reshaped in licentious metamorphosis according to human will, a prospect most frightening to Hopkins, the withdrawal of the divine Breath rendered creation deflated, without structure. The only sign of air in the "terrible sonnets"—elemental counterpart to God's "arch and original Breath"—is the tempest of "Carrion Comfort." Hopkins's frequent invocations of air, breath, the movement of clouds—in earlier poems such as "The Starlight Night" (1877), "The Sea and the Skylark," and "Andromeda" (1879)—have vanished. Equivalents of Wordsworth's "correspondent breeze"—the emblem of reciprocity that opens *The Prelude*—do not appear. "The fact," as St. Ignatius put it, "of God's being in every creature by essence, presence and power" [32] was no longer an emotional reality to Hopkins, though he sturdily maintained it in principle. His devastating grief of loss is unmistakable:

> Comforter, where, where is your comforting?
>
> ["No Worst"]

> And my lament
> Is cries countless, cries like dead letters sent
> To dearest him [Christ] that lives alas! away.
>
> ["I Wake and Feel"]

---

of infusing the thoughts and passions of man into every thing which is the object of his contemplation" (Coleridge, *Biographia Literaria*, 2:253).

[32] St. Ignatius Loyola, *The Spiritual Exercises*, trans. Thomas Corbishley (Westminster, Md.: Christian Classics, 1973), p. 27.

Christ's disappearance is the inescapable theological and poetic foundation of the "terrible sonnets." The most shocking aspect of the dual crisis, perhaps, is that Hopkins's sense of Christ's vanishing should have affected his poetry as much as it did, not only in the kind of images chosen, but in the kind of perception through which they were rendered. His perceptual habits, his techniques of analyzing phenomena, could not survive the loss of the metaphysic upon which they were ostensibly founded. Yet one remembers that those very modes of naturalistic observation had been fixed and well-developed for years —as the *Journal* entries between, say, 1864 and 1871 make plain[33]—before Hopkins subsumed them to a Christian theology specifically focussed on the Incarnation. Hopkins's crisis, that is, shows simultaneously the tremendous urgency of the need he felt in the early 1870s to give his delight in empirical observation a systematic, transcendental basis, and the substantial risks he took in doing so, as the aftermath of that effort in the "terrible sonnets" testifies. When he made his habits of perception depend upon a supernatural validation, he made them vulnerable, subject to damage *if* the metaphysic itself underwent stress. What Hopkins did not perhaps sufficiently realize was that, insofar as the metaphysic depended upon his continued exercise of the penetrative imagination in discovering Christ within things, his Incarnationist theology was in thrall to his temperament. As the world increasingly became God's book, its leaves lost something of their own existential character and became indices of God's hovering authorial Presence between the lines. For years the dangers in this double trade-off were not noticeable; indeed, it generated Hopkins's most jubilant and symbolically abundant poetry. But when God absconded, He not only blanked the leaves, giving Hopkins nothing to read; He took away as well both Hopkins's perceptual modes and his justification for seeing.

Hopkins's sense of Christ's absence, like his unwilling movement into "pathetic writing," is closely connected to his apocalyptic vision; on so delicate an issue, one hesitates to stipulate a precise causation. If nature were no longer a proleptic emblem of the redemption to come, but rather an image of human sin, the divinity that had previously informed its structure must have disappeared; as time and natural phenomena lost their sacred character, Hopkins's saving knowledge of Christ's indwelling in imperfect creation suffered great

---

[33] Not until 18 May 1870 did Hopkins specifically link his passion for inscaping with the recognition of Divine design in nature (*Journals*, p. 199); not until the summer of 1872, when he was reading Scotus, did he begin explicitly to see Christ immanent in all things (*Journals*, p. 221). For the secular and philosophical origins of Hopkins's conceptions, see Thomas A. Zaniello, "The Sources of Hopkins' Inscape: Epistemology at Oxford, 1864–1868," *Victorian Newsletter* 52 (1977): 18–24.

damage. Hopkins understood that the doctrines of immanence and of apocalypse were mutually exclusive; he could not simultaneously maintain them both. Belief in the first precluded the second, since it presumed the temporal world to be already infused with divinity; faith in the Apocalypse insisted that the desired immanence of the Holy Spirit was still distant, unachieved, and earth still wracked by corruption. Although the apocalyptic strain in Victorian culture had contributed much to his education, and although *The Wreck* represents a "complete Apocalypse,"[34] it was not until the 1880s that Hopkins's profound need for an apocalyptic resolution—a need which no literary fiction could gratify—began to dominate his work. Even in patently nonapocalyptic poems such as "Duns Scotus's Oxford," "Henry Purcell," and "To What Serves Mortal Beauty," the pronounced historicity of their imaginative form demonstrates Hopkins's new involvement in extended human time rather than in the sacred and eternal present. In these poems, notably, the celebration of a glorious past implies the destitution of the present: in "To What Serves Mortal Beauty," the conversion of England to Catholicism under Gregory the Great in 597 is an event that has yet, as *The Wreck* indicates, to happen again. Under the pressure of contemporary complexities in politics and religious history, Hopkins saw that an eschatology of final salvation was necessary; but in the process of accepting a linear model for Christian history, he was uncomfortably forced to revise the ontology upon which he had founded his earlier work: his keen sense of Christ's loss in the "terrible sonnets" measures the pain he experienced in sacrificing his immanental vision. The shift in his perspective is poignantly marked in "To Seem the Stranger" by the two definitions of Christ given in juxtaposition: "And he my peace / my parting, sword and strife." Mourning his lost vision, he nevertheless craved the conversion to Catholicism of both England and his family; these events he did not think possible without Christ's cataclysmic Second Coming. His situation in Ireland seemed to prefigure the final days: the Irish Catholic hierarchy, violently debating the Land Wars, Parnell, and Irish home rule, had become divided against itself; the third of these issues nearly resulted in schism from Rome; Hopkins himself was an Englishman in Ireland who was, thus, necessarily working against his deepest patriotic and imperialist instincts; and, in an exhibition of terrible self-contradiction, the instincts of this ex-Anglican Catholic priest were aligned with those of English Protestant culture.[35] His perturbations and ambivalences seemed so hopelessly complicated that only the Apocalypse might resolve them.

---

[34] Sulloway, *Hopkins*, p. 159; Sulloway's speculation (p. 169) that Hopkins joined the Jesuit order "partly because it offered him so legitimate a pulpit for his own apocalyptic sermons," however, dates prematurely the emergence of his apocalyptic vision.

[35] See Pick, *Hopkins*, pp. 113–14; Elisabeth W. Schneider, *The Dragon in the Gate: Studies in the*

Hopkins's active dedication to Christ's Second Coming might have adequately counterbalanced his loss of Christ's immanental presence had he been certain that the apocalyptic end he so much desired would come. But his apocalyptic writings during the period of the "terrible sonnets" show how gravely he doubted that imminent fulfillment of dogmatic belief. Even in "The Soldier" (1885), a poem which seemingly promises that final *parousia*, Christ speaks of His own Second Coming in a strangely hypothetical subjunctive mode, one which actually calls into question His supposed intention to return in judgment:

> Mark Christ our King. He knows war, served this soldiering through;
> He of all can reeve a rope best. There he bides in bliss
> Now, and séeing somewhére some mán do all that man can do,
> For love he leans forth, needs his neck must fall on, kiss,
> And cry 'O Christ-done deed! So God-made-flesh does too:
> *Were* I come o'er again' cries Christ 'it should be this'. [italics mine]

The Herbertian wit lacks assurance: Christ lovingly observes the human world, but merely speculates about assuming human form again. In "Patience," He remains equally elusive:

> And where is he who more and more distills
> Delicious kindness?—He is patient. Patience fills
> His crisp combs, and that comes those ways we know.

The speaker's answer to his own question, however much it appears to accept the grim period of trial prior to the Last Judgment, in fact evades his central concern: his definition of Christ's attribute is hardly a definition of His location, much less an assertion of His imminent return. The poem conceals not only Hopkins's difficulty in tolerating the experience of a Lord no longer visible in His created signs, but his anxiety in waiting for apocalypse.[36] So also "St. Alphonsus Rodriguez" (1888), an occasional poem whose highly nuanced language hints (through an allusion to John 10:9) at the Second Coming:

> there went
> Those years and years by of world without event
> That in Majorca Alfonso watched the door.

Poetry of G. M. Hopkins (Berkeley and Los Angeles: University of California Press, 1968), pp. 188–89. Hopkins's strong sense of the Englishness of the Catholic Church—a common extension from Anglo-Catholic polemics concerning the Apostolical Succession—derived (among many other sources) from Newman; see, e.g., John Henry Cardinal Newman, *Apologia Pro Vita Sua*, ed. Martin J. Svaglic (Oxford: Clarendon Press, 1967), pp. 240–41.

[36] Compare James Finn Cotter, *Inscape: The Christology and Poetry of Gerard Manley Hopkins*

Patience and duty may join here, but the closure is also touched by the empti-
ness of unfulfilled anticipation. The unsettling discrepancy between the mis-
givings latent in these poems and the extremity of Hopkins's desire is quickly
illustrated by comparing them with his blunt, breathless prayer of 1884:
"Wish to crown him King of England, of English hearts and of Ireland and all
Christendom and all the world" (*Sermons*, p. 255). Here Hopkins repeats, but
with far greater desperation, the same cry he had jubilantly uttered at the end
of *The Wreck*. In "That Nature Is a Heraclitean Fire" the need for apocalypse is
so pressing that the speaker, without preparation, simply asserts its sudden
happening: "*In a flash*, at a trumpet crash, / I am *all at once* what Christ is"
(italics mine). The extreme leap to faith from the earlier nihilism, sprung from
the speaker's sheer will to believe the world's transformation possible, has been
criticized as being poetically unsound: "The second part of the poem is more
an assertion of belief in traditional Christian eschatology than a recognition of
Christ within nature and human history. . . . The two halves of the poem do
not mesh; the comfort of the Resurrection does not grow organically out of
nature but is magically substituted for it." [37] Whether or not one accepts this
view, the poem surely shows an insurmountable antithesis between the realms
of nature and of grace. The resounding affirmations of the last eight lines func-
tion to banish entirely—not to integrate into a transformed vision—the
world of corruption where "vastness blurs and time ' beats level" all signs of
humankind. The hortatory subjunctive in "Flesh fade, and mortal trash /
Fall to the residuary worm; ' world's wildfire, leave but ash" encapsulates the
urgency of his desire. And the speaker, whose metamorphosis into "immortal
diamond" *will not* occur until the Apocalypse ("at a trumpet crash"), speaks as
if that great change were now happening. As Hopkins's demand for apocalypse
during these years intensified, his awareness both of earth's unregenerate emp-
tiness and of God's apparent refusal to fill that void was heightened; each expe-
rience of the divine silence, in circular fashion, produced a renewal of the plea
and an exacerbation of his frustration. Although Hopkins sought his own spir-
itual crucifixion, perhaps partly as a propitiatory magical act to hasten the de-
sired end"—"I saw how my asking to be raised to a higher degree of grace was
asking also to be lifted on a higher cross" (*Sermons*, p. 254), he knew that his
imitative sacrifice could not substitute for the historical realization of Chris-
tian eschatology. Having felt his world emptied of sacramental value, and hav-

---

(Pittsburgh, Pa.: University of Pittsburgh Press, 1972), pp. 266–67, who applies a "gnostic
reading" to the verb "know" and thus asserts the speaker's certitude of Christ's presence.

    [37] Fulweiler, *Letters from the Darkling Plain*, p. 161. Compare, e.g., Mariani, *Commentary*,
p. 289.

ing committed himself to an apocalyptic view of redemption, he was now confronted with an apocalypse that seemed not to happen.

Hopkins's altered conception of Christian history profoundly affected his entire procedure in the making of images; the evident connection between his use of pathetic fallacy and his consciousness of Christ's absence provides only one indication of the far-ranging ramifications that alteration entailed. In linguistic as well as eschatological terms, Hopkins's stress upon the Apocalypse left him waiting for the institution of a future relation between finite and infinite; it virtually cancelled his previous focus on the essential relation that the Incarnation, as incorporation of the Word, had established; it abrogated the original equation between Christ and His creation. That original equation, the theological form of what is loosely called metaphor, had been the earlier foundation of Hopkins's poetics; as such, it requires further elaboration, so that the dimensions of Christ's absence in the "terrible sonnets" can be clearly seen.

For Hopkins in his previous work, "the incredible condescension of the Incarnation"[38] enacts the principle of relation itself. By virtue of His assumption of a natural body, Christ elevates the natural and human realms to their true status as analogues of the divine. The world is His emanation; and He, its ultimate model or pattern. Immanent in all phenomena, which are thereby redeemed by His presence, He vouchsafes the specific and inimitable identity of each thing. Its *haeccitas* or "this-ness," to employ Scotus's concept, is its special uniqueness, created by God in His plenitude of imagination, through Christ, to differentiate it from all else. Christ is consequently the sole element that all things have in common, however various their particular inscapes or interior realities may be. As such, He makes possible the business of imaginative connection—through analogy, metaphor, simile—which is the poet's craft: "*under* the world's splendour and wonder" (*The Wreck*, stanza 5), He *is* the similitude between apparently disparate and unlike things—as Hopkins's approximate rhyme also shows.

Hopkins had interpreted Christ's Incarnation in things with a visionary literalism, and his empiricism was grounded in extreme faith. When he wrote, in a passage now famous, "I do not think I have ever seen anything more beautiful than the bluebell I have been looking at. I know the beauty of our Lord by it" (*Journals*, p. 199), he did not simply mean that the natural world was a means of intuiting the divine; nor did he construe the bluebell as an emblem of the infinite. Hopkins saw Christ *in* the flower; as Cotter observes, his "ac-

[38] Gerard Manley Hopkins, *Further Letters of Gerard Manley Hopkins*, ed. Claude Colleer Abbott, rev. ed. (London: Oxford University Press, 1956), p. 19.

companying sketch shows an Omega-shaped flower."[39] The flower's special inscape was not merely its Christ-given identity in its natural aspect but its actual participation in Christ's substance; it was not only the symbol of Christ's presence that, when realized, could be forgotten or disregarded but the symbolized presence itself.[40] Part of the exceptional rigor in Hopkins's neo-Romanticism is that, even beyond Keble's application of Biblical typology to the natural world in Tract 89, he transferred to the phenomena of nature the Tractarian doctrine of the Real Presence, the theological concept that the bread and wine of the Eucharist are not emblems or commemorations of Christ, but rather His mystical, and mystically real, substance; as Robert Wilberforce maintained in 1853, the doctrine posits neither the transubstantiation of the eucharistic elements into the divine Person, nor their consubstantial interrelation with Him, but rather a *"sacramental identity,"* a sameness, of the mystical Presence and the material objects.[41] The bread and wine *are* what they represent, by virtue of Christ's ghostly indwelling. To Hopkins, further, the bread and wine are also synecdoches of the natural world in the sense that Christ, celebrating the Incarnation of Himself in matter just prior to His Crucifixion, asserts the universality of His spiritual presence throughout creation. For this reason, as Peters has demonstrated, much of Hopkins's perceptual effort involves "impersonation," the imaginative recognizing, through intense concentration, of the person within the object yet not bound to it, a Person finally seen as Christ.[42] Between the theological vision of "impersonation" and the

[39] Cotter, *Inscape*, p. 290.

[40] See Leonard J. Bowman, "Bonaventure and the Poetry of Gerard Manley Hopkins," in *Jacques Guy Bougerol, ed., S. Bonaventura* (Rome: Collegio S. Bonaventura, Grottaferrata, 1974), p. 560, who uses St. Bonaventura's doctrine of nature as divine *vestige* (not mere symbol) to elucidate Hopkins's theological respect for natural things. Bowman's objection to Christopher Devlin's interpretation of Hopkins's Scotism is apt: "The concrete thing in its uniqueness would therefore [according to Devlin] be quite dispensable" after it had fulfilled its symbolizing function, "and that is something quite foreign to Hopkins' style" (p. 556).

[41] John Keble, "On the Mysticism Attributed to the Early Fathers of the Church," in *Tracts for the Times*, 6 vols. (Oxford: Parker; Rivington, 1841), 6: 162–86; Robert Isaac Wilberforce, *The Doctrine of the Holy Eucharist* (London: J. & C. Mozley; Oxford: Parker, 1853), p. 116. For the central role of this doctrine in the Oxford Movement, see Alf Härdelin, *The Tractarian Understanding of the Eucharist*, Studia Historico-Ecclesiastica Upsaliensis, 8 (Uppsala: Almqvist & Wiksells, 1965), esp. pp. 123–219; W[illiam] H[erbert] Mackean, *The Eucharistic Doctrine of the Oxford Movement: A Critical Survey* (London and New York: Putnam, 1933), esp. pp. 55–104; Yngve Brilioth, *The Anglican Revival: Studies in the Oxford Movement* (1925; rpt. London: Longmans, 1933), pp. 315, 317; Marvin R. O'Connell, *The Oxford Conspirators: A History of the Oxford Movement, 1833–1845* (London: Macmillan & Co., 1969), pp. 327, 342, 356, 382, 384–85; Miller, *The Disappearance of God.*, p. 312.

[42] For a fine exposition of Hopkins's practice of "impersonation," see Wilhelmus Antonius Maria Peters, *Gerard Manley Hopkins: A Critical Essay towards the Understanding of his Poetry* (London: Oxford University Press, 1947), pp. 7–13.

rhetorical trope of personification lies as apparent hairsbreadth that is really an abyss. The former is an empathetic acknowledgment of what actually is, an act in which the bluebell and Christ are perceived as being distinct yet the same; the copula between them is assumed by a metaphysic that eschews symbolism and metaphor. The latter is the parent of pathetic fallacy: to personify is to meddle with creation by transubstantiating it into a human—not divine—image; the implied copula (e.g., branches = fingers ["Ash-Boughs"]) is an act of appropriation instigated by the perceiver. Given the concreteness with which Hopkins saw Christ in things, it is hardly surprising that he should so assiduously have avoided using pathetic fallacy; for his constant aim in studying particular inscapes was to achieve a simultaneous comprehension of their natural *and* sacramental character, not an image of his own, or human, selfhood.

Christ's presence validated Hopkins's exercise of the "penetrative imagination," indeed made it the indispensable foundation of all other imaginative modes. Hopkins could dwell with prolonged and microscopic precision upon an object—"the very plain and leafy fact of it," as Ruskin says[43]—without fearing that his very concentration might distort its nature, because he knew that Christ objectively informed its structure. He was certain, moreover, that he could isolate and dissect phenomena, and understand their distinctiveness and utter uniqueness, without fearing that his analysis would ultimately condemn him to a void of atomistic perception in which, as Coleridge knew at the beginning of "Frost at Midnight," nothing was connected with anything else. Indeed, it was only by isolating particulars that connection and similitude could paradoxically be discovered; penetration of an object was necessary not only to perceive its analogous relation to the divine but to realize that Christ's Incarnation in the object also made it analogous to other phenomena, similarly understood. For Hopkins, as for Ruskin, Christ as the principle of relation allayed the submerged Victorian terror of a world so diverse and multitudinous in its particularity that no order could be discerned: "All the world is full of inscape and chance left free to act falls into an order as well as purpose" (*Journals*, p. 230); "the earth," Ruskin affirmed, "is full of splendour when God's hand gathers its atoms."[44] Thus, in "The Windhover," Hopkins could arrange in a mirroring alignment of curves the flight of the windhover, the sweep of the skate's heel, and the shape of the plough; the paralleling of these visible forms—which, in turn, suggest the elements of air, water, and earth—is made possible by the celestial fire that illuminates them all.

[43] Ruskin, *Works*, 5: 209.
[44] Ruskin, *Works*, 11: 41–42. See Carol T. Christ, *The Finer Optic: The Aesthetic of Particularity in Victorian Poetry* (New Haven, Conn.: Yale University Press, 1975) for a survey of the problem of discovering principles of order in diversity.

Hopkins's ebullient delight in discovering such systematic order in diversity is nowhere so clear as in "Pied Beauty" (1877). Here, the doubling and tripling patterns of phrasing in this miniature encyclopaedia of things climax in a quaternity ("All things counter, original, spare, strange") which also governs a multiplicity that would otherwise be mere flux. The poem then returns to triplings and doublings: the entirety is contained by initial and closing assertions of God's prevailing design. Beneath the pied unlikeness and extreme individuation of things, there lies a unifying principle of similitude, intimated not only by various parallelisms but by alliteration: "couple-colour," "swift, slow; sweet, sour; adazzle, dim." Analogy and pun also confirm the relatedness of phenomena: *this* poem, as a curtal or abbreviated sonnet, mirrors the proportions of a standard sonnet; the "Landscape plotted and pieced" by the farmer is also planned and organized by God. These poems give instances of Ruskin's "chordal variety"[45] pushed to the point at which the very displaying of analogy, as much as the significance of any specific analogy, becomes the primary meaning of the image or poem. In writing of "skies of couple-colour as a brinded cow," Hopkins plainly took an enormous pleasure in demonstrating that the most outrageously dissimilar phenomena were in literal fact linked; and both his pleasure and his method derived from the original equation which he understood the Incarnation to be.[46]

Hopkins's conception of Christ as the principle of relation is evident in more than his imagistic manipulation of natural things perceived as isolated phenomena. It affected as well his signal ability—damaged when he adopted a linear model for Christian history—to figure forth the stilled eternity that each transient moment, by virtue of the Incarnation, embodied. This Hopkins accomplished through the representation of simultaneous occasions: by analogy, mundane events rendered those in the Christian pattern; a finite occurrence could itself be seen to encompass, simultaneously, the chief points of demarcation in the Christian design and thus gain, through this cancellation of duration, an eternal character. Thus, in "Spring" (1877), the octave unwinds an exuberant but wholly secular vision of natural fecundity and dynamic activity that becomes, as the sestet compels reinterpretation, a version not only of "Eden garden" but of the Christian universe. The suppression of

---

[45] Ruskin, *Works*, 4: 96. The first intensive treatment of Hopkins's use of analogy was given by Herbert Marshall McLuhan, "The Analogical Mirrors," in [Cleanth Brooks, ed.,] The Kenyon Critics, *Gerard Manley Hopkins* (Norfolk, Conn.: New Directions, 1945), pp. 15–27.

[46] Compare Miller, *The Disappearance of God*, p. 299, who claims that the mundane world "lives in dynamic change" and action; but Hopkins has carefully suppressed the verbs in his description by transforming them into participles, and has reserved to God alone the power of full and continuing action: "He fathers-forth whose beauty is past change."

the simile in "Thrush's eggs look [like] little low heavens" stresses the radical equation; blue is Mary's color; the thrush itself traditionally prefigures the Crucifixion; the "echoing timber," in a punning taken from the "seasoned timber" of Herbert's "Virtue," is the Cross; the reciprocal greetings between earth and sky, rendered in natural movements, are the mundane correlatives both of the Incarnation and the Crucifixion: the "glassy peartree" suggests the perfect crystalline transparency of the New Jerusalem (Revelation 21 : 18). Remarkably, this typological transfiguration in the spiritual status and import of the scene does not seem superimposed by the poet upon his material. It emanates, instead, from the assumption that an analogy between finite and eternal is intrinsic to the particularities of the landscape itself; and that assumption governs, in turn, an exactitude of perception and phrasing that prepares with great tact for the sestet's revelation of true significance.

A comparable creation of simultaneities through the representation of the sacramental within the natural occurs in the octave of "As Kingfishers Catch Fire" (1877).[47] Here, the sacramental image that unifies the discrete identities of worldly phenomena is a church, subliminally suggested by the "hung bell" in its steeple and by the baptismal "roundy wells." The highly wrought parallelisms of the opening line combine, through a series of elaborate typological puns, the representation both of Satan's fall and of his final defeat at Armageddon; simultaneously embodying the Church militant and triumphant, Christ (the chief or "king" fisher) wars in fiery celestial raiment against the fleeing dragon whose sin "draws" divine wrath. Thus, a moment's quick meditation on the relation between mundane phenomena shows not merely the veiled suggestion but the direct enactment of the entire circle of Christian time. The analogical visions upon which both this poem and "Spring" are founded clearly derive from Hopkins's Scotist conception of the function of grace in the process of individuation: "For grace is any action, activity, on God's part by which, in creating or after creating, he carries the creature to or towards the end of its being, which is its selfsacrifice to God and its salvation" (*Sermons*, p. 154). As the "echoing timber" and the dragonfly become visible as Cross and Antichrist, each completes its teleology by assuming, without loss of phenomenological identity, its proper status in Christian iconography; achieving its true function as index of the total divine plan, it serves that design as it be-

---

[47] In Hopkins, *Poems*, 4th ed., pp. 280–81, Gardner and MacKenzie note that Hopkins's autograph is not dated. But MacKenzie has subsequently given 1877 as the poem's date, on the basis of handwriting analysis. See Norman H. MacKenzie, "Hopkins, Robert Bridges and the Modern Editor," in Eric W. Domville, ed., *Editing British and American Literature, 1880–1920* (New York: Garland, 1976), p. 29.

comes its most radical self, "Acts in God's eye what in God's eye [it] is." In Hopkins's aesthetic, this revelation of an object's teleology, through the "penetrative imagination," is the poet's primary business. The subsequent assertion of analogical relations does not involve the poet's superimposition of ciphers upon the things of nature: because of Christ's immanence, the relation preexists the making of a poem; it is objectively "there," in nature, to be discovered by the poet. As no more than God's humble scribe, the poet's task and moral responsibility then becomes the revelation of that truth to his audience.

Thus, construed theologically, metaphor does not exist in Hopkins's poetics prior to the "terrible sonnets." As a rhetorical trope, it of course flourishes; but a solely rhetorical analysis of a Hopkins metaphor will bypass its ultimate import, which is grounded in the dogma of the Incarnation. Hopkins's view of the Incarnation permits no comparison of terms, no transformation of one term into the other; it insists that both terms—God and man—are absolutely and simultaneously real, and that the copula between them is a literal metaphysical truth. The chief difficulty in Boyle's otherwise valuable consideration of Hopkins's metaphors is that it denies the reality of the second term: "I hold," he writes of metaphoric procedure, "that one real being is fused with a nature which is a concept and not a real being. . . . if metaphor is to be possible at all, the predicate noun must have no real existence of its own."[48] Whatever the linguistic and philosophic truth of such a view generally, it does not apply to Hopkins, for it contravenes his understanding of the Incarnation. It overlooks, too, Hopkins's purpose in metaphor: he uses metaphor rhetorically in order to negate its validity from a dogmatic perspective. Theologically, his equations express immanence: they show the identicality of Christ and humankind, Christ and the natural world. The poet does not "make" metaphors; he *sees* the dual identity of each thing as a reality already accomplished. As Brooke-Rose has said, summarizing much grammatical argument, Hopkins's "metaphoric changes are . . . either assumed as already changed and obvious . . . or breathlessly asserted by way of explanation, as it were apologetically and taken for granted."[49] The *"azurous hung hills"* in "Hurrahing in Harvest" do not constitute a rhetorical figure for Christ's "world-wielding shoulder / Majestic" but rather Christ's shoulder itself: through pun, the lateral protru-

---

[48] Boyle, *Metaphor in Hopkins*, pp. 180, 182. Nor does Miller's otherwise instructive account of "rhyme" and "chiming" in Hopkins take into account Hopkins's theological aversion to metaphor, as that term is commonly used; neither does it distinguish between metaphor and analogy (see especially *The Disappearance of God*, pp. 296–97, 313).

[49] Christine Brooke-Rose, *A Grammar of Metaphor* (1958; rpt. London: Secker and Warburg, 1965), p. 314.

sion of the hill (its "shoulder") is claimed to be identical with the anatomical "shoulder" of Hopkins's Lord. Tenor and vehicle are the same, and the effort of the poetry generally is constantly to gain a literal realization of such images of identity (as with "Thrush's eggs look little low heavens"). The final inscape of an object, its teleological fulfillment or "end of its being," is its identity with the body of Christ, a state in which the reliance upon metaphoric assertions of likeness becomes superfluous and thus dissolves. The achievement of that identicality is not a transformation of its nature but rather a transfiguration or revelation of itself, its *haeccitas*. Through Christ's grace, as Hopkins wrote in a passage that serves as a gloss to "As Kingfishers Catch Fire," "It is as if a man said: That is Christ playing at me and me playing at Christ, only that is no play but truth: That is Christ *being me* and me being Christ" (*Sermons*, p. 154; Hopkins's italics). The passage denies dramatic illusion and the mere fiction of seeming relation. Implicitly it rejects metaphor and simile; it ends in an image of equated identity—reciprocal Incarnation—in which each figure in the mutual personation remains distinct. Observe the difference here from common metaphoric procedure, which is predicated on the principle of altered identity, not its retention. Typically, *x* seemingly becomes *y* either through an imaginative conversion of its substance or through the establishment of a metonymic link, which then expands to imply a total transformation; in some cases, these alterations depend not upon a verifiable perception of likeness but upon nothing more than a metamorphosis in the poet's vision. Yeats's line "My wall is loosening" in "Meditations in Time of Civil War" (VI) is a good example of such a metaphor: in context, the crumbling wall of the speaker's tower becomes indistinguishable from his fleshly form. Eliot's feline "yellow fog that rubs its back upon the window-panes" ("The Love Song of J. Alfred Prufrock") or Yeats's "May she become a flourishing hidden tree" ("A Prayer for My Daughter") provides another obvious instance; so, also, does Donne's simultaneous transformation of himself into citadel and virgin in Holy Sonnet XIV or Marvell's extravagant fusion of brain and architecture at the outset of "Upon Appleton House." Hopkins abhorred this kind of transaction between terms. It involves an irreverent transformation of the created world that God has made out of Himself; it blurs the distinctions between things by which the *haecitas* of each is known and thus by which the true relation amongst things is perceived; and, finally, because such a practice of conversion recognizes no ultimate ontology and implies a merely fluid universe, it entails a metaphoric falsification of "the things that are" ("To What Serves Mortal Beauty") and thus denies both Christ's presence in them and the epistemological means of knowing Him through His vestiges. The evolutionary gradations of metaphor in "That Nature Is a Heraclitean Fire" by which the speaker climbs to his own Transfiguration are entirely atypical of Hopkins's work before the "terrible sonnets":

> This Jack, joke, poor potsherd,' patch, matchwood, immortal
>   diamond,
>   Is immortal diamond.

The passage, although it ends in the speaker's discovery of his identity in Christ's, does so only through irony. If it is true that the final equation ($x = x$, not $x = y$) denies the validity of metaphor and is thus consistent with Hopkins's earlier position, it is equally true that the reality of this copula is called into doubt because the effort to launch it has required so many intermediary steps. What is achieved here, with great bravura, is less a statement of identicality than an affirmation of possibility. The passage shows a transcendent Christ who *was* but *is not* immanent in the lower portions of the metamorphic spectrum; His absence is thus, ironically, the precondition for metaphoric transformations. For Hopkins generally, as for Ruskin, metaphor constituted the first irretrievable step towards the derangements of pathetic fallacy; and while Ruskin's conception of divine immanence was both less structured and less visionary than Hopkins's, his celebration of Homer is based precisely on Homer's refusal to countenance metaphoric conversions:

> Homer *had* some feeling about the sea; a faith in the animation of
> it much stronger than Keats's. But all this sense of something liv-
> ing in it, he separates in his mind into a great abstract image of a
> Sea Power. He never says the waves rage, or the waves are idle.
> But he says there is somewhat in, and greater than, the waves,
> which rages, and is idle, and *that* he calls a god.[50]

For Hopkins, Christ's Incarnation—the original "conversion" by which "Heaven once [is / was] Earth" ("Ash-Boughs")—made metaphor both superfluous and meretricious.

Hopkins's aesthetic thus implies a hierarchy of linguistic comparisons. It is founded on two criteria: (1) accuracy of perception in determining the teleological inscape of things and in delineating the ordered analogies between the particularities of God's creation, and (2) intensity of religious involvement in recognizing and praising God's design. Chief and most revered among his modes of analogy is that in which analogy virtually disappears, ceding place to an image of sacramental identity that embodies the original equation made

---

[50] Ruskin, *Works*, 5: 222–23.

possible by Christ's Incarnation. There follows analogy itself, the establishment of parallel but not identical structures in which each term retains its self-distinctive character. Metaphor and simile are both degraded approximations of images based on identity or analogy; each distorts revealed religious truth in different ways. Metaphor can convey an intensity of perception that may yet falsify the nature and true relation of things. Simile may offer accuracy in likening, but without intensity of religious awareness; it is a distanced recognition of similitude that lacks the consciousness of immanence.

In the "terrible sonnets," therefore, the perceptible fact that the few remaining images from nature are either metaphors or similes constitutes direct evidence that the "penetrative imagination," in all its ramifications, has failed. The analogical imagination has faded; images of identity have virtually disappeared; and the Incarnation, the original equation and principle of relation between things, no longer dominates Hopkins's poetics.[51] Hopkins had written of Christ in 1879, "the only person that I am in love with seldom, especially now, stirs my heart sensibly";[52] that destitution now recurred. Without Christ, Hopkins could not see the outer world, much less imitate the divine design through an act of coherent perception; unable to perceive "the glories of the earth," he could not know "the hand that wrought them all," Christ immanent within it ("Nondum" [1866]). As Hopkins circled back to repeat aspects of the crisis preceding his conversion, the "desert ways" of Mosaic exile lost their rhetorical blankness and assumed a new and startling truth: none of the natural metaphors or similes in the "terrible sonnets" appears to emerge from direct observation en plein air. This is so, in part, because the breathless world of these poems offers no more possibility for the perception of true relation than the enclosed, ramshackle hovel implied in "No Worst." Although Hopkins may actually have been remembering specific scenes—a visit to Netley Abbey, for example, may have generated the image of "Natural heart's-ivy Patience"—the connection between experience and metaphoric transformation is tenuous at best (Journals, p. 215).[53] If the image of the "cliffs of fall /

---

[51] See Miller, The Disappearance of God: "In Hopkins' last poems natural images appear only as indirect metaphors for an experience which is transnatural" (p. 353). See also Hallgarth, "A Study of Hopkins' Use of Nature," commenting on natural images in "That Nature Is a Heraclitean Fire": "These references are used metaphorically as part of the argument and not, as in the earlier poems, analogically . . ." (p. 92). Neither critic, however, explores or demonstrates the positions thus asserted.

[52] Hopkins, Letters to Bridges, p. 66.

[53] See also Hopkins, Journals, p. 263, for Hopkins's account of his visit (1875) to the ruined castle at Denbeigh; the earlier memory (1871) of Netley Abbey, however, is a more likely source for "Patience" because its ecclesiastical architecture—by which Hopkins was much impressed—embodies more fully his consciousness of his own religious failure.

Frightful" in "No Worst" resulted from Hopkins's visit to the "cliffs of Moher on the coast of Clare," the relation remains oblique, abstract; the actual occasion of seeing has been lost in generalization.[54] Hopkins's speaker in the "terrible sonnets" appears to conjure images from nothing. Compare the precise, concrete evocations of "Duns Scotus's Oxford" and the immediacy of self-dramatizing perceptions in "Hurrahing in Harvest": "Summer ends now; now, barbarous in beauty, the stooks rise / Around." With the possible exception of the mountains in "No Worst," moreover, the metaphors and similes are local and undeveloped; they are but the brief shadows of Hopkins's characteristic practice of exfoliating analogous relations throughout an entire poem. In consequence, they seem decorative, superimposed by the poet upon his material. Explicitly in "Patience" and "My Own Heart," these figures portray no present scene but signal, instead, the speaker's desire for peace with God; in "No Worst," the mountains mirror an internal terror. Thus partaking of fantasy rather than acting as realizations of observed reality, they are imaginative fictions whose true referent is the speaker's mind. As such, they approximate the self-reflexiveness of pathetic fallacy and solipsism.

The decorative and ornamental component in these images is most plainly manifest in "Patience" (lines 5–8), with its superbly bucolic, nearly Virgilian surface:[55]

> Rare patience roots in these, and, these away,
> Nowhere. Natural heart's-ivy Patience masks
> Our ruins of wrecked past purpose. There she basks
> Purple eyes and seas of liquid leaves all day.

The passage is problematical, and not simply because Hopkins's compound noun in line 6 has never been correctly printed. In the sudden, quasi-metaphoric collocation of the heart's-ivy with Patience, the natural object itself disappears. It serves but a modifying function, in particularizing the special kind of patience for which the speaker longs; and it gives, as well, a distinct emotive coloration to the abstract virtue. As a phenomenon with its own identity, however, it is nothing; the "penetrative imagination" is here held in abeyance. Although the verb "roots" eases the transition into this cumbrous, difficult compound noun, the structure of the image is by no means clear. Presumably Hopkins means that the ivy conceals architectural ruins in the same

---

[54] Hopkins, *Letters to Bridges*, p. 193. Compare Kathleen Raine, "Hopkins, Nature, and Human Nature," *Sewanee Review* 81 (1973): 205–6, who bypasses Hopkins's late poetics in claiming that "it is likely that he had real cliffs in his mind's eye."

[55] Mariani, *Commentary*, p. 235.

way that Patience masks "Our ruins of wrecked past purpose," but the analogy is imperfectly achieved. Furthermore: does "Natural" modify "heart's-ivy" or "Patience"? Is a distinction made between "natural Patience" and patience celebrated as a cardinal virtue, the "Rare patience" of the preceding line? That Hopkins should thus have confused both the form of his image and its theological import attests a mind which, despite an apparent clarity in the invention of picture, has lost that precision in delineating relationships which typifies the earlier work.[56] Patience, moreover, hovers uncomfortably between natural phenomenon (ivy) and figural form. Doubtless Hopkins's personification of Patience in "Nondum" ("with her chastening wand") lacks individuation and force; but it avoids the dysfunctional ambiguity evident here. It is likely that Hopkins, in this image, sought to render something like the tantalizingly uncertain status of Keats's Autumn, who / which vacillates between temporal concept, experience of season, and personified embodiment. But the telling hiatus after "basks" ("in"? "as"?) shows how little the last line in the quatrain can actually satisfy both the natural and the figural requirements of the personification. Instead of adhering to his previous method of paralleling the natural, human, and abstract realms, Hopkins here attempted—and failed—to fuse them. As this structural tension indicates, moreover, the image constitutes an elaborate version of pathetic fallacy: it seeks to project an interior human disposition upon an exterior landscape. But because the poem merely hypothesizes that landscape through the subordinated, adjectival image of the ivy, the effort backfires and the metaphor of Patience ends in reflecting only the speaker's soul. As such, in accordance with Hopkins's own aesthetics, it travesties the proper order and use of things in God's design.

The lack of transition to the end of the sestet demonstrates again how much this localized image has become a mere counter for the poet's manipulation:

> And where is he who more and more distills
> Delicious kindness?—He is patient. Patience fills
> His crisp combs, and that comes those ways we know.

Patience, once defined by "Natural heart's-ivy," has been transformed into the honey of Christ's grace: nothing but an abstract idea of virtue and an exceedingly tenuous similitude based on "liquidity" connects the two metaphors.

[56] Compare Alfred Thomas, "Gerard Manley Hopkins: 'Doomed to Succeed by Failure,'" *The Dublin Review* 240 (1966): 171, n. 3: "It is not only possible to read this sonnet autobiographically in a general sense, but to see in the rejection for publication by *The Month* of the 'Deutschland' and the 'Eurydice', part at least of Hopkins's 'wrecked past purpose.'" The autobiographical reading should not obscure the poetic characteristics of the image.

The abrupt alteration in the imagistic vehicles for nominally similar concepts evinces Hopkins's inordinate difficulty in realizing—i.e., both making real, and understanding—the *haeccitas* of natural things; so much less coherent than the shift between octave and sestet in "Spring," it conceals both the craving and the nagging doubt that underlie the speaker's apparently calm certitude of Christ's perpetual guardianship.

"My Own Heart" closes in the same fashion: a future-oriented image of nature masks the present absence of God's informing spirit:[57]

> let joy size
>
> At God knows when to God knows what; whose smile
> 'S not wrung, see you; unforeseentimes rather—as skies
> Betweenpie mountains—lights a lovely mile.

After the mind's claustrophobic self-torment, the triumphant spaciousness conferred by this return of sight must come as a relief. But as with Hopkins's speculation on Christ's Second Coming in "The Soldier," the simile invokes a hypothesis, not a reality; although the natural image is obviously remembered, it is used to figure but a flash of future possibility.[58] Note the hortatory "let," and compare Hopkins's declarative, assured conviction in "God's Grandeur" that "the Holy Ghost over the bent / World *broods*" (my italics). Nor, significantly, does the relation between God's smile and the sun's appearance constitute an image of identity in which Incarnation is made manifest: both the metonymy and the simile negate His immanence. In the manuscript, indeed, Hopkins had originally evoked God's presence and power more fully:

> whose smile
>   who
> 'S not wrung, see: [it] unforeseen times rather, as skies
> Betweenpie mountains, lights a lovely [?] mile.

This earlier version directly identifies God as the cause of natural light; observe the revision of "it" to "who." In addition, by implicitly predicating

---

[57] The closure of "Nondum," to which this ending is parallel, makes the future orientation obvious. See also *Sermons*: "It is as if one were dazzled by a spark or star in the dark, seeing it but not seeing by it: we want a light shed on our way and a happiness spread over our life" (p. 262). While both Cotter (*Inscape*, p. 231) and Mariani (*Commentary*, p. 240) cite this passage as a gloss on "My Own Heart," neither deals with the anticipatory element in interpreting the poem. MacKenzie (*Hopkins*, p. 94) also misses the future orientation because, citing an apparently corresponding passage in the *Journals* (p. 210), he reads the closing image as a "comforting reminiscence."

[58] See the hypothetical phrasing of a passage in *Sermons*: "Certainly God *could* make us most happy without our knowing what we were happy about" (p. 207, Hopkins's italics).

"who" as the object of "see" Hopkins crosses the colon to posit the speaker's
unmediated, visionary capacity to see or know God; the "greeting" here is like
that found in *The Wreck* (stanza 5). In the final version, however, these intima-
tions of immanence are cancelled. The omission of the relative personal pro-
noun in nominative form diminishes God's active presence in history; dashes
emphasize the mere similitude of the relation between the speaker and God,
God and nature; and Hopkins attempts, through gnarled syntax, to make this
weakened similitude embody immanence. Although Gardner has argued that
the "unnatural claustrophobic tension of the grammar" in the octave is finally
"broken up into short colloquial ejaculations" suggestive of freedom,[59] Hop-
kins has only produced a mixed metaphor betokening God's distance. As in
"Patience," the image from nature bears slight visual or structural relation to
God's smile; compare the corresponding contours of the hills and Christ's
shoulder in "Hurrahing in Harvest." One might argue that Hopkins sought
through this disjunction to render linguistically the consciousness of miracle;
but whereas Eliot's "White light folded" (*Ash Wednesday*, IV) is a deliberately
unnatural image designed to reveal the supernatural quality of divine grace,
the false parallelism and muddled fusion of terms here—so contrary to Hop-
kins's earlier exactitude—cannot be thus justified.

The natural images in "Patience" and "My Own Heart"—however hypo-
thetical and fictive, however subject to the speaker's inconstant vision—still
imply some definite relation, if only in the past or future, between perceiver
and perceived scene. But in "No Worst," fantasy dominates:

> O the mind, mind has mountains; cliffs of fall
> Frightful, sheer, no-man-fathomed. Hold them cheap
> May who ne'er hung there. Nor does long our small
> Durance deal with that steep or deep. Here! creep,
> Wretch, under a comfort serves in a whirlwind: all
> Life death does end and each day dies with sleep.

As the mind creates far more than it perceives, the objective world virtually
vanishes.[60] The mountains appear solely as interiorized emblems of private
moral and emotional states. Turned against itself, converting God's creation

---

[59] W. H. Gardner, *Gerard Manley Hopkins: A Study of Poetic Idiosyncrasy in Relation to Poetic Tra-
dition*, 2 vols. (1949; rpt. London: Oxford University Press, 1966), 2: 347.

[60] See Sister Mary Humiliata, "Hopkins and the Prometheus Myth," *PMLA* 70 (1955): 67.
Patricia A. Wolfe, "The Paradox of Self: A Study of Hopkins' Spiritual Conflict in the 'Terrible'
Sonnets," *Victorian Poetry* 6 (1968): 96, softens the passage: "In the sestet the poet reflects on the
vast complexity of the human mind. 'O the mind, mind has mountains' expresses with simple
majesty the twofold nature of man's consciousness. It enables him to reach for the sky, yet at the
same time humbles him through an awareness of its own inadequacy."

into a mirror of the natural self, the mind distorts normal categories of space, scale, relation: in a metaphor of extraordinary emotive force, the skull bursts to encompass images of the earth's gigantic formations. As imagination becomes fearfully and destructively measureless, "no-man-fathomed," and enters an interior territory that not even Odysseus (who gave "No Man" as his name to the Cyclops) understood, structure dissolves, interchanges between perceiver and object become blurred, the perceiver loses grasp of his own modes of sensory perception. Hopkins had once been able, in "Hurrahing in Harvest," to approximate, through an image of identity, the sacramental character of mountains as described by Ruskin: "these great cathedrals of the earth, with their gates of rock, pavements of cloud, choirs of stream and stone, altars of snow, and vaults of purple traversed by the continual stars." But he consciously fell prey here to the "weakness of mind" and "feebleness of intellect" with which Ruskin associated a fixation on the terror of mountain scenery.[61] Hopkins considered such perceptual madness or *deordinatio* to be "the soil of sin" and linked it with "a want of subordination, of obedience to God's order" (*Sermons*, p. 135). That lost sense of order, in turn, suggests another pun in "no-man-fathomed": the phrase hints that the "no-man" who *did* fathom the "cliffs of fall" was Christ. Once accepted, the pun shows Hopkins's speaker toying with the Monophysite heresy (discussion of which Newman had recently revived) by denying Christ's humanity; and in rejecting His dual nature, he simultaneously loses the divine Presence who, incarnate in mundane things, substantiates their form and being. When Christ's immanental presence fades out of ken, the mind—as the solipsistic metaphor demonstrates— incorporates the world in a parody of Incarnation.

At the same time, however, as Hopkins indicated in his contemporaneous commentary on St. Ignatius, Christ's presence would have forestalled the disaster rendered in this poem:

> The divine Persons see the whole world at once and know where to drive the nail and plant the cross. A 60-fathom coil of cord running over the cliff's edge round by round, that is, say, generation by generation, 40 fathoms already gone and the rest will follow, when a man sets his foot on it and saves both what is hanging and what has not yet stirred to run. Or seven tied by the rope on the Alps; four go headlong, then the fifth, as strong as Samson, checks them and the two behind do not even feel the strain. [*Sermons*, p. 169]

---

[61] Ruskin, *Works*, 6: 425, 398. See Sulloway, *Hopkins and the Victorian Temper*, pp. 173–78, for a useful discussion of apocalyptic mountain imagery in the nineteenth century.

But in "No Worst," as in Hopkins's late apocalyptic writings generally, Christ's saving power to regulate the deranged imagination is known only by its absence. The consequence is a poem that, more than any of the other "terrible sonnets," achieves its anguish through repeated, and apparently uncontrolled, synaesthesia. The deracination begins with the fusion of sound, color, and bodily movement in "Pitched." With "My cries heave," this self-distanced self-awareness underscores other (con)fusions: the speaker experiences his screams as if they were emitted by another creature; and he apprehends the sound not audibly, but through muscular spasm (in the manuscript, "heave" was originally a neutral "come"). In the compound adjective "herds-long," the imagined sight of cattle merges with auditory consciousness of their echoing bellowings; the faculty of sight is itself confounded through the dazzling contraction from "long" to "huddle," and the sentence buried in this apposition—"Herds long [for Christ]"—connects the perceptual dislocations of the entire poem with Christ's disappearance.[62] It is thus hardly surprising that, after the directional uncertainties of "steep or deep,"[63] the final designation of place—"Here!"—loses all power of spatial signification and dissolves, in this wholly interior landscape, into an insubstantial linguistic structure, an axiom whose actual import, for all its overt pessimism, is itself ambiguous.

It is plain that Hopkins here could not sustain his earlier capacity for generating images of identity and analogy from natural phenomena. But as "No Worst" intimates, the deracination attendant upon Christ's absence also gives rise to a self-conscious bodily imagery that is unique in Hopkins's work; it marks a definite stage in the history of modern English poetry. This is the imagery of primitive and distorted sensation, grotesque bodily deformity verging on shapelessness, decreation into animality; it delineates Hopkins's speaker as a nearly composite form: a man who slides into beast down an untempered and variable scale of metamorphosis that effectually denies the existence of a stable ontology. The metamorphosis is the consequence of a world made metaphoric; the dehumanization is the consequence of the personifying process that projects human attributes out from the self.

The opportunities for employing a composite form as emblem of chaos, psychic and moral confusion, had not been much exploited since Milton had created his amorphous figure of Death:

> The other shape,
> If shape it might be call'd that shape had none

---

[62] Wolfe, "The Paradox of Self," p. 96, unaccountably identifies the animals as "Lucifer's discordant herd."

[63] Hopkins was evidently concerned to intensify the spatial ambiguities of the whole poem as

Distinguishable in member, joint, or limb,
Or substance might be call'd that shadow seem'd,
For each seemed either; black it stood as Night,
Fierce as ten Furies, terrible as Hell,
And shook a dreadful Dart; what seem'd his head
The likeness of a Kingly Crown had on.

[*Paradise Lost*, 2. 666–73]

Over a century of Cartesian dualism intervened before the modern version of this figural indefinitude recurred, in benign form, in Wordsworth's vision of the leech-gatherer:

As a huge stone is sometimes seen to lie
Crouched on the bald top of an eminence;
Wonder to all who do the same espy,
By what means it could thither come, and whence;
So that it seems a thing endued with sense:
Like a sea-beast crawled forth, that on a shelf
Of rock or sand reposeth, there to sun itself[.]

["Resolution and Independence," stanza 9]

This naturalized heroic simile raises central questions about the leech-gatherer's intellectual faculties, his figural shape, and his relation to the cosmos. Though ennobling the leech-gatherer by endowing him with an elemental wholeness, its underlying ambiguities again made feasible a more negative and disturbing treatment of similar materials. Tennyson (in "The Kraken" and "The Mermaid") and Arnold (in "The Forsaken Merman") verged on such a handling; but it was chiefly Browning in Victorian poetry before Hopkins, who understood this potential for the imaging of chaos as he wrote out his phantasmagoria, "Childe Roland to the Dark Tower Came" (stanza 21):

—good saints, how I feared
To set my foot upon a dead man's cheek,
Each step, or feel the spear I thrust to seek
For hollows, tangled in his hair or beard!
—It may have been a water-rat I speared,
But, ugh! it sounded like a baby's shriek.[64]

---

he revised, for the initial version of line 10 reads: "Frightful, sheer[,] *down*, not fathomed . . ." (italics mine).

    [64] See William Clyde DeVane, *A Browning Handbook* (New York: Appleton Century Crofts, 1935), pp. 205–6 and n. 48, for the influence of Gerard de Lairesse's *The Art of Painting in All its Branches* on Browning's conception of the grotesque.

Such concern with indeterminacy of identity is not solely a matter of figural shape. As Wordsworth's passage indicates, it also entails questions about the origin of phenomena—"By what means it could thither come, and whence"— that directly touched the most basic of Victorian anxieties. It is obvious that metamorphic imagery and the recourse to composite forms, in their fluidity and indefinite history, are the apt, if not inevitable, aesthetic correlatives to Lyell's investigations of fossil life and geological time, Darwin's hypotheses about human evolution, and the theological furor caused by Jowett and others in *Essays and Reviews* (1860). Whether as techniques or as themes, they constitute emblems of trauma for a culture that no longer knew the duration of time, the nature of its own biological (and thus moral) ancestry, or the certitude of Biblical revelation. Hopkins had reviled the "first slime" of evolutionary corruption in "The Sea and the Skylark"; when he tapped this imagery that obscures previously accepted boundaries, he provided one of the essential poetic transitions to modernism. The "terrible sonnets" (in this respect) are the chief antecedents of Yeats's "shape with lion body and the head of a man" ("The Second Coming") and his vision of bestialized "Trooper belabouring trooper, biting at arm or at face" ("Meditations in Time of Civil War," VII).[65] They prefigure as well the ghastly, dumbly satiric protagonist of Hughes's *Crow*, a composite man/bird who is simultaneously hatched from an egg and delivered from the womb of a woman/bird whose breasts then "wept blood" ("Two Legends," II; "Examination at the Womb-Door"; "Crow and Mama").[66]

Hopkins's imagery of corporeal dissolution, however, does not function primarily as an expression of cultural uncertainty; nor, surely, does it embody, as in Wordsworth, a beneficent vision of the soul's expansion. It remains, as it was for Milton, an imagery of freakish and heinous mutation that assumes, however fitfully, a standard of bodily perfection by which the aberrations themselves may be judged. That standard, of course, is Christ, Blake's "human form divine" and Yeats's "divine architecture of the body."[67] Hopkins's imagery thus renders, in the most intimate terms possible, his experience of dis-Incarnation. It is the logical inward consequence of his grief that Christ

[65] Gustave Moreau's painting "Oedipus and the Sphinx" (now in the Metropolitan Museum of Art, New York) is only Yeats's most obvious source for this composite beast (see also A. Norman Jeffares, *A Commentary on the Collected Poems of W. B. Yeats* [Palo Alto, Calif.: Stanford University Press, 1970], pp. 243–44). But compare the earlier painting by Ingres on the same subject (National Gallery, London) for a treatment that minimizes the composite nature of the sphinx.

[66] The composite nature of Hughes's Crow is made especially plain in Leonard Baskin's line drawings for the folio edition; see Ted Hughes, *Crow: From the Life and Songs of Crow*, with twelve drawings by Leonard Baskin (London: Faber and Faber, 1973).

[67] William Blake, "The Divine Image" (*Songs of Innocence*); W. B. Yeats, *Mythologies* (New York: Macmillan Co., 1959), pp. 332–33.

had withdrawn Himself from the natural world. So carefully nurtured an ana-
logical intelligence as Hopkins's, moreover, hardly permitted him to acknowl-
edge the loss of the divine spirit without also positing a corresponding deterio-
ration in the form that Christ had assumed. It is no accident that, in "No
Worst," it is the mind—human shelter for the divine reason—that explodes.
The poems provide no foundation for the claim that Hopkins perceived this
process of his deformation as an ultimate trial constituting an *imitatio Christi*.
Rather, they suggest his recognition of the process as a self-parody based on
the Crucifixion, when Christ experienced the departure of the Holy Ghost
most acutely, or an ironic reversal of the Incarnation, as the divine breath
leaves—instead of enters—the human form. While self-parody of this kind
may bear a certain structural kinship to the *imitatio Christi*, in that both de-
pend on the model of Christ to be interpreted, it functions in an entirely op-
posite manner. In its masochistic self-loathing, it is the appropriate generic
counterpart to the chasm, not the closeness, Hopkins felt between himself and
Christ when he wrote that "now my action leads from . . . the Incarnation"
(*Sermons*, p. 263).

The imagery of bodily dissolution in these poems is frankly infernal, and
sometimes demonic.[68] It results not from a self-imposed bending to humilia-
tion but from the acute sense of active participation in original sin that Hop-
kins's own preoccupation with apocalypse had fostered. It accords entirely
with St. Ignatius's instructions for the composition of place in meditating on
"The Triple Sin":

> Where the subject-matter is not something visible, as in the pres-
> ent case of sins, the "picture" will be the idea, produced by an
> effort of the imagination, that my soul is a prisoner in this cor-
> ruptible body and that my whole self, body and soul, is con-
> demned to live amongst animals on this earth, like someone in a
> foreign land.[69]

The bestial imagery accords as well with Hopkins's own late commentary on
St. Ignatius's "Meditation on Hell":

> *2nd. Prelude*—To ask for what we want, which here is such an
> inward feeling of the pain the damned suffer that if we ever come
> to forget the love of the eternal Lord, through our faults (our ve-
> nial sins, lukewarmness, worldliness, negligence), the fear of

---

[68] Miller, *The Disappearance of God*, pp. 339, 355, and Chevigny, "Instress and Devotion in the
Poetry of . . . Hopkins," p. 151, have also commented on the infernal elements in these poems.
[69] St. Ignatius Loyola, *Spiritual Exercises*, p. 30.

hell-pains at least may help us then and keep us from falling into
mortal sin. [*Sermons*, p. 241]

The "terrible sonnets," however, deviate significantly from the commentary in
that their imagery of bodily dehumanization is not consciously adapted as a
self-monitory and vicarious experiment in the experience of damnation. Like
the poems themselves, it seemingly comes "unbidden and against my will."[70]
Compare the mind's active self-direction in "Hurrahing in Harvest,"

> I walk, I lift up, I lift up heart, eyes,
> Down all that glory in the heavens to glean our Saviour,

with the passive victimization evident in "I am gall, I am heartburn" ("I Wake
and Feel"). The infernal imagery is an immediate, uncontrolled reality.

The very manner of Hopkins's intense fascination with his body's degenera-
tion is part of his speaker's derangement. Hopkins had previously heeded the
bodies of others, but not his own. He had celebrated (though morally he had
condemned) the manly stature of the sailor in *The Wreck* (stanza 16)—with
"dreadnought breast and braids of thew"—and Felix Randal's "mould of man,
big-boned and hardy-handsome." In portraying his own speaker, however, he
had hardly shown the concern with bodily placement and movement that typ-
ifies Coleridge's "conversation poems" and Browning's dramatic monologues.
He had largely restricted himself to delineating the capacities of ear and eye,
had only occasionally suggested the motions of his body, and had never im-
plied his entire physical form; in "The Windhover," he had intimated his
physical position only by evoking an emotion: "My *heart* in hiding" (italics
mine). Hopkins's clinical and hyperconscious observation of his whole body in
the "terrible sonnets" springs from his recognition (1880) that

> Part of this world of objects, this object-world, is also part of the
> very self in question, as in man's case his own body, which each
> man not only feels in and acts with but also feels and acts on. . . .
> A self then will consist of a centre *and* a surrounding area or
> circumference, of a point of reference *and* a belonging field.
> [*Sermons*, p. 127; Hopkins's italics]

If Hopkins's dissection of himself into component areas helped him to rebut
sensationalism and to clarify the phenomenology of perception, it also fore-
shadowed the process of "dismémbering" that he associated with apocalyptic
upheaval in "Spelt from Sibyl's Leaves." Such fragmentation, although it ap-

---

[70] Hopkins, *Letters to Bridges*, p. 221.

pears to enhance a sense of the body's interconnectedness and thus the indi-
viduation, "that taste of myself" (*Sermons*, p. 123) Hopkins so valued, ends by
playing directly into the mood of self-enclosed solipsism that governs the "ter-
rible sonnets." With the body as depersonalized object, as well as undifferen-
tiated subject, the speaker enters into a relationship with his physical form
rather than with the external world. Living, like Joyce's Mr. Duffy, "at a little
distance from his body,"[71] he substitutes a wholly private system of communi-
cation for the earlier reciprocity in which he had been able to "greet" the di-
vine spirit in things. Like Ruskin's "squirrel in its circular prison,"[72] the
speaker studies his "belonging field" as if in dialogue—"My cries heave" ("No
Worst"). Yet the body, a false interlocutor, cannot respond: as object, it is as
mute as Earth in "Ribblesdale"; as subject, it but echoes the knowledge of the
perceiving self. Nor, in this perceptual closed circuit, can the speaker commu-
nicate with his body save by isolating its parts or sensory apprehensions;
through this atomizing and self-dismemberment he must negate the unity he
seeks to form. As object, moreover, his body compels him to recognize that he
himself is his own stranger; in himself, he lives in what St. Ignatius, defining
the realm of the damned, calls a "foreign land." Hopkins's efforts to animate
his parts through the language of territory—"belonging field," "circum-
ference"—come at exactly the time when his sense of his integral or bounded
wholeness dissolves. The situation, indeed, closely parallels the dynamics of
pathetic fallacy evident in Hopkins's images from nature. Panicked by the loss
of Christ's spirit in external reality, Hopkins sought to fill the void in nature
through anthropomorphizing self-projections; having failed, and having made
blank or self-reflexive what had once been live and independently reciprocat-
ing, he turned inward from this larger territory to that of his own body,
sought similarly to animate it, and thus made it foreign.

　　This dis-Incarnation begins with the felt collapse of his human anatomical
structure. What he had feared as early as 1873 becomes his own experience:
"nature . . . like a clod cleaving and holding only by strings of root." That
structure Hopkins had construed, from the outset of his major work, as a vital
armature whose elements were held together and manipulated by the liga-
ments or strands of Christ's grace; alternately, his armature was the skeletal
model upon which the divine sculptor molded human clay. In *The Wreck*, God
is the "World's strand": "Thou hast bound bones and veins in me, fastened me
flesh" (stanza 1). The speaker is "laced with fire of stress," Pentecostal and
prophetic (stanza 2); he is

---

[71] James Joyce, *Dubliners* (1916; rpt. New York: Viking, n.d.), p. 108.
[72] Ruskin, *Works*, 4: 288.

>   . . . roped with, always, all the way down from the tall
>   Fells or flanks of the voel, a vein
>   Of the gospel proffer, a pressure, a principle, Christ's gift.
>
>   (stanza 4)

The imagery derives most obviously from Job (10 : 11): "Thou hast clothed me with skin and flesh, and hast fenced me with bones and sinews." As late as "The Soldier," perhaps recalling Herbert's "The Collar" and "The Pulley," the speaker can still claim of Christ, "He of all can reeve a rope best." But by the time of "Carrion Comfort," as the speaker characterizes his imminent destruction, the imagery has become nearly secularized:

>   Not, I'll not, carrion comfort, Despair, not feast on thee;
>   Not untwist—slack they may be—these last strands of man
>   In me . . .

Yet the despairing soul's effort to forestall the collapse of structural support fails. God's overwhelming power leaves him not only prostrate and paralyzed but formless, "heaped"; the word invokes the Biblical image of Damascus levelled into a "ruinous heap" by God's wrath (Isaiah 17 : 1).[73] In "Patience," his "wrecked past purpose" is explicitly called "ruins," an architectural rubble lacking articulation of interior spaces. In "I Wake and Feel," he observes his body as a naturalized counter-structure, "Bones built in me, flesh filled, blood brimmed the curse"; the "vein / Of the gospel proffer" is significantly omitted. The structure of the Christian self, which had once been formed to put on "the whole armour of God" (Ephesians 6 : 11), now breaks into fragments. The "scaffold of score brittle bones" ("The Shepherd's Brow" [1889]) is transformed into an amorphous mass approximating shapeless clay, the "squandering ooze" of "That Nature Is a Heraclitean Fire." With the collapse of God's temple and "bone-house" ("The Caged Skylark"), the strands of Christian self-definition lie in a slack coil. "A coil or spiral," Hopkins had written in "The Great Sacrifice" (1881), "is then a type of the Devil, . . . a type of death, of motion lessening and at last ceasing" (*Sermons*, p. 198). This is the basic bodily emblem of spiritual negativity from which the "terrible sonnets" begin.

   Startling metamorphoses in sensory apprehension accompany the body's collapse. As the radical decrease in frequency and potency of visual images indicates, the speaker undergoes a suppression of sight, the faculty which Western philosophical and religious traditions have since the Renaissance ven-

---

[73] Marie Cornelia, "Images and Allusion in Hopkins' 'Carrion Comfort,'" *Renascence* 27 (1974): 53. See also Isaiah 25 : 2; Jeremiah 26 : 18, 49 : 2.

erated above all others; it is a measure of the cultural shift these poems represent that, in this reversal of hierarchy, the "baser" senses are ironically elevated to a new preeminence. The extreme handicap becomes his fixation. Only in "My Own Heart" does sunlight appear, and then as part of a simile; "basks" in "Patience" perhaps suggests sunlight, but that, too, is realized only in a fiction. Elsewhere, the lowering "whirlwind" of "Carrion Comfort" and "No Worst" or the "dark" heaven of "To Seem the Stranger" enshrouds him. Mocking his own blindness, the speaker uses the verb "to see" in surprising or inappropriate contexts ("I Wake and Feel," "My Own Heart"). More striking still, he loses comprehension of the eye's identity and function. In "Patience," the ivy's berries become "Purple eyes," nonhuman and strangely displaced from himself to the landscape; they satirize the very organ whose dysfunction he suffers. In "My Own Heart," as Boyle has noted, the speaker "does not compare himself to a blind man. He compares himself to blind eyes" that "through some internal defect . . . do not receive the light effectually." [74] The synecdoche, in a distortion of relation typical of these poems, diminishes the self to its most valued part, now incapacitated. The organic deformity, counterpart to original sin throughout the "terrible sonnets," leaves the speaker in futile and self-reflexive struggle against his own incapability. God's eyes alone have power, but these are "darksome devouring" ("Carrion Comfort"). As God becomes composite, nearly theriomorphic, thus corresponding with the speaker as bestialized prey, His eyes are metamorphosed into engulfing mouths. In this synaesthetic transformation, the animality of God's eye / mouth marks a considerable intensification over the imagery of disgorgement in Roothan's *De Ratione Meditandi*, a commentary on St. Ignatius's *Spiritual Exercises* that Hopkins knew intimately; Roothan writes, with a clearly anthropomorphic deity in mind, of "the threats of God against the tepid that He will vomit them forth from His mouth." [75] Hopkins's fusion of senses, as in "No Worst," is but another evidence of the dissolution of discrete epistemological functions, known categories, and defined modes of thought.

Hopkins explores this horrific condition of deformed vision most fully in "I Wake and Feel":

> I wake and feel the fell of dark, not day.
> What hours, O what black hours we have spent
> This night! what sights you, heart, saw; ways you went!
> And more must, in yet longer light's delay.

[74] Robert Boyle, *Metaphor in Hopkins*, pp. 147–48.

[75] John Roothan, *How to Meditate (De Ratione Meditandi)*, trans. Louis J. Puhl (Westminster, Md.: The Newman Bookshop, 1945), p. 36. Roothan was Superior General of the Society of Jesus from 1829 to 1853.

The steady iambs of the opening conclude with a highly sprung "not day" emphasized by an abrupt and rare caesura *within* the alliterative unit; the dulled knowledge that consciousness offers no reprieve from a moral darkness made strangely tactile quickens into shocked outcry against loss. Unable to define the nature of his vision, the speaker can only reiterate the emotion of hellish torment to which his fantasies, lacking outward reference, have given rise. The echo of Shakespeare's Sonnet 97—"What freezings have I felt, what dark days seen!"—stresses not only the speaker's implicit separation from his beloved Christ but also the confusion of temporal categories that here corresponds to the indeterminacy of sensory functions. Paralyzed in a timeless vacuum, he is caught waiting—either for "longer light" (an ironic periphrasis on his totally blackened state and, again, a synaesthetic attribution of shape to insubstantial air) or for the "longer delay" of light to come to an end. But "This night" imitates the apocalyptic confounding of diurnal pattern; it "is not of so many hours, a number known beforehand; it is of quite uncertain length; and there is no dawn, no dayspring, to tell of the day coming, no morning twilight" (*Sermons*, p. 40). With Christ absent, the speaker proceeds in the sestet to define himself demonically as "gall," an instrument of Christ's torture (Matthew 23:34); he thus becomes one of those who "banishes, excommunicates God" (*Sermons*, p. 133). The speaker's punishment for such rebellion, the darkness itself, is analogous to that of the fallen angels; Hopkins analyzed it in his commentary on St. Ignatius's "Meditation on Hell" (1881):

> This throwing back or confinement of their energy is a dreadful constraint or imprisonment and, as intellectual action is spoken of under the figure of sight, it will in this case be an imprisonment in darkness, a being in the dark; for darkness is the phenomenon of foiled action in the sense of sight.

The unmistakable self-reference follows:

> But this constraint and this blindness or darkness will be most painful when it is the main stress or energy of the whole being that is thus balked. [*Sermons*, p. 137).

This, Hopkins cannot but have known, was his own doom. He obediently assumed that the punishment was necessarily caused by his own sin, even though "I Wake and Feel" specifies no particular sin as the catalyst for meditation; the corruption was in his generic human nature. The poem's bitter irony, however, is that God's punishment itself goads the speaker to further sin; as he acknowledges his corruption, he also defines himself infernally as the "gall" of bitterness (see Acts 8:23) and thus invites further punishment. The cycle aptly illustrates the language of inescapable frustration in Hopkins's commentary: "This throwing back," "foiled action," "balked." Because of the intimate relation between physical and intellectual behavior in Hopkins's life, moreover, the cycle of frustration operates aesthetically and perceptually as well as morally. The imprisonment in "blindness or darkness," not a generalized emblem, is a private revelation to the speaker of the final isolated solipsism that is the result of his gradually deteriorating vision, his failure to see "the things that are." Indeed, the punishment *is* the condition of solipsism, an imitation of the sin. It blocks Hopkins's "main stress or energy," thwarts absolutely the "penetrative imagination" whereby he had been able to know God's presence in things and to imitate His design through visual analogy. But if the very nature of this divine retribution keeps Hopkins trapped in the solipsistic vacuum he himself has unwillingly entered, then how can he escape it to return to God's world of significant and reciprocal relation?

Barred from sight, the speaker must rely on his other faculties for whatever diminishing contact with exterior reality he can maintain. But that new dependency becomes another measure of his dehumanized incapability to delight:

> Sight does not shock like hearing, sounds cannot so disgust as smell, smell is not so bitter as proper bitterness, which is in taste. . . .
>
> And still bitterness of taste is not so cruel as the pain that can be touched and felt. Seeing is believing but touch is the truth. [*Sermons*, p. 243]

Hopkins understood the process not only as a mortification but as the progressive curtailment of human cognition: "sight is a continuous sense, but hearing is intermittent mostly" (*Sermons*, p. 175). Auditory perception, which had once enabled his speaker to think the skylark's song identical with the "rash-fresh re-winded new-skeinèd score" of angelic harmony, now yields him only the reverberating noises of his own anguish:

> My cries heave, herds-long . . .
>
> ["No Worst"]

> And my lament
> Is cries countless, cries like dead letters . . .
>
> ["I Wake and Feel"]

> We hear our hearts grate on themselves . . .
>
> ["Patience"]

The voice is animal; sound has the thinness of paper; as the heart becomes metallic, the metaphor implicitly expresses his discordant relationship with God: "Are we his pipe or harp? we are out of tune, we grate upon his ear" (*Sermons*, p. 240). It is indicative of Hopkins's underlying theme of rebellion here that it was to Pilate that he first ascribed the warped capacity to hear his own voice as a foreign sound: "My several moans come distant in their tones / As though they were not from within" ("Pilate" [1864]). These hyperconscious anatomies of the qualities of sound, for all that they reveal of Hopkins's brilliant musicianship, are instances of "foiled action"; leading nowhere, they demonstrate the failure of Hopkins's effort to communicate spiritually with his body as object. As auditory phenomena become entirely self-referential, the sound *of* the poems (apart from the sounds represented *in* them) becomes obsessively monotonic. Internal rhyme gives way to a stalled repetition, both in vocabulary and in syntax, which signals not only the speaker's "relentless cycle of woe"[76] but his ceasing to make analogies between things. This isolating repetition is not at all an application of Roothan's advice that the words in meditation should "be simple and few, but frequently repeated and dwelt upon for greater length"[77] in order to achieve religious depth; it is the evidence of fixation, balked narrative. In the most extreme of these repetitions, akin to the imprisoning patterns of chiasmus elsewhere,

> My own heart let me more have pity on; let
> Me live . . .
>   . . . not live this tormented mind
> With this tormented mind tormenting yet [,]

the repeated words nearly lose their syntactic and lexical meanings, begin to function as nonlinguistic signifiers in which the sheer self-hypnotic noise itself assumes chief importance. Ultimately, the fixation, like the imagery of sound in "No Worst," embodies the speaker's sense of himself as an animal, unable to use human language. Compare the variety of literary terms—"psalm," "prayer," "hymn"—that the speaker of "Nondum" (stanza 1) uses to designate his appeals to God. Here, however, literary capability seemingly fails; the connections between emotion, language, and public articulation break:

>   Only what word
> Wisest my heart breeds dark heaven's baffling ban
> Bars or hell's spell thwarts.
>   ["To Seem the Stranger"]

[76] Louis Rader, "Hopkins' Dark Sonnets: Another New Expression," *Victorian Poetry* 5 (1967): 17.

[77] Roothan, *How to Meditate*, p. 45.

The incisive pun on "baffling"—enigmatic or confusing; absorbing or deflecting sound [78]—epitomizes the auditory imagery of the "terrible sonnets"; the world has become a ghostly echo-chamber, preventing prayer as well as verbal recognition of exterior reality.

Touch reduces the speaker's possible range of awareness to his material body and thus gives him intimate knowledge of his decreation into animal. With "continuous sight" and "intermittent" hearing blocked, he can no longer depend upon automatic apperception; he must deliberately utilize his body if he is to recognize his shrunken world. Thus, defining space by touch and gesture, but without the normal reinforcement of visual perspective, he finds himself —like "old Earth" in "Ash-Boughs"—"*groping* round my comfortless" ("My Own Heart"; italics mine); he cannot grasp the invisible comfort of the Paraclete which his phrasing ironically converts into tactile form. As he remembers his conversion, in "Carrion Comfort," he first thinks that it was his hand, not his heart, that "lapped strength, stôle joy . . ."; notably, the confusion did not appear in the poem's first draft. His heart's present pain he understands not only as noise but as "bruise" ("Patience"). He wakes to "*feel* the *fell* of dark," experiences time synaesthetically through its seeming texture, as if by animal instinct. "Fell," superbly connoting the material weight of time and temporality, defines the previous falling of darkness as the Fall: humankind's entrance into mortality. In his commentary (1881) on St. Ignatius's "Meditation on Hell," Hopkins remembered

> St Teresa's vision of hell, to this effect: 'I know not how it is, but in spite of the darkness the eye sees there all that to see is most afflicting'. Against these acts of its own the lost spirit dashes itself like a caged bear and is in prison, violently instresses them and burns, stares into them and is the deeper darkened. [*Sermons*, p. 138]

This equation of the "lost spirit" with a "caged bear" makes the emblematic substance of animal "fell" or "pelt" explicit: the speaker, *vetus homo*, now wears original sin as his natural clothing; "Unto Adam also and to his wife did the Lord God make coats of skins, and clothed them" (Genesis 3:21).[79] This, the most extreme of tactile enclosures in the "terrible sonnets," also typifies the group in its use of shrunken space as sign of the soul's inability to exercise its original Christian liberty to choose God. The "fell," a sardonic symbol for the

---

[78] The OED gives 1881 as the first date for this usage, as in "baffle-plate"; see Hopkins's pun in "The Blessed Virgin compared to the Air we Breathe," lines 66–67.

[79] See MacKenzie, *Hopkins*, pp. 89–90.

enclosed vaults of heaven,[80] is the tactile counterpart to "dark heaven's baffling ban." The skin of darkness perhaps also suggests the uterine casing for the speaker's regression into his embryonic sin of birth, for in "I Wake and Feel" Adam's sin becomes his biological inheritance: "Bones built in me, flesh filled, blood brimmed the curse" is an irrevocably organic image of gradual imprisonment during the gestation process, an unyielding Christian version of Wordsworth's "prison-house" imagery in the "Ode: Intimations of Immortality." The exiled speaker of "To Seem the Stranger" envisages his heart as a womb that can only "hoard," not release, its fruit; compare with this forced constriction the emotion of alluring privacy and interior wealth in the much earlier image of the "first and vital candle in close heart's vault" ("The Candle Indoors" [1879]). In "No Worst," the speaker must "creep" towards a hovel as ruined as his body; his posture signifies neither awe nor humility but animal nature. Even the beneficent image of grace in "Patience"—the honeycombs—reveals the same persistent habit of thinking in terms of confinement. No wonder that the imagined liberation in "My Own Heart" takes the form of spatial expansion: "let joy size."[81] Yet this expansion, in which emotion might gain tactility and shape, is the only one of its kind in poems otherwise dominated by a claustrophobic incoiling of self.[82]

It is in the body's own enclosure, the mouth, that the speaker knows his fallen nature most acutely; through taste—the most passive, private, and self-referential of the senses—he recognizes the extremity of his animal perversion. In "The Habit of Perfection" (1866), Hopkins had clearly defined the mouth's antithetical functions: either it is the secular organ of material sustenance, immoderate sensuality, and (by extension) false language; or it is the sacred organ of prayer, Communion, and the mystical Presence of spirit in matter.

> Palate, the hutch of tasty lust,
> Desire not to be rinsed with wine:
> The can must be so sweet, the crust
> So fresh that come in fasts divine.

---

[80] Ibid., p. 89.

[81] Elisabeth W. Schneider, "My Own Heart Let Me More Have Pity On," *The Explicator*, 5 (1947), item 51, traces Hopkins's use of "size" here to Keats's description of the whale in *Endymion*: "'twould size and swell / To its huge self." But Hopkins had already used the verb as a present participle in "Lines for a Picture of St. Dorothea" ("the sizing moon"), and it is more likely that he derived the word from Herbert's "The Size," whose last line also provided him with the title for "Heaven-Haven."

[82] Miller, *The Disappearance of God*, p. 354, argues that in the "terrible sonnets," "This experience of the infinity of finite human time is matched by an experience of the infinity of space." But it is only "No Worst" whose imagery supports his contention, and there only sporadically; the rest of the "terrible sonnets" are very plainly marked by images of constriction.

Neither such quaint diction nor such arch wit graces the Johannine tempta-
tion, in "Carrion Comfort," to parody that Communion by making it a grue-
some cannibalism. The sickly lure of such autophagy is revealed in the first
draft: the second line shows "carrion comfort" metamorphosed into "carrion
sweetness." In the parallel between "not feast" and "Not untwist," moreover,
the speaker equates his self-mutilation with the destruction of Christ within
him. Both the horror and the self-destructiveness of sin are what Hopkins
called "proper bitterness": "the worm of conscience, which is the mind gnaw-
ing and feeding on its own most miserable self" (*Sermons*, p. 243).[83]

The parodic element in "I Wake and Feel" is yet more pronounced. The
power of refusing to blaspheme, not by word but by the mouth's mere bodily
action, has been taken away; indeed, God compels the speaker to recognize his
parodic nature in the same manner that He punishes him with solipsism:

> I am gall, I am heartburn. God's most deep decree
> Bitter would have me taste: my taste was me;
> Bones built in me, flesh filled, blood brimmed the curse.

By association with the crucial verb "brimmed," the material body itself be-
comes original sin and thus the profaned chalice of Communion. Both as chal-
ice and as acrid "gall" he torments Christ on the Cross. At the same time, in
his very aversion to tasting from the impure chalice of his own identity, he
mimics Christ in Gethsemene—and thus renders his most intimate experience
of Christ's disappearance, as Christ experienced God's:

> And [Christ] went a little further, and fell on his face, and prayed,
>   saying, O my Father, if it be possible, let this cup pass from me:
>   nevertheless, not as I will, but as thou wilt. [Matthew 26:39]

Hopkins's conception of the parallel—together with the raging viciousness,
the gross sensual asceticism of his speaker's language—suggests his passionate
self-chastisement for all his earlier delectations. This transformation in taste-
perception, now "sour with sinning" ("Spring"), involves a change not so
much in the power or object of taste as in the theology of sensory apprehen-
sion. The change corresponds exactly with the one embedded in Hopkins's
commentary (1882) on St. Ignatius's "First Principle and Foundation." Ini-

---

[83] See Alan M. Rose, "Hopkins' 'Carrion Comfort': The Artful Disorder of Prayer," *Victorian
Poetry* 15 (1977): 215, for an extreme and admittedly "blasphemous" reading of the poem's open-
ing: "The poet is being driven by the devil to eating the devil's food, to the very action of a black
mass, a devil's eucharist." Rose also notes that "in the sestet, the poet *is* an animal, lapping
strength" (p. 214).

tially he had instanced his own sense of taste as evidence of God's transcendent genius in creating so utterly distinctive a human self:

> For human nature, being more highly pitched, selved, and dis-
> tinctive than anything in the world, can have been developed . . .
> only by one of finer or higher pitch and determination than it-
> self. . . . And this is much more true when we consider the
> mind; when I consider my selfbeing, my consciousness and feel-
> ing of myself, that taste of myself, of *I* and *me* above and in all
> things, which is more distinctive than the taste of ale or alum,
> more distinctive than the smell of walnutleaf or camphor, and is
> incommunicable by any means to another man. [*Sermons*, pp.
> 122–23]

The passage has been much quoted; later in the essay, however, he threw aside such aesthetically pleasing comparisons in order to acknowledge the realities they masked:

> But these things and above all my shame, my guilt, my fate are
> the very things in feeling, in tasting, which I most taste that self-
> taste which nothing in the world can match.[84] [*Sermons*, p. 125]

Hopkins here severely qualified his definition of that unique distinctiveness of which commentators have made so much. His radical insistence on original sin as being intrinsic to his body's normal functioning points not to his abso-lute individuation but to the specialness with which he shared in the general condition of fallen humankind.

Hopkins's selftaste, in "I Wake and Feel," not only parodies the wine of Christ's blood, retained in a besmirched chalice; it defiles the bread of Com-munion as well:

> Selfyeast of spirit a dull dough sours. I see
> The lost are like this, and their scourge to be
> As I am mine, their sweating selves; but worse.

"Selfyeast" inscapes and energizes his rebellious pride of spirit, aligns him with the damned: he sees his natural man's satanic illusion of self-creation. Puffing up the "dull dough" of his body, it emblematizes his breaking of cove-nant with God: it inflates into a distorted Communion wafer the self that God

---

[84] Mariani, *Commentary*, p. 221, does not distinguish between these two self-definitions; nei-ther Miller, *The Disappearance of God*, p. 271, nor Robert H. Goldsmith, "The Selfless Self: Hopkins' Late Sonnets," *Hopkins Quarterly* 3 (1976): 71, comments on it.

had commanded to remain unleavened (see Exodus 12 : 19–20).[85] As bread, he becomes his own self-consuming, self-consumed sustenance; without Christ's kneading hand to create his bodily freedom and perfection, he becomes like formless clay, shapelessly "heaped." Hopkins's self-abasing mockery continues brilliantly: "sweating," he becomes Adam as yet unredeemed (Genesis 3 : 9); sweating like bread in the oven's heat, he feels that unregeneration and psychic torment as a fiery infernal pressure. Between sin and damnation comes the final element in this self-parody on a Crashavian theme: in the garden of Gethsemene, Christ's "sweat was as it were great drops of blood falling down to the ground" (Luke 22 : 44); Hopkins had earlier (1881) identified those redemptive "drops of sweat or blood" with "the blissful agony or stress of selving in God" that created the world (*Sermons*, p. 197). Here, however, there is nothing but helplessly disobedient perversion, and one that, through the compressed allusion to the Fall and the Crucifixion, encompasses all of Christian history save the Apocalypse.

Sensation of taste, then, provides the true index of the self's corruption. Simultaneously, it generates the most radical metaphor of bodily dissociation in all of the "terrible sonnets": "I am gall, I am heartburn." To read these metaphors only for their emblematic value, as blunt symbols of humankind's indwelling antagonism to the Lord, is to miss half the point. Although they derive from Ignatian imagery of diseased sin ("Let me see myself as an ulcerous sore running with every horrible and disgusting poison"),[86] these self-definitions are not based on discrete analogy: they involve metaphoric conversions, they alter the body. The equations shrink the rational and conscious self, housed in an entire bodily shape, to separate and unconscious sensory phenomena; Eliot's bodily synecdoches in "Preludes" disorient similarly. With "heartburn" (perhaps a parody of the flaming Sacred Heart as well as a metaphor of sorrow), the body is transformed into an evanescent process of pain. As such, the metamorphoses render in extreme form the speaker's experience of diminished space and lessened, dehumanized cognition. As with the indirect equation of self and "blind / Eyes" in "My Own Heart," the self is reduced to isolated and seemingly dismembered points of agony; these phenomena then engulf the original self, define the whole by means of the part—much as "Self-yeast," the morally salient and identifying feature of the entire loaf, "sours"

[85] For alternative, but not antithetical readings of this image of yeast, see Boyle, *Metaphor in Hopkins*, p. 155, and Mariani, *Commentary*, pp. 221–22. The immediate source for Hopkins's image may well be Keats's statement to Benjamin Bailey (23 January 1818): "The best of Men have but a portion of good in them—a kind of spiritual yeast in their frames which creates the ferment of existence—by which a Man is propell'd to act and strive and buffet with Circumstance" (*The Letters of John Keats*, ed. Rollins, 1 : 210).

[86] St. Ignatius Loyola, *Spiritual Exercises*, p. 34.

the bread completely. As the pain draws all psychic energy to itself, it seems unnaturally enlarged; the original self loses proportional awareness, and the normative hierarchy of bodily relations is destroyed. Not the entirety of the speaker's "belonging field," but a particular sensation in one of its areas becomes the only means of defining the self.

This engulfing of the whole by the part is not so much an emotional hyperbole as a kind of anti-synecdochic imagery: instead of implying the whole, the sharply constricted focus functions mainly to demonstrate the whole self's disappearance, irrelevance, or absorption into its part. With less derangement than appears here, Hopkins had explored this anti-synecdochic imagery in his 1880 Retreat Notes as he attempted, through his Scotism, to understand his relation to the divinity of which he was a part. From Ruskin he took, first, a passage analyzing the Greek view of immanence:

> . . . the Greek reasoned upon this sensation [of animated nature], saying to himself: "I can light the fire, and put it out; I can dry this water up, or drink it. It cannot be the fire or the water that rages, or that is wayward. But it must be something *in* this fire and *in* the water, which I cannot destroy by extinguishing the one, or evaporating the other, any more than I destroy myself by cutting off my finger; *I* was *in* my finger,—something of me at least was; I had a power over it, and felt pain in it, though I am still as much myself when it is gone.[87]

Hopkins's handling of Ruskin's image is based on the same analogy: God is to myself as I am to my finger. But—more faithful to Ruskin's source in Locke,[88] and with an imaginative complexity greater than Ruskin's—he realized his finger as a person and endowed it with volition, personality, powers of moral discernment distinct from those that he himself possessed:

> Put it thus: suppose my little finger could have a being of its own, a personal being, without ceasing to be my finger and my using it and feeling in it; if I now hold it in the candle-flame the pain of the burning, though the selfsame feeling of pain, experienced by me in my finger and by my finger in itself, will be nevertheless

---

[87] Ruskin, *Works*, 5 : 224.

[88] "Thus every one finds that, whilst comprehended under that consciousness [the self], the little finger is as much a part of himself as what is most so. Upon separation of this little finger, should this consciousness go along with the little finger, and leave the rest of the body, it is evident the little finger would be the person, the same person; and self then would have nothing to do with the rest of the body" (John Locke, *An Essay Concerning Human Understanding*, ed. Alexander Campbell Frazer, 2 vols. [New York: Dover, 1959], 2 : 459).

unlike in us two, for to my finger it is the scorching of its whole
self, but to me the scorching only of one finger. And beyond this,
taking it morally, if I have freely put my finger into the flame and
the finger is unwilling, but unable to resist, then I am guilty of
my folly and self-mutilation, but my finger is innocent; if on the
other hand my finger is willing, then it is more guilty than I, for
to me the loss of a finger is but mutilation, but to my finger itself
it is selfmurder. Or if again it were selfsacrifice the sacrifice would
be nobler in the finger, to which it was a holocaust, than in me, in
whom it was the consuming of a part only. [*Sermons*, p. 126]

The theological discriminations behind this imagery should not obscure its
psychic import: five years before the "terrible sonnets," at a time roughly cor-
responding to the introduction of pathetic fallacy in his poetry, Hopkins was
writing of self-mutilation, murder, suicide, holocaust by flame. The extraordi-
nary clinical curiosity, as well as empathy, in the passage barely masks the fas-
cinations of masochism. Nor does the language of philosophical distinctions
much conceal this most elaborate of Hopkins's attempts to establish an auton-
omous system of communication between himself and his body. Unlike the
self-reducing metaphors of "I Wake and Feel," however, the prose passage
maintains in distinct but simultaneous perspectives both the embracing self of
the "I" (Hopkins) and the newly postulated "self" of the finger; without that
simultaneity, it would not render such a sense of odd dislocation. The passage
is not in itself anti-synecdochic, though it certainly moves in that direction
both through Hopkins's virtuosity in ascribing intellective attributes to the
finger alone and through his creation of a dramatic antagonism between dis-
junct forces and moral perspectives. Even so, there is no suggestion that the
finger engulfs the original self, only the hypothesis that the finger possesses its
own individuality—not merely as object of the self's contemplation but as
conscious being in its own right. Indeed, more than any other passage in
Hopkins, this extended image manages successfully to transfer to the body's
various parts that sense of reciprocity, shared relation, which Hopkins had
once, much earlier, considered to be the central sacramental value in his per-
ception of nature.

It is against this passage that the metamorphoses of "I am gall, I am heart-
burn" must be weighed. The balance postulated between self and finger van-
ishes; the self loses both identity and hierarchical control, is engulfed by its
properties, gall and heartburn. The absorption of the self by its parts marks
Hopkins's failure to sustain what he had barely achieved in the prose passage,
the interior connectedness that, however solipsistic its primary focus, was nev-

ertheless an important index of his own coherence. One must turn to one of Hopkins's most careful students, Plath, in order to find a comparable capacity for extravagant fantasy about parts of the body and sensory phenomena. In Plath, although the emphasis is more on dismemberment than on the kind of amorphous dissolution characteristic of Hopkins, the imagery similarly attests the fragility of ego-structure. Thus, the poem "Cut," from *Ariel*:

> What a thrill—
> My thumb instead of an onion.
> The top quite gone
> Except for a sort of hinge
>
> Of skin,
> A flap like a hat,
> Dead white.
> Then that red plush.
>
> Little pilgrim,
> The Indian's axed your scalp.
> Your turkey wattle
> Carpet rolls
>
> Straight from the heart.
> . . . .
>
> Out of a gap
> A million soldiers run,
> Redcoats, every one.
>
> Whose side are they on?
> O my
> Homunculus, I am ill.

For Hopkins, as for Plath, the obsessive fixation on an isolated sensory occasion is so intense that the rest of the "belonging field"—not to speak of the exterior world—all but ceases to signify. In becoming the sensory experience itself, the speaker of "I Wake and Feel" loses the last of those capacities that distinguish his human nature: the capacity to feel consciously, to interpret and reflect, to keep the self's dual aspect as self and object in balance. If the rest of the sestet suggests a certain recovery of cognitive functioning, it but measures the extremity of this darkest of self-annihilations.

III
IGNATIAN STRUCTURE: HOPKINS'S FAILURES IN COLLOQUY

Suffer me not to be separated

And let my cry come unto Thee.

T. S. ELIOT, *Ash Wednesday*, VI (1930)

It is a bitter proof of Hopkins's creative integrity and wholeness of sensibility that his personal suffering of Christ's withdrawal should have manifested itself in the actual structure of the "terrible sonnets," as well as in the imagery rooted in pathetic fallacy and dehumanization. While it is again difficult to establish the causal relations between religious disposition and poetic form, it is nevertheless plain that the structure of the "terrible sonnets" differs markedly from that of the earlier poems. This change correlates directly with Christ's disappearance, both from nature and from the self, and with the emergence of Hopkins's solipsism. As he had lost the sacramental reciprocity between himself and nature, so, too, he became estranged from God; in chapter 4 I show the social ramification of these losses in Hopkins's broken relationship with the implied audience of his poems. The "terrible sonnets" show, formally, an explicit and unalleviated psychomachia, an inturning of design through which contact with exterior reality is blocked or evaded: these are the structural counterparts to Hopkins's effort to generate an entirely closed system of communication between himself and his body. In its most significant manifestation, as I shall presently explain, this introversion of design eliminates, curtails, or distorts the climactic colloquy with Christ that is the center of the Ignatian meditative pattern: the poems are dismembered, theologically unfinished. Thus, although the "terrible sonnets" may be complete as sonnets (that is, as conventionally constructed *literary* artifacts), their structure is psychically and religiously incomplete when compared both with Hopkins's earlier work and with traditional Ignatian design. Their incompleteness, particularly because it is of so organic a kind, is telling evidence of Hopkins's inability to wrest free of the "fell of dark" that enshrouded him.

The radically changed structure of the "terrible sonnets" is quickly signalled in the opening lines. Whereas poems like "The Starlight Night," "Spring," "Pied Beauty," and "Hurrahing in Harvest" (and even "Ribblesdale," among the late nature poems) begin with a spontaneous, sensuous apperception of the exterior world and Christ's immanence therein, the "terrible sonnets" commence by positing internal anxiety and conflict. Three of them expressly announce the soul's warfare against itself:

> Not, I'll not, carrion comfort, Despair, not feast on thee . . .
>
> ["Carrion Comfort"]

Patience, hard thing! the hard thing but to pray,
But bid for, patience is!

["Patience"]

My own heart let me more have pity on . . .

["My Own Heart"]

In microcosmic form, these self-debates concern the central Christian tension between what Hopkins called the "affective will" (the desire or impulse of the natural, fallen man) and the "elective will" or *arbitrium*, the Christ-directed choice or election to perform God's bidding that figures so prominently in the *Spiritual Exercises*. The implications of this psychomachia involve the polarities of Christian history. "The irremediable divorce between desire and choice," Devlin has written, "is the state of the damned in hell. The complete and utter union of desire and choice is true love, a pledge of heaven" (*Sermons*, p. 118).[1] Thus, in "Carrion Comfort," against the threat of suicide and the damning temptation to profane the Eucharist, the speaker heroically determines to remain God's creature. In "Patience," against distempered lethargy or *accedia*, and against the natural man's frustrated inability to endure God's "humiliations" (*Sermons*, p. 253), he quests for that Christian patience which is, ultimately, a faith in the Apocalypse. And in "My Own Heart," against a masochistic scrupulosity in ferreting out his sins, he seeks for the discipline of charity, the self-pity that Hopkins called the "disavowal of our past [sinning] selves" (*Sermons*, p. 135). The alternatives are dreadful. But these initiating conflicts are still purposive; they at least offer a choice between possibilities. The self still senses itself as having sufficient elective will to achieve a Christian identity. "And it is in the presence of the alternatives," Hopkins remarked, "that the elective will has this freedom [to choose the good], for after their withdrawal it remains as fast as if it were frozen in its last choice" (*Sermons*, p. 152).

By comparison, the openings of the remaining "terrible sonnets" reveal no such freedom of possibility; the elective will suffers atrophy, and psychic as well as physical space is reduced. Hopkins had commented that "when there is but one alternative, that is / no alternative, when there is no choice, no free-

[1] Gerard Manley Hopkins, *The Sermons and Devotional Writings of Gerard Manley Hopkins*, ed. Christopher Devlin (London: Oxford University Press, 1959). Devlin's entire treatment of Hopkins's conception of the affective and elective wills is extremely valuable (*Sermons*, pp. 115–21), particularly his questioning "whether Hopkins was right in sometimes taking for granted an inevitable opposition between the two" (p. 116). Note also his brief indication (p. 120) of Hopkins's debt to Romantic psychology in positing a "naked, anti-natural" *arbitrium*.

dom of field, the elective will always, without effort, passively ratifies the spring of the affective will to action" (*Sermons*, p. 152). But these openings, far less optimistic than the prose, show a self-division that is neither the condition of choice nor the elective will's ratification of the affective will's mere uncontrolled impulse towards "whatever has the quality and look of good" (*Sermons*, p. 152). They show instead a fruitless conflict whose anguish is wholly self-enclosed and unbreachable. "No worst, there is none"—as the flanking negatives suggest—evokes the stark recognition of an inhuman pain the speaker lacks power to mitigate. "I wake and feel the fell of dark, not day" combines thwarted hope of reprieve with doomed acceptance of continued disaster. "To seem the stranger lies my lot, my life / Among strangers" exhibits in its incoiling chiasmus that oddness in self-regard, that hypersensitive awareness of being a trapped spectator of one's debility which defines the speaker's characteristically doubled, sometimes antiphonal, voice within these poems. Yeats may have found such self-distance advantageous in questing for his own self-completion, organizing his experience—as in "Lapis Lazuli"—into tragedy; but Hopkins did not, and nowhere do these poems resonate with those firm tonalities, reflecting an interior faith in his own indivisible coherence, that distinguish the openings of his earlier poetry. The self-divisions here are, of course, Hopkins's versions of a typically Victorian mode. Tennyson's "The Two Voices" and "The Palace of Art," Clough's "Dipsychus," Arnold's "The Buried Life" and "Resignation," Yeats's "A Dialogue of Self and Soul," and Eliot's "The Love Song of J. Alfred Prufrock" and "Gerontion"—all show certain affinities. The salient issue, however, is the relative place that these poems of self-division have in each poet's development: whereas Tennyson and Eliot, for example, began in self-division and subsequently sought to overcome or reconcile the tensions thus explored, Hopkins found himself assailed by self-division only as his brief career neared its close. Nor could he then find energy, time, or spiritual strength either to recover the wholeness he had lost or to achieve a new integration.

The technical, and theological, concomitant of such enclosed self-debate is that the vocative mode nearly vanishes.[2] Christ absent, He cannot be addressed save in the bereft cries of "No Worst"; nor does He appear as an understood Presence who, although silent, overhears and guides His servant's tormented devotions. With the exception of "Carrion Comfort," the "terrible sonnets" generally do not substantiate Hartman's claim that "Hopkins's style is as voca-

---

[2] For a discussion of the Omega-symbolism in Hopkins's vocatives prior to the "terrible sonnets," see James Finn Cotter, *Inscape: The Christology and Poetry of Gerard Manley Hopkins* (Pittsburgh, Pa.: University of Pittsburgh Press, 1972), pp. 287–90.

tive as possible."[3] When a vocative does occur, it ironically refers to a part of the speaker's own body—"what sights, you, heart, saw" ("I Wake and Feel") —and thus becomes an aspect of the imprisoned self-address he cannot escape. Even in "No Worst," as he names the Comforter directly, he gains only the rude knowledge that the Name no longer betokens His function. Most typically, however, the poems constantly turn a potential vocative—"O"—into a mere exclamation or intensifier:

> O the mind, mind has mountains . . .
>
> ["No Worst"]

> England, whose honour O all my heart woos . . .
>
> ["To Seem the Stranger"]

> What hours, O what black hoūrs we have spent . . .
>
> ["I Wake and Feel"]

Compare Hopkins's use of "O" as an integral part of invocation in his earlier work:[4]

> O Father, not under thy feathers nor ever as guessing
> The goal was a shoal . . .
>
> [*The Wreck of the Deutschland*, stanza 12]

> AND the fire that breaks from thee then, a billion
> Times told lovelier, more dangerous, O my chevalier!
>
> ["The Windhover"]

Hopkins's practice of transforming the invocatory "O" into an emotional interjection that posits no audience is actually visible in his revisions of "Carrion Comfort":

Yet why, thou terrible . . .	(1st draft)
O yet, thou terrible . . .	(2nd draft)
But ah, but[,] O thou terrible . . .	(3rd draft)

---

[3] Geoffrey H. Hartman, "Hopkins Revisited," in *Beyond Formalism: Literary Essays, 1958–1970* (New Haven, Conn.: Yale University Press, 1970), p. 237.

[4] Wilhelmus Antonius Maria Peters, *Gerard Manley Hopkins: A Critical Essay towards the Understanding of his Poetry* (London: Oxford University Press, 1947), pp. 73–74, does not distinguish between the "O" as "inarticulate cry" and as ritualized invocation. I do not mean to argue that Hopkins, in the poems prior to the "terrible sonnets," did not use the "O" as an emotional intensifier; see, e.g., *The Wreck of the Deutschland* (stanza 2): "I did say yes / O at lightning and lashed rod." Rather the opposite: in the "terrible sonnets," the use of "O" as invocation of divinity does not occur. See commentary below on "O thou terrible."

Blunt address is gradually diffused. In the final version, the comma originally functioned to set off "O thou terrible" as an entire invocation, preceded by a gasped pause; the cancellation reconstitutes "O" as part of the chromatic cry, "But ah, but O . . . ." This weakened vocative, signalling the speaker's failing ability to "greet [God] the days I meet him," epitomizes many of Hopkins's revisions of the "terrible sonnets." "Patience" originally opened,

> Patience, hard thing! the hard thing but to pray,
> But bid
> [Ask God] for, patience is!

Eradicating the Name of his audience, adding a "but" that interferes with the implicitly vocative mode of "Ask God," Hopkins proceeds in the sestet to modify severely the central—and now despairing—hope of his prayer:

> Yet the rebellious wills
> bend
> Of us wé dö bid God [bring] to him even so.

What is bent, however flexibly, may here never touch; the distance created by sin may be finally immitigable.[5] In "I Wake and Feel," Hopkins makes that sin seem nearly Calvinist in its deterministic force as, in the sestet, he changes his verbs from present tense to past:

> was
> my taste [is] me;
> t   ed   med the
> Bones buil[d] in me, flesh fill[s], blood brim[s]   [a] curse.

If the past tense erases the impression of ongoing sinfulness, it also suggests that creation and divine energy have ended, leaving the speaker in an unalterable state. As with the change from "see: who" to "see you" in "My Own Heart," the sense of God's active intervention in history is diminished.

The suppression of direct or implied vocatives in the revisions is systematic if not complete; and it is doubtful that Hopkins thus stressed the breach between himself and God for literary reasons alone. Precisely why he cancelled these few traces of a spiritual kingdom that he might still have contacted cannot be known. The revisions may well represent Hopkins's masochistic tendency to mortify himself by denying himself the possibility of the divine relief

---

[5] Paul L. Mariani, *A Commentary on the Complete Poems of Gerard Manley Hopkins* (Ithaca, N.Y.: Cornell University Press, 1970), p. 236, observes a pun on "bend": "There is no other way to gain patience (*patiens* = suffering, and also the Passion of Christ) but by bending (crisp = *crispus* = *curvus* = curved) the stubborn, grotesquely twisted heart to God." The verb "bend," however, implies a less complete motion towards God than "bring."

he so craved. At the same time, he may have eliminated these vocatives be-
cause they belied his real understanding that such reciprocal relations had ac-
tually been broken. In any case, the revised poems suggest, far more than the
initial versions, a world in which the vocative has lost its propitiatory and
summoning functions; prayer is curtailed, the deity is absent, and the speaker
—without any audience but himself—must wrestle in his own vacuum.

The self-debate with its attendant suppression of the vocative mode, how-
ever, is itself symptomatic of a much larger alteration in Hopkins's procedure.
Translated into the terms of Ignatian meditation, the elimination of the voca-
tive amounts to an omission of colloquy with God, the central and climactic
occasion towards which the entire meditative exercise should move. Indeed,
the "terrible sonnets" diverge so sharply from the design of Ignatian medi-
tation to which Hopkins had previously adhered that neither Downes nor
Bender (both of whom have analyzed St. Ignatius's influence on Hopkins) has
been able to account for the structure of the "terrible sonnets" in Ignatian
terms at all.[6] Hopkins's deviation cannot be construed in aesthetic terms as a
conscious effort at formal experimentation, an invention of new forms through
variation on traditional pattern; for it emerges from a faltering he could not
entirely control. The deviation is chiefly theological, a sign of the extremity of
Hopkins's crisis; and its dimensions can only be understood by comparing the
poems with their Ignatian model. Properly speaking, the "terrible sonnets"
constitute failures in Ignatian meditation. Some of the poems omit colloquy
altogether, others distort it; that the poems correspond in other respects to the
meditative structure set forth in the *Spiritual Exercises* is sufficient proof that
the deviation, however untoward, was not accidental. Although Downes has
cleverly juxtaposed portions of Hopkins's poems with selected texts of Ignatius
and Thomas à Kempis in order to create an impression of spiritual dialogue,[7]
his arrangement cannot obscure the absence of colloquy with God that marks
the "terrible sonnets" as thwarted works whose partial nature prevents them
from achieving their fullest spiritual efficacy.

Briefly put, the Ignatian exercise is a consciously Trinitarian structure. Its
three main episodes—the composition of place, the moral analysis, and the
colloquy—correspond to the chief faculties of Augustinian psychology, the
memory, the understanding, and the will.[8] The Trinitarian structure makes

[6] David A. Downes, *Gerard Manley Hopkins: A Study of His Ignatian Spirit* (New York: Book-
man Associates, 1959), chap. 5, passim; Todd K. Bender, *Gerard Manley Hopkins: The Classical
Background and Critical Reception of His Work* (Baltimore, Md.: Johns Hopkins University Press,
1966), pp. 146–58.
[7] Downes, *Hopkins*, pp. 138–44.
[8] See Joseph de Guibert, *The Jesuits: Their Spiritual Doctrine and Practice*, trans. William J.

completion of the exercise—in the soul's willed movement towards God—
essential for the recognition of its sacramental nature. Hopkins, as a novice at
Roehampton, had listened in refectory not only to readings from St. Ignatius
but to Luis de la Puente's *Meditations upon the Mysteries of our Holie Faith, with
the Practise of Mental Prayer touching the same*,[9] and he cannot but have under-
stood the critical failure of the "elective will" that his omission of colloquy
entailed. His deviation is all the more surprising because, from a strictly liter-
ary perspective, it is plain that in all but three of his previous sonnets ("The
Sea and The Skylark," "Felix Randal,"[10] and "Ribblesdale"), he had concluded
with a colloquy—and thus successfully meshed Ignatian meditative pattern-
ing with the requirements of sonnet-form. The incompletion of the "terrible
sonnets"—as meditative structures—is evidence of spiritual and psychic de-
bility. Hopkins well knew that St. Ignatius himself, acknowledging that "in
time of distress it is very hard to finish" the meditation, firmly counselled the
exercitant "to counter the distress and overcome the temptation" by continu-
ing "a little longer than the full hour."[11] He knew, too, that Roothan, in *De
Ratione Meditandi*, while urging that the exercitant's feeling of base unworthi-
ness "should be entertained as long as there is sincere affection and some relish
in keeping the thought before our mind,"[12] counselled colloquy with God as
the proper conclusion to such mortification. And he understood the justice of
Roothan's comment on the indivisibility of the components in Ignatian medi-
tation: "We know that no means St. Ignatius has prescribed for the success of
our meditation is superfluous. All his recommendations fit together like the
links of a chain; if even one of them is removed or broken, the chain becomes

Young, ed. George E. Ganss (Chicago: The Institute of Jesuit Sources and Loyola University Press,
1964), p. 549: "In the *Exercises*, therefore, the method of the three faculties occupies only a highly
restricted place. Consequently it is an error, no less serious than frequent, to regard this method as
the peculiar and exclusive type of all mental prayer made according to the Ignatian *Exercises*. . . .
Outside the first week there are a few meditations, such as that on the Three Classes of Men,
which take up again this method of the three faculties; but by far the largest place is taken up by
the contemplation of the gospel events."

[9] Alfred Thomas, *Hopkins the Jesuit: The Years of Training* (London: Oxford University Press,
1969), p. 215. It is not certain which edition of Puente's *Meditations* Hopkins used (p. 72, n. 6).
Thomas's Appendix 2 (pp. 214–45) gives an extremely valuable list of books and articles read in
refectory during Hopkins's period of training.

[10] Cotter, *Inscape*, p. 211, however, sees a movement towards Incarnation at the end of this
poem that might be taken as a version of colloquy: "The literal level yields to the spiritual one in
the final unifying object of the poem. The inscape comes in the semicircular sandal, the mark of
Christ—capital Omega—held and glowing with fire."

[11] St. Ignatius Loyola, *The Spiritual Exercises*, trans. Thomas Corbishley (Westminster, Md.:
Christian Classics, 1973), p. 15.

[12] John Roothan, *How to Meditate (De Ratione Meditandi)*, trans. Louis J. Puhl (Westminster,
Md.: The Newman Bookshop, 1945), p. 48.

either entirely useless for its purpose or at least less serviceable."[13] Thus under-
standing the unity of mental prayer, Hopkins would not have subscribed to
the view of Ignatian meditation advanced by Martz in *The Poetry of Meditation*:
"In other meditative poems we may find only 'some part' of the total action [of
meditation] set down in poetical form; and yet the poem may contain an im-
plied relation to the total process of meditation."[14] Hopkins would have dis-
missed this synecdochic argument as a violation of St. Ignatius's intent. He
had sought, in his earlier poetry, to make each sonnet a complete exercise; and
when he found, in his private meditations of 1888, that he could not progress
beyond feelings of "loathing and hopelessness" (*Sermons*, p. 262), he bitterly
preferred to cease meditating altogether rather than suffer the continued pain
of incompletion. There is some basis in the Ignatian tradition for considering
the self-debate of moral analysis as a kind of colloquy; but that element in the
entire exercise cannot substitute for completion of the whole. Thus, Puente,
citing the psalms of David as an instance of the soul's legitimate colloquy with
itself, urges "conference with our owne soule. Sometimes our selves (as S. Paul
saieth) exhorting our selves, and reviving our selves in the affections, and peti-
tions rehearsed. Other times reprehending our selves for our faultes, and for
our want of zeale, and being ashamed of our selves that we serve almightie
God so negligentlie." But Puente then goes on to reject the synecdochic view
of meditation. He concludes, "from these colloquyes we must next proceede to
speake to God himselfe, as did the prodigall sonne."[15] Hopkins could not pro-
ceed. Nor did he feel that his self-debates had the status of legitimate interior
colloquy. Robert Parsons, whose *Christian Directorie* (1585) Hopkins knew
well, had called mental prayer "nothing els but an elevation of our spirite unto
almightie God, & an exercise of our soule wherin she debateth [in] the pres-
ence of her Creator the affaires which appertaine to her owne salvation."[16] But

[13] Ibid., p. 62; Roothan's ellipsis.

[14] Louis L. Martz, *The Poetry of Meditation: A Study in English Religious Literature of the Seventeenth
Century*, rev. ed. (New Haven, Conn.: Yale University Press, 1962), p. xxiv. See also John Donne,
The Divine Poems, ed. Helen Gardner (Oxford: Clarendon Press, 1952), pp. l–liv: Gardner sim-
ilarly believes that a partial meditation implies the whole. The position may well hold true for
Donne, who, as Gardner says, "made extended and highly original use of the tradition of medita-
tion" (p. 1); but not for Hopkins.

[15] Luis de la Puente, *Meditations upon the Mysteries of our Holie Faith, with the Practise of Mental
Prayer touching the same*, trans. John Heigham, 2 vols. (St. Omer, France, 1619), 1:9. I have si-
lently normalized the use of *v, u,* and *s* in the orthography. Martz, *The Poetry of Meditation*, p. 37,
quotes the first passage, but not the second; he thus, perhaps, creates a misleading impression of
the real demands of meditative structure.

[16] Robert Parsons, *A Christian Directorie* ([Rouen,] 1585). The section from which this citation
is taken—"A Breefe Method How to Use the Former treatises, chapters, and considerations"—is
unpaginated; again, I have normalized the use of *v, u,* and *s*. See Thomas, *Hopkins the Jesuit*, pp.
215, 217, for the readings from Parsons in the refectory of Manresa House, Roehampton.

Hopkins felt no such invisible, divine encouragement. Prayer, according to Puente, "in its perfect degree embraceth union with God;"[17] the "terrible sonnets," lacking proper colloquy, were imperfect, could achieve no such union. It is not sufficient to say that self-debate, in the "terrible sonnets," drives out colloquy with God. Hopkins's failure to generate colloquy is the exact structural counterpart to major issues treated in the subject-matter, the breakdown in images of nature and the blocked communion with Christ. As Christ, the mediator between the divine and the human, disappears from sight, the mediation of prayer itself is structurally curtailed.

It is important to understand more fully what it is that Hopkins has omitted or distorted. St. Ignatius, incorporating into the *Spiritual Exercises* the atmosphere of dialogue he had found in *The Imitation of Christ*, considered colloquy to be the imaginative, dramatic, and theological center of the entire meditation. The nearly mystical significance he ascribes to colloquy is indicated by the particular point in the *Spiritual Exercises* at which he first describes it—at the end of the meditation on "The Triple Sin" (in the First Week):

> Let me picture Christ our Lord hanging on the Cross before me, and speak to Him in this way: how has He, the Creator, come to be man? Knowing eternal life, how has He come to this temporal death, this death for my sins? Then, turning to myself, I will ask: what have I done for Christ? What am I doing for Christ? What must I do for Christ?
>
> Seeing the state Christ is in, nailed to the Cross, let me dwell on such thoughts as present themselves.
>
> The colloquy is really the kind of talk friends have with one another, or perhaps like the way a servant speaks to his master, asking for some kindness or apologising for some failure, or telling him about some matter of business and asking for his advice.
>
> The colloquy ends with an *Our Father.*[18]

The passage follows a long meditation on the history of sin—in the angels, in Adam and Eve, and in the exercitant himself. Through the colloquy, however, the ineffable gulf between the human and the divine—created through sin— is mediated. For the first time, as the centripetal structure of the meditation reaches its climax in the individual consciousness, the exercitant recognizes the cosmic implications of his own sins in the scheme of salvation history; he understands, beyond discursive reasoning, both what Hopkins called the "incredible condescension of the Incarnation" and the mystery of redemption

[17] Puente, *Meditations*, 1:12.
[18] St. Ignatius Loyola, *Spiritual Exercises*, pp. 32–33.

which is the Crucifixion. Both the vision and the intimacy of colloquy consti-
tute the exercitant's attainment, through grace, of an imitation of Christ. Ac-
cording to Rahner, St. Ignatius ascribes "such intimate awareness of sin to
prayerful colloquy alone"; "only through contemplation of Christ crucified is
it possible to find out the ways and means by which the divine order may be
restored." [19] In this greeting of the divine and the human, the colloquy thus
has nothing to do with "intellectual self-knowledge in the merely psychologi-
cal sense;" [20] indeed, the implied interchange of voices in the exercitant's self-
questioning—"What have I done for Christ?"—points to his transfiguring
adoption of a divine perspective. The centrality of self-transfiguration here is
the wholly personal counterpart to the transfigurations of nature Hopkins at-
tempted to achieve by revealing Christ immanent within it. Although the col-
loquy maintains the distinctions of traditional hierarchy (e.g., between ser-
vant and master), the knowledge it imparts amounts to a mystical infusion and
thus an elevation. Puente, while cautioning that the capacity for colloquy is
partly a learned skill, insists that the grace of the Holy Spirit is always present
during colloquy:

> . . . for with his inspiration hee teacheth us, and mooveth us
> to aske, ordering our petitions, and stirring up those affections
> wherewith they are to bee made.

> . . . as our Lord is very courteous, and gentle, and inspireth us to
> pray, hee speaketh to us when wee speake to him; and converseth
> familiarly with those, that enter into their heart to treat, and
> converse with him. . . . For God to speake, is to communicate
> guiftes infusing his graces, and vertues upon them to whome hee
> speaketh, filling them with that spiritual joy that cannot be ex-
> pressed, and with that peace that passeth all understanding. [21]

Thus, a meditation that begins in contemplation of the angels' refusal of divine
grace ends (if successful) in a colloquy whose very occurrence, by grace, cancels
the linguistic confusion of Babel and prefigures the ultimate redemption of
humankind. The obvious assumption of colloquy, as Puente's description makes
plain, is that, at this privileged level of contemplation, the exercitant's medita-
tion itself both evokes and embodies God's participation in human discourse.
By evoking a dialogue with divinity, it implies God's response; by implying
God's response, it assumes His activity within its form. From the perspective

[19] Hugo Rahner, *Ignatius the Theologian*, trans. Michael Berry (London: Geoffrey Chapman,
1968), pp. 86, 88.
[20] Ibid., p. 89.
[21] Puente, *Meditations*, 1:9, 11.

of a religious linguistics, colloquy does nothing less than incarnate the Word within the word. As Barthes has hinted in his treatment of Ignatian meditation, the central incertitude of colloquy—and the incertitude that makes colloquy dramatic—is whether or not this simultaneity of human and divine speech will occur;[22] but there is never any question about the fundamental necessity of continuing to strive for such transfiguration in prayer.

The exercitant's theological recognition of God's design is no less essential to colloquy than the attainment of transcendent inner speech. In the closing meditation on "The Triple Sin," this recognition prompts a movement towards Christian action, one which directly anticipates the climactic election of Christ that comes at the end of the Second Week and thus, as with colloquy itself, foreshadows redemption. But the soul's awareness of future action is eschatological as well as ethical: the exercitant examines his past and present to discern his future function in the constant warfare against satanic dominion. Thus, the recognition of God's design is simultaneously a recognition of his own role in that scheme. As this understanding surfaces, the fundamental alteration that St. Ignatius implicitly posits in the status of the exercitant—from observer to participant—is completed. For both the dramatic intimacy of colloquy and the personal realization of the individual function of the "elective will" result from a meditative process that is, throughout, dramatic: the careful disciplining of the memory and the understanding has as its chief goal the transformation of exercitant into actor.

Through the memory, which operates here in both its personal and historical aspects, the exercitant forms an "imaginative representation" or composition of place appropriate to the particular subject of the meditation.[23] As he applies his senses in making and elaborating the representation of scene, he reconstitutes past events—his own sins, for example, or an event in Christ's life—as immediately present actualities: this dissolution of linear time is clearly a first step towards the timelessness of colloquy. In "this writing of Christ's life in the heart,"[24] the aim of imaginative visualization is the transcending of imagination itself: the exercitant must transmute the initially

<hr />

[22] Roland Barthes, *Sade/Fourier/Loyola*, trans. Richard Miller (1971; American edn. New York: Hill and Wang, 1976), pp. 42–44. Barthes's semiotic approach to the *Spiritual Exercises* produces a fascinating essay, but one that overlooks (or consciously disregards) the position of virtually all commentators on the *Exercises*, namely, that in colloquy the divine response *is intrinsic in* the human prayer; instead, Barthes poses the divine response as a problem within linear time: "Will the Divinity accept the language of the exercitant and offer him in return a language to be deciphered?" (p. 44).

[23] St. Ignatius Loyola, *Spiritual Exercises*, p. 30.

[24] Hugo Rahner, *Ignatius the Theologian*, p. 193. Rahner takes his phrase from the *Meditationes Vitae Christi*, once attributed to St. Bonaventura, but now thought written by an unknown fourteenth-century Franciscan.

quasi-fictional composition of scene and *dramatis personae* into literal reality. As Roothan remarks,

> In meditating upon an historical fact, we must be careful not to represent it as a painting or something that happened long ago. We should imagine it as though we were present and saw it enacted before us, as though we were there in the cave of Bethlehem or on Mt. Calvary. We see all with our eyes, hear all; the events actually take place now before us.[25]

Hopkins, commenting on St. Ignatius and following Roothan exactly, is yet more extreme: "The composition of place is always a reality, even when the story, the *historia*, is not history" (*Sermons*, p. 179). He would have taken sharp exception to Barthes's opinion that "The Ignatian image [in the composition of place] is not a *vision*, it is a *view*, in the sense this word has in graphic art."[26] As he illustrated elsewhere, knowledge of external facts must always cede place to spiritual illumination:

> Not that the exercitant, if he has not been over the ground [i.e., from Nazareth to Bethlehem], will make much of it, but that, even by the realising—I mean more as we speak of realising a sum, a fortune—his ignorance or the small knowledge he has, he may reach the reality of the facts; something as to have been on pilgrimage to Jerusalem in the dark would be more full of devotion than to see it in the best panorama. [*Sermons*, p. 173][27]

As the scene becomes present, so does the perceiver or exercitant; the space between perceiver and "painting" or "panorama" dissolves, much as the speaker of *The Wreck*, "Away in the loveable west, / On a pastoral forehead of Wales" (stanza 24), enters empathetically into the "Wiry and white-fiery and whirlwind-swivellèd snow" (stanza 13) of the disaster. Perceptual immediacy entails moral involvement, recognition of one's own responsibility, and thus the activation of the whole self. Hopkins's emphasis on "small knowledge" or lack of imaginative capability is instructive: the imagination has value not in itself but only in its capacity to show the exercitant, through the very nature of his imagining, his spiritual condition. As the entire meditation on "The Triple

[25] Roothan, *How to Meditate*, p. 14; see also pp. 19, 21.

[26] Barthes, *Sade/Fourier/Loyola*, p. 55.

[27] See Thomas, *Hopkins the Jesuit*, p. 178, n. 3, for the tantalizingly incomplete account, all that survives, of Hopkins's essay (1877) on "The Composition of place in the Spiritual Exercises," in which Hopkins maintained that the function of the composition "is not principally intended to keep the mind from wandering or to assist the imagination."

Sin" demonstrates, the spiritual adequacy of the imaginative faculty is judged wholly according to the exercitant's interior apperception of the mystery of the Crucifixion and thus his fitness for colloquy; particularly in the meditations on Christ's life during the Second Week, as Rahner indicates, the *"dramatization of the mysteries . . .* can only be properly appreciated in the light of the Election to which it is leading."[28]

This imaginative actualizing of the persons as if they were real is analogous to the "penetrative imagination," which "affirms from within"; Roothan calls such "application of the memory . . . the foundation on which the reflections and acts of the will during the remainder of the meditation must rest."[29] The exercitant, having constituted himself a participant in the composed scene, enters next into what Hopkins called "pious *reasoning"* (*Sermons*, p. 173), a moral and rational analysis of the scene whose aim is the exercitant's discovery of his proper action within it. The analysis focusses simultaneously on the exercitant's individual condition and on his relation to the design of universal redemption. This process of understanding is closely allied with the cultivation of the affections, here purged of false desire; the sestet of "Hurrahing in Harvest" presents "pious reasoning" as a fusion of perceptual understanding with awe:

> These things, these things were here and but the beholder
> Wanting: which two when they once meet,
> The heart rears wings bold and bolder
> And hurls for him [Christ] . . .

The passage brings the exercitant to the verge of Christian action. As the devout intellect converts composition into moral type, moral type into individual crisis, the exercitant understands the nature and purpose of his "elective will"; significantly, Hopkins considered that "will" a virtually separate faculty and called it "the faculty of fruition" (*Sermons*, p. 174), the means by which the exercitant enacts his Christian choice. Lorenzo Scupoli, whose *Spiritual Combat* Hopkins studied, simply made St. Ignatius's directions explicit when he recommended that the exercitant combine the conscious preparation of his "elective will" with "the meditation of the life and passion of Christ, applying always his actions to that vertue, which thou most desireth."[30] Thus, in

---

[28] Rahner, *Ignatius the Theologian*, p. 103.

[29] Roothan, *How to Meditate*, p. 23.

[30] Lorenzo Scupoli, *The Spiritual Combat: Written in Italian by a devout Servant of God, and lately translated into English out of the same language* (Rouen: Cardin-Hamilton, 1613). Hopkins may have read Scupoli as early as 1865, in the 1846 translation by Edward Bouverie Pusey; see Gerard Manley Hopkins, *The Journals and Papers of Gerard Manley Hopkins*, ed. Humphrey House, completed by Graham Storey (1959; rpt. London: Oxford University Press, 1966), p. 56 and n. 1.

"Hurrahing in Harvest," the very action proposed—"The heart rears wings" —is very nearly an *imitatio Christi*; certainly it involves a transfiguration of the exercitant's affections. Finally, in colloquy, the exercitant recognizes Christ's incarnate presence within him and thus becomes entirely an actor who participates directly in the divine drama; here, all imaginative and temporal distinctions between exercitant and Biblical event vanish. As in "As Kingfishers Catch Fire,"

> Christ plays in ten thousand places,
> Lovely in limbs, and lovely in eyes not his
> To the Father through the features of men's faces.

The dramatic metaphor, which denies dramatic illusion through the stressing of Incarnation, is an apt summary not only of colloquy but of the process and end of Ignatian meditation.

This, then, is the structure of Ignatian meditation whose entire pattern, including the climactic colloquy, Hopkins so dextrously and faithfully observed in his sonnets prior to the "terrible sonnets" of 1885. Indeed, Hopkins's adherence to the form, whatever his flexibility in emphasis, is so exact—the demarcations between episodes so neat, the sense of progressive design so clear —that the Ignatian influence is virtually unmistakable.[31] To postpone momentarily the problem of colloquy in the "terrible sonnets" themselves: it will be helpful, by way of review, to demonstrate Hopkins's typical practice of integrating the whole Ignatian pattern with sonnet-form. As a text for exposition, "God's Grandeur" (1877), although no more pristine an instance than other sonnets that might be selected, has the advantage of showing, in its content as well as its form, how explicitly involved Hopkins was in contemplating the representation of colloquy even before his later aridity made colloquy with Christ a desperate matter.

The poem opens—"The world is charged with the grandeur of God"—

---

[31] Several sonnets written prior to Hopkins's reception into the Society of Jesus, however, also appear to have a meditative structure that might be called Ignatian—the poems numbered 11, 13, 16, and 19 in Gardner and MacKenzie's 4th edition. The date of Hopkins's first reading of the *Spiritual Exercises* has not yet been ascertained, and future accounts of his debt to St. Ignatius—a full version of which we still require—must squarely face the problem, posed by the chronology of Hopkins's development, of whether St. Ignatius was his initial source for the meditative form. For the prominent role of Catholic devotional and mystical literature in the piety of the Oxford Movement, see, e.g., Yngve Brilioth, *The Anglican Revival: Studies in the Oxford Movement* (1925; rpt. London: Longmans, Green, 1933), pp. 296–98; Hubert Northcott, "The Development and Deepening of the Spiritual Life," in N. P. Williams and Charles Harris, eds., *Northern Catholicism: Centenary Studies in the Oxford and Parallel Movements* (New York: Macmillan Co., 1933), p. 320.

with an Ignatian prelude announcing the subject. The apparently abstract statement contains, in its central pun on "charged," the basic material from which the composition of place evolves. The verb defines, in electrical terms, God's indwelling energy in the natural world; it posits humankind's consequent obligations to heed Him through His designs in creation; in recalling that initial injunction, it invokes the faculty of memory to station the poem within its proper temporal frame, that of Christian history. The composition proceeds in parallel sensory images to proclaim the variety of God's theophanies in nature. These images simultaneously enact Ruskin's "penetrative imagination" and Hopkins's own Ignatian stress on understanding the composition as "a reality, even when the story . . . is not history"; they function to intensify the speaker's private involvement in the glory he meditates. That consciousness of an intimacy with the concretized idea thus evoked—evident in verbs that show his acute awareness of God's continuous activity—emanates in "pious reasoning": "Why do men then now not reck his rod?" This stern lament for perpetual ("then now") human disobedience poses a debased human history against the design of sacred history and includes within it the speaker's own consciousness of sharing the responsibility for failure. It culminates in a darkly satiric understanding of profanation: "nor can foot feel, being shod." The central meaning of this image is anagogical: evoking Moses barefoot before God immanent in the burning bush (Exodus 3 : 1–5), it absorbs the earlier image of flame, links one of God's first theophanies with those of Pentecost,[32] and thus frames the entire octave in sacred time. More significantly yet, the allusion embraces colloquy—and colloquy of a very specific kind: not only does it concern the establishment of covenant, but it is God who initiates the colloquy. Both the numinosity and the privilege of Moses's colloquy become the speaker's standard for criticizing his present world. The breach of immediate contact between foot and ground is a naturalized version of broken colloquy. It enacts in bodily form, moreover, the religious failure to satisfy the conditions necessary to divine colloquy. If humankind cannot recognize holy ground (which in fact the whole world is), then it certainly lacks the awe to perceive God within it, much less the devout capacity to invoke Him; thus, "the soil / Is bare now"—the burning bush has vanished.

Hopkins has thus constructed a "pious reasoning" whose primary focus is the proper response to God's creation. Between the antithesis of colloquy achieved (by Moses) and colloquy indifferently refused (by the present world) falls the desire for colloquy that is the speaker's aim. The very meditation on

<hr />

[32] See Cotter, *Inscape*, p. 172, for a full examination of the Pentecostal imagery in "God's Grandeur." See also Mariani, *Commentary*, p. 95.

the nature of colloquy stirs his affections, motivates him to overcome the dismal sacrilege of human history by regaining the perception of miracle. It is thus the "elective will" that here directs the "penetrative imagination" in the last phase of the "pious reasoning":

> And for all this, nature is never spent;
>   There lives the dearest freshness deep down things . . .

This is a rational analysis of the eternity of God's handiwork, based on the metaphysical logic that humankind ultimately lacks the power to destroy (though it may defile) the presence of God in His creation. But the analysis is infused with a richly observant piety, as the syntactical ambiguity suggests:

> There lives the dearest freshness deep down [in] things . . .

> There lives the dearest freshness [in] deep down things . . .

Both versions distinguish between surface and core, a tension that develops the earlier images of crushed oil and bare topsoil. In both cases God's informing presence, like Christ's in *The Wreck*, is conceived to be "*under* the world's splendour and wonder" (stanza 5; italics mine); together the two images are analogous to the definition of God as both the center and circumference of His own circle.

The renewed faith in God's redemptive design that this recognition prompts appears immediately in the speaker's final achievement of colloquy:

> And though the last lights off the black West went
>   Oh, morning, at the brown brink eastward, springs—
> Because the Holy Ghost over the bent
>   World broods with warm breast and with ah! bright wings.

The speaker has become a participant in the divine drama: his images are neither generalizations nor similes used as examples; they are direct and visionary perceptions, in fixed space and time, of a natural phenomenon, dawning, whose explicit analogue, in the concluding image of the Paraclete, is that of the apocalyptic Second Coming. Notably, the night of dark anguish prior to Christ's return to majesty appears to pass (by enjambment) with an instantaneous suddenness; it is an image buoyed by the resurgence of joy—an image wholly lacking the anxiety and desperation of "I Wake and Feel." But what graces these images with the status of colloquy is not only the present observation of mystery but the use of the vocative. "Oh, morning," though it slides into declarative statement, has the initial impact of joyous direct address, an apostrophe whose true religious energy comes from the implied recognition that it is Christ within the sun of morning who "springs," ascends from "deep down." If this colloquy is made ambiguous by the dubious syntactic status of "Oh," there is no question that the final line—with its intimate stressing of the *non*-alliterated "ah!"—renders a direct visionary invocation. In this awed and tender colloquy, the superbly sensuous apprehension of the mystery of Incarnation in "bright wings" encompasses the restitution, within Christian history, of broken covenant; for the Holy Ghost, burning in supernatural flame, answers the miracle of the burning bush. It is not necessary to argue that the speaker, vouchsafed such a vision, finds his own analogue in Moses; it is enough to see that both nature and his natural eyes have been transfigured and that, in this realizing of Incarnation, the fulfillment of colloquy is attained.

No such colloquy informs the "terrible sonnets." Because the Ignatian design presumes an ending known in advance and embodies a plot whose central narrative question concerns not the mandatory ending but the means of reaching it,[33] the failure in the "terrible sonnets" to attain that conclusion must be read as a pervasive irony of structure whose spiritual bleakness cannot be overestimated. Only "Patience" and "My Own Heart" approximate the complete Ignatian pattern; and even here, the nature and psychodynamics of colloquy differ considerably from those of the earlier poems. God, as Puente counsels, "*is riche towards all that invocate him*";[34] but the "terrible sonnets" cannot reach that state of colloquy.

"Patience" plainly has its basis in St. Ignatius's advice for dealing with periods of spiritual desolation: "In this state [the exercitant] should also strive to abide in patience, which is the antidote to the trials that beset him. He should also reflect that he will soon be comforted, and should put forth all his efforts against this distress."[35] Scupoli repeats the counsel and then, celebrating the finally tranquil endurance of distress, urges the exercitant to "suffer the burden of thy Aridity and drinesse with patience and humble resignation, for this above all others is praier most acceptable to God."[36] "Patience" exhibits a dialectical structure that in part duplicates the psychic tension implicit in St. Ignatius's paradoxical injunction, "*strive* to abide in patience"; but it never reaches the pacific acceptance of desolation that Scupoli likens to prayer. The quatrains are violently contradictory in mood, rhythm, and imagery; the tercets war against each other similarly. The transitions between the initial petition (lines 1–4), the composition of place (lines 5–8), the "pious reasoning"

[33] See Barthes, *Sade/Fourier/Loyola*, pp. 60–61, for an analysis of narrative movement in the *Spiritual Exercises*.

[34] Puente, *Meditation*, 1:8.

[35] St. Ignatius Loyola, *Spiritual Exercises*, p. 109.

[36] Scupoli, *The Spiritual Combat*, chap. 28.

(lines 9–11), and the indirect colloquy (lines 12–14) are extremely abrupt. The poem's structure, in fact, offers the same antithesis repeated twice: the affective will's shrinking from the struggle for patience vs. the elective will's effort to visualize its achievement.[37] Thus, though the poem concludes in apparent calm, as the speaker intuits in reflective colloquy Christ's abiding patience as model for his own, it hardly progresses in any common manner; certainly it does not move easily and continuously towards its climax. Given this established structure of radical vacillation between units, there is no reason not to think that the alternation between the affective and elective wills may indeed continue beyond the poem's ostensible closure. If the ending provides any resolution, its peace is temporary; and the shakiness of this peace results not only from the imagistic inconsistencies analyzed in chapter 2 but from the fact that the poetic structure itself disputes this apparent conformity with Ignatian principles.

The implied continuation of conflict, moreover, has a thematic bearing on the hesitant, limitary nature of the speaker's colloquy. "Patience" is an apocalyptic poem: the context for its exploration of the cardinal virtue is not only the speaker's individual endurance of suffering but the epochal time of tension, the waiting for Christ's Second Coming—and it is this apocalyptic incertitude that the indefiniteness of the poem's closure renders. While Christ epitomizes the patience the speaker seeks to emulate, the clause "He is patient" also defines Christ as the Lord who Himself patiently awaits the time of His reappearance; the honey imagery is thus proleptically paradisal as well as pastoral. The implicit analogy between the speaker and Christ as they simultaneously await the same event has a tender poignancy typical of Hopkins; but it must not obscure the fact that the poem's foundation in future apocalypse necessarily postpones the realizing of Incarnation that is the substance of Ignatian colloquy. Christ's absence is thus rationalized as a consequence of Christian eschatology; but compare "God's Grandeur," in which the apocalyptic structure does not damage in the least the speaker's capacity, in colloquy, for direct invocation of the Godhead.

Postponed as well is the fulfillment of St. Ignatius's counsel that the exercitant "will *soon* be comforted."[38] Although the speaker comes to understand the relation of his own patience to salvation history, he gains no alleviation of his pain: this withholding of relief, of course, is part of the ascetic discipline and

---

[37] Mariani, *Commentary*, p. 235, also observes both the abrupt transitions and the repetition of the main antithesis; he sees these elements, however, as creating "The two themes of the severity and serenity of patience" and does not consider their import for poetic—as opposed to religious—structure.

[38] St. Ignatius Loyola, *Spiritual Exercises*, p. 109.

submission that the poem's theme demands. Nevertheless, in the last tercet, the speaker asks for divine response, but must do so—"where is he?"—by referring to Christ in the third person, so great is the grim sense of unmediated distance created by Hopkins's late apocalyptic vision. He must, moreover, answer his own question. The apocalyptic framework accounts, too, for the curious discontinuity between question and answer. For the question as posed, addressing the central issue of Christ's second Incarnation, cannot be answered save through faith in mystery and through imagery which, if it is to remain orthodox, must patiently deflect the chief anxiety. The concluding faith in the coming of sufficient grace to "abide in patience," however, is qualified by a suspiciously blank phrasing: "that comes those ways we know." However intimate the knowledge implied, this is a statement of probability based on doctrine and past experience, not a realizing of present grace proffered. By comparison with the colloquy of "Peace" (1879), one that is also oriented towards the future,

> O surely, reaving Peace, my Lord should leave in lieu
> Some good! And so he does leave Patience exquisite,
> That plumes to Peace thereafter [,]

the colloquy of "Patience" lacks conviction, visual clarity, and a concrete representation of agency. What this poem does not elaborate, though the other "terrible sonnets" certainly indicate its undercurrent, is the speaker's pained straining to have the time of tension ended.

"My Own Heart," both in its general context and in the nature of its colloquy, shows yet another weakening in the speaker's capacity for Ignatian meditation. St. Ignatius offers the following counsel to the exercitant who experiences desolation:

> When in distress, a man should reflect that God is testing him by leaving him to his own resources in his struggle against the different assaults and temptations of the enemy; he can succeed with the help of God, which is always there, even though he is not clearly aware of it. God has indeed withdrawn any great warmth of feeling, intensity of love and extraordinary grace, but He has left grace enough for the man's eternal salvation.[39]

But as the apocalyptic faith of "Patience" dwindles, the speaker knows only the bitterness left by God's withdrawal: he cannot recognize the operation of sufficient grace; nor, more significantly, can he construe his suffering within

[39] Ibid.

the context of a divinely-imposed trial, itself a microcosm of Christian war-
fare, which the speaker of "Patience" still finds available. The poem opens in a
context of pain so secularized, so bereft of eschatological framework, that its
self-debate between the affective and elective wills betrays no apprehension of
the supernatural order at all. Clearly this self-referential colloquy occurs pre-
cisely because traditional Ignatian colloquy with Christ, considered here as an
intiating petition or, more loosely, as a general "examination of conscience,"
does not seem possible. The interior wrestling results entirely, in the poem's
psychological structure, from a composition of place (ll. 3–8) that defines the
spirit's demoniac torment, its futile quest for baptismal sacrament, its be-
reaved recognition that Christian solace is utterly inaccessible. The surrogate
attempt at self-comfort in the initial resolution—to "live to my sad self hereaf-
ter kind, / Charitable"—is one that all but dispenses with the notion of divine
assistance. If the consciousness of abandonment is tonally less frantic and ni-
hilistic than that of "No Worst," and less despairing of the self's capacity to
gain its own regeneration, the recourse to an enforced self-reliance still par-
takes of the same grim minimalism: it intimates no reflection whatsoever "that
God is testing him by leaving him to his own resources." The speaker of "My
Own Heart" thus diverges noticeably from Hopkins in his commentary on St.
Ignatius's Third Exercise of the First Week, in which the exercitant's cultiva-
tion of self-comfort is explicitly deemed both an *imitatio Christi* and a prepara-
tion for a more exalted and therapeutic consolation through grace:

> [We are to pray] for that feeling towards past sin which our Lady
> felt or would feel when sins were presented to her and shrunk
> from them instantaneously and which our Lord feels in His mem-
> bers and God Himself, who means us to copy His nature and
> character as well as we can and put on His mind according to our
> measure. For they turn from sin by nature . . . [and] find it in-
> finitely piteous: 'O the pity of it!' . . . So that we may pity our-
> selves in the same way, that such a thing as sin should ever have
> got hold of us. This pure pity and disavowal of our past selves is
> the state of mind of one whose sins are perfectly forgiven. [*Sermons*,
> pp. 134–35]

As the beginning of a meditation, the octave of "My Own Heart" is less suc-
cessful than this. The religious value of pity as an attitude towards repentance
barely surfaces, even when viewed in conjunction with charity. Christ, the ul-
timate type of such piteous self-regard, is too dimly distant—as the imagery
of organically deformed sight makes plain—to be perceived as a model to be

copied. However much the opening appears to implement the self-injunctions of "Patience," which aim at a purified serenity, it offers no evidence that the speaker deliberately and consciously undertakes his own self-comfort as a discipline informed by the faith that a greater, divine easement may follow.[40]

Thus slumped in desolate frustration, the speaker turns in the sestet to an apparently "pious reasoning" on the subject of self-mercy; but the transition from the octave is so abrupt that, even if the metaphorical continuity can be explained,[41] the new banter, the light and cajoling, somewhat cynical wit must be considered the consequences of a superimposed reversal of attitude, not one which emerges naturally from the previous material. The first version of the sestet's opening is more consonant in mood with the octave than the second:

> [Come self,]
> Now, poor self, poorJa Jack Self, I do advise
> You . . .

> Soul, self; come, poor Jack self, I do advise
> You . . .

Beset by vacillation as in "Patience," the speaker reverts to his initial mode of self-debate, but intensifies that indirect colloquy by apostrophizing the split voices of the octave in an address that implicitly emphasizes the absence of the encouraging Paraclete: "Soul, self; come, poor Jack self." The voice that thus reintegrates the contrary energies of his affective and elective wills, however, is different from either. In calling for the end of "thought," it asks for more than the cessation of torment: it rejects the warfare of Christian psychology and recognizes the dangers of religious meditation that Hopkins himself acknowledged. As such, this voice stands apart, distanced, with the same disembodied self-regard that characterizes Hopkins's own uncertainty of self-conception; the resulting multivocity of the passage, though it appears to end in temporary unity, shares much with the self-divided cacophony of "No Worst."

As the speaker rejects his earlier masochistic indulgence in deprivation and substitutes compassion for self-pity, God's beneficence unexpectedly and inexplicably emerges. Both the tone and the *dramatis personae* of the colloquy change instantly:

---

[40] Compare both Mariani, *Commentary*, pp. 237–38, and Patricia A. Wolfe, "The Paradox of Self: A Study of Hopkins' Spiritual Conflict in the 'Terrible' Sonnets," *Victorian Poetry* 6 (1968): 101; both view this poem as an attempt to enact the discipline of patience outlined in "Patience."

[41] See Robert Boyle, *Metaphor in Hopkins* (Chapel Hill, N.C.: University of North Carolina Press, 1960), p. 147.

                    leave comfort root-room; let joy size

At God knows when to God knows what; whose smile
'S not wrúng, see you; unforeseentimes rather—as skies
Betweenpie mountains—lights a lovely mile.

But if the poem thus renders an influx of sufficient grace and ultimately dem-
onstrates that Christian "comfort comes from within,"[42] it is nevertheless in-
structive that God first enters the speaker's consciousness through idiomatic
throwaway phrases—the most casual, unpremeditated introduction of God in
Hopkins's entire canon. The sudden inspiration, though it enacts the desired
end of meditation, does not emanate from the deliberate discipline of medita-
tion itself. Indeed, the exasperated, flamboyant tone of "At God knows when
to God knows what" all but submerges in abandoned wit the theologically
precise evocation of God's omniscience; the exasperation itself, moreover, im-
plies that the advice to "let joy size" has no more justification than a sense of
absurdity, no more cause of joy than the minimal "comfort" of "No Worst."
Clearly the rendering of grace comes in the speaker's capacity to see beneath
his own irreverent tone, take his accidental phrasing literally, and thus submit
to God's design; but the enlightened colloquy which follows is not the tri-
umph which commentators have supposed. As indicated in chapter 2, the nat-
ural simile falls short of immanence; the original vocative mode is diluted; the
coming of joy remains a future possibility and thus a present fiction. Just be-
fore the end, moreover, the speaker is still debating himself over the nature
of divine justice and the quality of God's disposition towards His creation:
"whose smile / 'S not wrúng, *see you*" (italics mine). The awareness of God,
instead of cancelling the debate, merely gives it a new twist. To convince the
dubious "Jack self" who, in the octave, had sought his own consolation, the
speaker resorts to the oldest of substitutes for discursive argument, figurative
language. And, as in Tennyson's "The Two Voices," the poem ends without
providing that natural self with the chance to object: the choice of Christian
action or disposition that culminates Ignatian meditation is here foreshadowed
but not achieved. The poem's apparent resolution through an indirect colloquy
with God is, finally, no more conclusive than that of "Patience"; were the
poem considered apart from Hopkins's character and total *oeuvre*, its closure
would seem superimposed if not meretricious.

The colloquies of "Patience" and "My Own Heart" are tentative, sus-
pended, suffused by lush, redolent images of possibility. By comparison, those
of "Carrion Comfort" appear direct, unmistakable, and overwhelming. The

[42] Wolfe, "The Paradox of Self," p. 102.

entire poem, including the composition of place in the octave, is made of colloquies; it is Hopkins's most elaborate and intricate study of different types of colloquy. The poem subsumes *each* of the meditative units to the form of colloquy;[43] that Hopkins should thus have varied the Ignatian pattern—which stipulates, at each successive stage, an increasingly close linguistic contact with God—bespeaks his desperate determination to attain Communion no matter what the means. Simultaneously, the colloquies depart markedly from the tone of civilized gentility and trusting friendship that St. Ignatius, in describing colloquy, intended as a sign of the soul's final tranquility. Their violence iterates the poem's context, which, as in "No Worst," is far more Judaic than Christian. The images of Aaron accepting the rod of the priesthood, Jacob wrestling with the stranger,[44] and Job scarred in his suffering—all attest a spiritual world that, since it preexists the Christian dispensation, virtually precludes on historical grounds any colloquy with Christ as merciful intercessor. While Hopkins certainly considered these images typologically as prefigurations of the Christian epoch, their analogical aspect is not nearly so evident as in "Andromeda" (1879), another poem founded upon the typological interpretation of a foreign mythology. These Judaic images function primarily to characterize a theological universe in which grace is often brutal, God manifests Himself in bravado displays of sheer power, the nature of His justice is not yet clarified, and the act of covenant can occur through disaster. The poem's oral imagery—feasting, "darksome devouring eyes"—defines the semibarbaric nature of colloquy: the communication of messages is accomplished through cannibalism, not language. Only in the sestet, as the speaker remembers using his lips to signify his submission, does the poem approach the Ignatian spirit of civilized colloquy.

No wonder, then, that in the octave the speaker twice evades colloquy, however different in kind. In the first refusal, he quells his own dehumanized animal instinct to feast upon his despair, counters his temptation to suicide not with an untoward pride in the preservation of self[45] but with a supreme

---

[43] Compare the provocative analysis of this poem's structure by Alan M. Rose, "Hopkins' 'Carrion Comfort': The Artful Disorder of Prayer," *Victorian Poetry* 15 (1977): 207–17. Rose contends that "the poem presents the reader with the three powers of the soul [memory, understanding, and will] in reversed order; . . . And thus, precisely because the poet is in sin, the reverse of grace, and precisely because his mind is in turmoil, the poem reflects by its inverted structure that the poet is overturned spiritually, unbalanced mentally" (p. 215). Rose's essay is particularly valuable for its emphasis on the poem's demonic undercurrent.

[44] Devlin remarks that this image "is somehow alien to Catholic spirituality" (*Sermons*, p. 118).

[45] Compare Wolfe, "The Paradox of Self": "But, ironically, in not choosing not to be, he is pitting himself against the Almighty. Taking pride in the invincible human spirit, Hopkins is coming dangerously close to denying man's essential dependence on God" (p. 91). The argument here does not take into account the Catholic position on suicide. David Anthony Downes, "Be-

stuttering effort of the elective will to use his mouth properly, in the articulation of his identity as God's temple. Having refused to parody Communion, however, he is shockingly smitten by divine bestiality, cyclonic tempests of breath against which his own remonstration in human speech-acts is powerless. In this ironic opposition—rather than Ignatian similitude—between human and divine sound, the speaker finally drops his Job-like mask of self-justification and confesses an absolute terror of confrontation: "me frantic to avoïd thee and flee." It is instructive to note that Hopkins could not drop that mask immediately; the phrasing in his first draft—"me frantic to arise and flee"— shrinks from the emotion of dread. The sestet continues in this strain of resistance; the concluding colloquy is presented not as the desired result of his choice but as a divine intervention forced upon him:

> That night, that yéar
> Of now done darkness I wretch lay wrestling with (my God!) my God.

Whether or not the speaker here sees God face to face and is renamed Israel, a prince of God (Genesis 32:27–28), all of these resistances evince a psychology of colloquy far more conflicted than that found either in the other "terrible sonnets" or in the rest of Hopkins's work: alone, "Carrion Comfort" is rooted in aversion to colloquy, the truncation of the Ignatian design. That aversion is not a response to the special violence of God peculiar to this poem; for in *The Wreck* (stanzas 24–30), the speaker reveals a passionate empathy for the nun who, dying amidst terrific disaster, cries out to Christ and is answered by the violent triumph of His Passion visited upon her. The aversion comes, instead, from a dread that is both primordial and inexplicable. What complicates the aversion, of course, is that it is part of a dynamic paradox of attraction/repulsion: these repeated instances of resistance to colloquy occur in a poem whose very form, deliberately varied from Ignatian practice, is comprised of colloquies.

None of these colloquies, however, and particularly not the last, can be adequately interpreted without attention to the poem's dual time-scheme. Cotter, rightly observing the odd dislocation in temporal design that the last sentence thrusts upon the poem, has argued that "In this conclusion the poet

---

atific Landscapes in Hopkins" (part 2), *Hopkins Quarterly* 1 (1975): 195, however, gives credence to Wolfe's contention and claims that the poem is "Hopkins' Lucifer poem. The poet struggles to hold himself together after being pitched from the paradise of dwelling on his own beauty and power. . . . Lucifer, self-beauty, clings to some assertion of self-existence, . . . finds a joy in his own capacity for utter destruction. This sonnet is Lucifer's song in Hopkins' soul: love destroys." But the poem offers no concrete evidence for Downes's interpretation. The allusion in line 3 to Dante, *Purgatory*, 10.139, suggests not pride, but rather the quest for patience to endure distress and suffering.

puts in the past tense what was described in the present tense in the octave."[46]
Thus construing the poem as a self-contained unit whose time-shift implies no
exterior reference, he presumes Hopkins extremely conscious (more so than I
think he was) of the linear, successive nature of writing: the past poem (the
octave) becomes identified as past experience. But the reference of "That
night, that yéar" comprehends more than the violent debates of the octave
taken as present experience; and even in the octave itself the speaker refers to
himself as "me heaped *there*" (italics mine), the distancing adverb implying
not only a spatial dislocation between the perceiver and his body but also a
temporal distinction between present narrative and past event remembered.
The distinction was not part of Hopkins's original conception for the poem;
the salient passages appear as follows in the first draft (italics mine):

> . . . me heaped *here* . . .
>
> [line 8]

> . . . in *the* toil and coil . . .
>
> [line 10]

> I know *this* night, *this* year
> Of darkness done, that I wretch wrestled, I wrung with God.
>
> [lines 13–14]

The allusion in the final sestet to Hopkins's conversion and reception into the
Jesuit order—"since (seems) I kissed the rod"—reinforces the suspicion that
the octave, too, even as it manifests the terrible confrontation as present expe-
rience, is actually transforming a specific past event into present occasion.
That event, regained in the process of revision, is the center of Hopkins's own
personal *historia*, the experience of conversion which he had earlier narrated—
as simple past event—in *The Wreck* (stanzas 2 and 3).[47] Doubtless "Carrion
Comfort" would have been less ambiguous had Hopkins not introduced the
time-shifts; but he would also have made a narrower work. Here, the Ignatian
memory—re-creating the scene, realizing its *dramatis personae*—has done its
work so thoroughly before this compressed meditation actually begins that the
traces of its processes remain barely perceptible. Through the concentrated
pressure of a memory so vivid that past and present have fused, the composi-
tion of place (the octave) represents Hopkins's nearly abreactive recovery of his
decisive moment of choice.

[46] Cotter, *Inscape*, p. 223.
[47] Ibid. Cotter has noted this allusion to *The Wreck* but has not observed its relation to the
poem's time-scheme.

In alluding to the conversionary experience as portrayed in *The Wreck*, "Carrion Comfort" joins "That Nature Is a Heraclitean Fire" (lines 17–18) as the only Hopkins poems which advert to his earlier poetry in the manner of Yeats. For the compressed reference, far from reiterating the earlier account, is also a revision, one that demonstrates, even as it recovers the past, the devastating interference of present agony in the process of remembering. In "Carrion Comfort," the speaker realizes the "hurtle of hell" far more fiercely than in *The Wreck* (stanza 3); the whole of the first quatrain deals with his warfare against Despair. Yet he does not flee that evil to rush, "dovewinged," "with a fling of the heart to the heart of the Host" (stanza 3); instead, he is "frantic to avoïd" God's awful visitation. Nor does he "confess" in reverence "Thy terror, O Christ, O God" (stanza 2)—partly because the figure of Christ as intercessor is absent, and partly because "Carrion Comfort" defines God in a manner foreign to *The Wreck*, as animal force capable of cruelty. The discrepancies, in brief, are marked: the speaker of "Carrion Comfort" is pinioned between damnation and disaster, not damnation and grace. The psychic and spiritual complications produced by this transmuted memory of the conversionary experience are immediately evident in the second quatrain. Apparently unable to remember "accurately" a conversion in which terror of divinity was ultimately lost in joy, the speaker now protests to God his "frantic" opposition to divine intervention. The present remonstration certainly attributes to his past experience a shuddering aversion one would hardly have expected. But is this seemingly false memory really the accurate version? Does the remonstration also serve as a long-belated, now uninhibited, and *true* expression of attitudes—defiance and dread—previously harbored but unspoken? And is the remonstration, surely a recoil from confrontation in the present, also an effort to revise the initial decision, that primary submission to God's will upon which Hopkins founded his life? The point is not that the answers cannot be known, but rather that the poem broaches the questions at all and that, in so doing, it calls into doubt the whole of his priestly vocation. In addition, the octave takes as its "text" for meditation the central colloquy of Hopkins's life and examines it afresh in yet another colloquy; but it does so not only by seeking a breach of colloquy in the present but by questioning the truth of the colloquy he had held with God in the past. The tensions here are manifold: through the dual time-structure and the intersection of its colloquies, Hopkins managed a colloquy in "Carrion Comfort" that is more violently wrenched between affective and elective wills than any other in his poetry.

These complexities recede somewhat in the "pious reasoning" that opens the sestet. As the speaker turns from colloquy to self-examination, he offers a standard justification for inexplicable suffering which temporarily resolves the conflict:

Why? that my chaff might fly; my grain lie, sheer and clear.

Such a justification, however, is unique in the "terrible sonnets." But it is impossible to discern whether this explanation constitutes a present analysis of the "present" composition or a remembered analysis made earlier; and the ambiguity forces yet another question: if the speaker accepted this justification in the past, does he still think it valid? In any case, as the sestet in its spoken progression increasingly separates past and present, the speaker suddenly doubts his own self-comfort and scrutinizes the adequacy of his catechetical response:

Nay in all that toil, that coil since (seems) I kissed the rod,
Hand rather, my heart lo! lapped strength, stôle joy, would laugh, cheer.
Cheer whóm though?

Significantly, the first line in this citation (line 10) initially read (italics mine):

Nay, in the toil and coil, *because* I kissed the rod—[.]

In the final version Hopkins plainly shied away from establishing a causal relation between his vocation and his pain. But the crucial question—"Cheer whóm though?"—still asks if God's servant is but a miserable pawn to whom God, in His prosecution of a total design, is personally indifferent. It evolves from the lacklustre drudgery and agitation of Hopkins's Dublin years:

> I do not waver in my allegiance, I never have since my conversion
> to the Church. The question is how I advance the side I serve on.
> This may be inwardly or outwardly. Outwardly I often think I am
> employed to do what is of little or no use. . . . Meantime the
> Catholic Church in Ireland and the Irish Province in it and our
> College in that are greatly given over to a partly unlawful cause,
> promoted by partly unlawful means, and against my will my
> pains, laborious and distasteful, like prisoners made to serve the
> enemies' gunners, go to help on this cause. I do not feel then that
> outwardly I do much good . . . and this is a mournful life to lead.
> . . . Yet it seems to me that I could lead this life well enough if I
> had bodily energy and cheerful spirits. However these God will
> not give me. The other part, the more important, remains, my
> inward service. [*Sermons*, pp. 261–62]

Notably, Hopkins temporarily ceased writing here, without elaborating at all upon the nature and value of his "inward service." Gardner believes that the last sentence gives, "as always with Hopkins, something which may be called, with theological precision, a saving grace."[48] But Hopkins's continuation of his writing, some hours later, lends no support to such an interpretation. It indicates, instead, that although he was able to mention his "inward service," he was unable to contemplate its rewards, could not counterbalance his dismal sense of outward failure, and thus found that "saving grace" inaccessible; indeed, his mind seems to have reverted almost immediately to brooding frustration:

> I was continuing this train of thought this morning when I began to enter on that course of loathing and hopelessness which I have so often felt before, which made me fear madness and led me to give up the practice of meditation except, as now, in retreat and here it is again. . . . What is my wretched life? Five wasted years almost have passed in Ireland. I am ashamed of the little I have done, of my waste of time, although my helplessness and weakness is such that I could scarcely do otherwise. . . . what is life without aim, without spur, without help? All my undertakings miscarry: I am like a straining eunuch. I wish then for death: yet if I died now I should die imperfect, no master of myself, and that is the worst failure of all. O my God, look down on me[.] [*Sermons*, p. 262][49]

This passage, like the question in "Carrion Comfort," stops short of unwilling rebellion against God's demand for a service Hopkins could not give; both ask, instead, whether God, in flaying the chaff, has not also bruised the kernel irredeemably. In *The Wreck* (stanza 30) the speaker marvels that Christ "hadst glory of this nun" and finds that triumph analogous to his own conversion. Here, however, as he reconsiders his case, he foregoes both the divine perspective and the salvific analogy: doubting the mutuality of endeavor, he asks if God's servant should not also have benefit:

Cheer whóm though? The héro whose héaven-hand|ling flúng me, fóot tród
Me? or mé that fóught him? O whích one? Is it éach one?

[48] W. H. Gardner, *Gerard Manley Hopkins: A Study of Poetic Idiosyncrasy in Relation to Poetic Tradition*, 2 vols. (1949; rpt. London: Oxford University Press, 1966), 2: 344.
[49] Although this passage is taken from the Retreat Notes that Hopkins made at Tullabeg in 1888, it is an accurate—although obviously more extensive—version of his thinking both before and during the period of the "terrible sonnets" as well. See, e.g., the Retreat Notes made at Beaumont, 1884–85 (*Sermons*, pp. 254–60).

The queries have no conclusive answer.[50] The chiasmic structure in the first pair of questions suggests, in its mirroring effect, a continuity of relation between the Lord and the speaker that masks the adversary content. In the second pair (added in the second draft), the approximate rhyme of "which" and "éach" implies both an identity and a reciprocity between the two contenders —as if all uncertainties had been resolved. It thus gives the questions a rhetorical quality that disguises the real import of the questions themselves. The evasions here bear distinct resemblances to those in "Patience" and "My Own Heart."

The introduction of this present questioning into the reflective and partly remembered analysis of the teleology of suffering, together with the recapitulation of past experience, turns the octave into a metaphor of the speaker's present condition: the speaker defines his present agony in terms of his revised memory of past grace. By extension, his present is *only* his past; the hints of future beneficence that mark "Patience" and "My Own Heart" have been cancelled. But although his past supplies his present with meaning, he is left, as he reviews the grim personal history that followed from his conversion, with the sense of a "lonely" and now embittered "began" ("To Seem the Stranger"). This superimposition of the past upon the present clearly intimates the speaker's awareness that the thrill of religious dedication has waned; although it recurs in memory, analogous awakenings no longer happen. The colloquy with God in the second quatrain, a privileged if dreadful occasion of direct and unmediated confrontation, derives from the past; in the present, it is mediated by memory. The speaker's consciousness of the grievous discrepancy between his past and present religious experience closes the poem:

> That night, that yéar
> Of now done darkness I wretch lay wrestling with (my God!) my God.

If the passage expresses a certain relief that the time of trial is passed, the relief is subsumed to an emotion of great loss: for here the speaker understands with absolute certainty the vital and authentic relation with God he once knew. This self-revelation especially heightens his loss because it contains the recognition that he had wrestled with a type of Christ and thus gained physical knowledge of the Incarnation. And as he comprehends his past experience, he can name his Adversary without recourse to the epithets and attributes he had employed in the second quatrain. It is against the immediate knowledge his past experience conferred that the crucial parenthesis "(my God!)" must be

---

[50] Compare J. Angela Carson, "The Metaphor of Struggle in 'Carrion Comfort'," *Philological Quarterly* 49 (1970): 553: "With the suggestion that he wished to cheer each one, the struggle of indecision seems to have been resolved."

weighed. This briefest of invocations, however much diluted by its merely ex-
clamatory quality, is the only genuine and direct colloquy with God in the
poem's present. Not added until the third draft of the sestet, it is all Hopkins
could salvage. A gasped, awed recognition of past grace extended, it is also an
acknowledgment of grace now lost, a submission to the present trial of dep-
rivation, and a whispered plea for the return of Incarnation. Paradoxically,
too, the speaker initiates his colloquy with the knowledge that God now with-
holds response. Hopkins has here built a poem that, like its partial source,
Herbert's "Jordan" (I), climaxes in a vocative address that, despite its brevity,
constitutes the sole substantive content of the poem; its tone, however, carries
no such dignity or confidence of answer. And although Mariani has argued of
the speaker that "his has been the privilege of being crucified with Christ, and
he echoes the agonized words of the dying Christ in his '(my God!) my God',"[51]
the echo is really split, as if in parody, both between two time-periods and
between second- and third-person reference. Nor, given the poem's Judaic ori-
entation, does the speaker's final sense of foresakenness occur in the context of
an *imitatio Christi.* Even if these difficulties are disregarded and the conclusion
is taken as an imitation of the Last Words, it must mean chiefly that colloquy
has become its own opposite, the very negation of the concept that divine and
human voices can speak together.

Like "Carrion Comfort," "No Worst" juggles time-structure and plays with
opposed voices to achieve the defeat of colloquy. But instead of pitting past
against present colloquy, instead of postponing direct colloquy until a future
time, the poem concatenates the voices in various kinds of colloquy to such a
degree that the end result is cacophony, sound without meaning. As Hopkins's
parody of his contemporaneous studies in musical counterpoint, "No Worst"
should be compared with "The Sea and the Skylark": the speaker of the earlier
poem can still absorb the polyphony of the natural world and integrate its
contrary voices into so coherent a pattern that the skylark's song can be repre-
sented as an actual musical score. Here, the speaker himself has two voices,
human and animal. In addition, he hears himself, in uncanny self-distance, as
an anvil struck; yet the anvil is not that upon which, in "St. Alphonsus
Rodriguez" (1888), Christ will "forge his glorious day," but rather the me-
dium of noise. The voices—not heard, but evoked—of Christ and the Chris-
tian God contend not only against that of Jahweh (figured in the whirlwind)

[51] Mariani, *Commentary*, p. 233. Compare also Rose, in "Hopkins' 'Carrion Comfort': The Art-
ful Disorder of Prayer," p. 217, who sees in the "final ambiguity of the sestet" a sharp division
between profane and sacred: "Hopkins has committed the blasphemy expressed by the epithet
'(my god!)' and the act of faith expressed by his acknowledgment in the last words of the poem,
'my God'."

but against the shrieks of a pagan Fury. These voices intimate radically op-
posed conceptions of humankind, divergent visions of suffering, and contrary
theologies of redemption; their parts are written, so to speak, in different keys
and thus cannot be harmonized. Consequently, and of necessity because they
coexist within a single poem, the voices reverberate uncontrollably within the
speaker's mind. In its equalization of discordant voices, the chaos renders "No
Worst" a poem that balances Christianity against other modes of belief in a
nearly relativist fashion; its manner, anticipating the polyglot world of *The
Waste Land*, is unique in Hopkins's work. Clearly this relativism, this dissolu-
tion of the proper hierarchy of voices, is not desired. The real point, however,
is that the speaker is incapable of hearing the Christian voice alone; and the
closest he can come to reconciling the discord is the virtual cessation of sound
in the sestet—a relief from auditory violence, to be sure, but not the resolu-
tion of cacophony.

Alone among the "terrible sonnets," "No Worst" opens with explicit imag-
ery of sound; but the communication is nonverbal:

> No worst, there is none. Pitched past pitch of grief,
> More pangs will, schooled at forepangs, wilder wring.

The homophone ("wring"/"ring") identifies sound with excruciating bodily
pain and bodily contortion; the chaos of that pain, the sole content of utter-
ance, perhaps parodies the chiming of church-bells and thus inverts the sacra-
mental imagery of "As Kingfishers Catch Fire."[52] "Pitched," tuned beyond
the scale of human emotion, the speaker cannot articulate prayer; he himself
sees that his animal nature blocks colloquy. Yet this visceral realization, elabo-
rated in the second quatrain, prompts a tremendous effort to regain human
speech and Christian sensibility:

> Comforter, where, where is your comforting?
> Mary, mother of us, where is your relief?

Here is the most extended invocation of the heavenly host in all of the "terrible
sonnets." Yet what is it but a desperate, pleading, angry parody of the Triple
Colloquy with which Ignatius concludes the Third Exercise of the First
Week?[53] For, as in "Nondum," "No answering voice comes from the skies";
God is not mentioned; the attempt at colloquy itself comes prematurely, with-

---

[52] Alison G. Sulloway, *Gerard Manley Hopkins and the Victorian Temper* (London: Routledge &
Kegan Paul, 1972), p. 177, perhaps extrapolating from a passage in the *Sermons* (p. 170), associ-
ates the pain with "the mounting torture of a woman in prolonged and difficult labour"; but the
implied sex-shift in this reading, while relevant to "I Wake and Feel" and "To Seem the Stranger,"
does not seem pertinent here.

[53] St. Ignatius Loyola, *Spiritual Exercises*, p. 35.

out preparation or evidence of self-control. Indeed, Hopkins has made his composition of place—the agony of unanswered suffering—out of the very absence of colloquy that, formally and spiritually, is its cause.

The dramatic failure of this effort to achieve colloquy drives the speaker back into renewed, and now exaggerated, self-definition as beast and thing; Hopkins's structuring insists that humankind deprived of Christ has no humanity. In place of the desired answer from Christ or God, the speaker hears only a terrific pagan voice, void of redemptive power or concern, which cruelly counsels further purposeless suffering if not suicide:

> Fury had shrieked "No ling-
> Ering! Let me be fêll: force I must be brief."

The demonic parody of the Triple Colloquy is thus complete.[54] In the poem's linear progression, the voice of the sadistic Fury replaces the healing comfort of Christ or God; its demented anger is a degenerate version of the presumably just and principled wrath of the Judeo-Christian God. It is evidence of Hopkins's extreme commitment to the Incarnation that, with the disappearance of the traditional Christian intercessors Christ and Mary, his speaker's conception of God should so radically regress to pagan form. As in "Carrion Comfort," moreover, the time-scheme reveals an additional psychological dimension to Hopkins's galling revision of Ignatian colloquy. "Fury *had* shrieked" (italics mine):[55] it is the echoing resonance of that pagan cry, before the poem opens, that initially prompts the speaker to call on Christ and Mary to give witness that the world is not governed by mere vengeance, that the universe has both purpose and redemptive order. But the attempt to superimpose Christian colloquy on pagan noise fails; the speaker is helplessly subject to the memory of Fury, a memory that simultaneously distracts him from his Christian focus and comes at precisely the point where it can complete the parody of the Triple Colloquy. Fury's shriek is now the *recurrent* index of a world without design, ruled by frivolous and tyrannical deities. So radical is the dichotomy between the voice of Fury and the desired response from Christ that it is hardly reasonable to maintain that the self-evident Prometheus myth underlying the poem's imagery is allegorically complementary to the Christian vision of suffering;[56]

---

[54] See Marcella M. Holloway, "No Worst, There is None," *The Explicator* 14 (1956), item 51: "The voice in the poem turns to the Comforter (the Holy Spirit) and then to the Mother of God. But the only voice that replies is that of Fury, closing the octave of the sonnet in his shrieking, mocking, strident tones."

[55] Sister Mary Humiliata, "Hopkins and the Prometheus Myth," *PMLA* 70 (1955): 65, sees the past-tense recollection chiefly as saving the octave from "melodrama."

[56] Compare Humiliata, ibid., passim, who argues that "the secret motivation of the cry of anguish found in Sonnet 65" has its source in the speaker's assumption of vicarious suffering for

what the speaker undergoes in his agony, dominated as it is by pagan forces from which the speaker asks God to rescue him, is the exact opposite of an *imitatio Christi*. Indeed, wrenched between two worlds, the speaker dreads the power of the Greek ethos to supplant the later dispensation; the poem enacts, in psychomachia, a nearly Yeatsian conception of the alternating recurrence of antithetical historical epochs.

The failed colloquy with Christ ends, as the solipsistic imagery of the mountains indicates, in the total vacancy of the sestet. Although there is "no turn in the argument,"[57] the abrupt spatial shift from valley to mountains marks a mind wholly unhinged by the dissolution of value it confronts: the panoramic sweep of space suggests an utter soundlessness that is the exact inversion, yet the central meaning, of the earlier cacophony. The "cliffs of fall / Frightful, sheer, no-man-fathomed" image the abyss of nothingness, "Being's dread and vacant maze" ("Nondum"), which gapes when discordant systems clash without resolution. The typological reference to Christ's Temptation is clear enough; but in the speaker's moral analysis it is significantly treated without "pious reasoning." If Christ's "throwing of himself from the pinnacle was to be a safe act," the speaker can only think himself a forlorn and mocking parody of the Divine Presence who has not appeared; if Satan's "best hope was that his victim would kill himself" (*Sermons*, p. 182), the speaker recoils from the abyss and sin of suicide with no greater motive than self-preservation, and with no apparent fear of tempting God:

> Here! creep,
> Wretch, under a comfort serves in a whirlwind . . . .

As the natural man acts to salvage his own most bitter and minimal consolation, he finds in self-address a new surrogate for colloquy; but his response to his own injunction is no more satisfying than the voice of Fury:

>   all
> Life death does end and each day dies with sleep.

The self's action is neither ethical nor Christian; the election of Christ that culminates Ignatian meditation does not occur, nor does the speaker refuse

---

the sake of Christ and the fallen world. It is "a cry which issues as one voice from the tortured figure of Prometheus and from the Christian soul which has given itself as victim for sinners. The first is a prototype of Christ suffering to assist mankind; the latter is His close follower in His redemptive mission" (p. 64). The poem offers no evidence that the speaker suffers voluntarily. That Hopkins was familiar with the standard typological interpretation of Prometheus is no argument that he automatically adhered to it in this poem; indeed, as in "That Nature is a Heraclitean Fire," the Greek material is wholly antithetical to the Christian.

[57] Mariani, *Commentary*, p. 227.

suicide on religious grounds. What he perceives, as Hopkins again injects his poem with noise, is Jahweh's most inchoate theophany, a whirlwind whose spiralling (in Hopkins's iconography) cannot easily be discerned from that of Satan. Having lost a divinity whose justice is tempered with mercy, terrified by deities who dismiss both, the speaker remains alive to be assaulted—his barren reward—by a God whose justice is inscrutable. As he cowers (as in "Carrion Comfort") from the terrible privilege of theophany and seeks to contract the fearful spaces of his imagination, he provides himself a "comfort" that is no more than submission to the obliteration that closes each natural cycle.[58] Despite the passivity, distancing, and generality of phrasing, the death-wish is evident: the speaker all but assents to a mild form of Fury's temptation and comes as close as possible to the blasphemy of choosing "not to be" ("Carrion Comfort") without actually saying so. How bleak this "comfort" is can only be judged by comparing it with the bare surviving kernel of Christian belief embedded in the ambiguous syntax: "all Life [an epithet for Christ] does end death."[59] But this buried sentence—intimating the Resurrection and salvation, rather than the muted suicidal longing—remains buried, a mockery of his earlier faith. And while the voices of the Christian and the natural man still contend in irresolution (as at the end of "My Own Heart"), it is the mundane world, not the supernatural, that now lures him.

The irony of this "comfort serves in a whirlwind" emerges in its fullness only when juxtaposed against the opening of "I wake and feel the fell of dark, not day." Here, the grim faith that mere diurnal cycle may provide easement from inexplicable suffering is immediately quashed as the speaker enters, from night, into nothing more than his own continued interior darkness; demarcations of time and light dissolve as he meditates upon a memory of his recent agony. The central mark of this unwilled solipsistic imprisonment is that this poem—unlike the other "terrible sonnets"—patently *assumes* colloquy to be impossible. Its very mode—a joyless parody of Matins—implies the defeat of any effort to attain the proper culmination of Ignatian meditation. The speaker acknowledges the seeming permanence of Christ's absence and accepts his banishment:

> my lament
> Is cries countless, cries like dead letters sent
> To dearest him that lives alas! away.

In "No Worst" and "Carrion Comfort," direct address to the Lord, although unrequited, is a feasible verbal act; here, however, Christ is distanced into the

---

[58]Compare Cotter, *Inscape*, p. 225; Humiliata, "The Prometheus Myth," p. 68.

[59]Mariani, in *Commentary*, sees an ambiguity only in the word "all": "Since it receives a stress,

third person, beyond summoning, and entirely removed from the reciprocal relation the speaker silently craves to stave off the endless debate between himself and his "belonging field." Skillfully, Hopkins's description of his unanswered communications reveals a progressive deterioration in both force and rhetorical effect. The deepest desire of his elective will cannot be uttered: "lament" is a verbal symbol of grief, not the grief itself. This inclusionary word of sorrow is first altered and broken down into a metaphor of fragmentation, "cries countless"; next, the disordered multivocity itself is compared—as simile—to a mode of communication even less direct and nonverbal: "dead letters." And these, despite an idiomatic usage which defines "dead letters" as those whose destination is finally discovered to be unknown, are considered to be "dead" even before they are "sent": that is, the downcast speaker issues his indirect pleas with no real expectation of response. The sequential degeneration in this image shows an extremely keen, albeit negative, apprehension of the imaginative relation between Christ and the speaker that ought to obtain: it is Christ whose felt presence is mandatory to inspire the speaker to prayer and colloquy; without that divine encouragement, the human imagination fails. There is little doubt, either, that in "dead letters" Hopkins was characterizing at least some, if not all, of the "terrible sonnets"; in making this pun, he was plainly revising his attitude towards whichever of the sonnets he had composed before "I Wake and Feel," and claiming that, whatever their flashes of recovery and joy, they were futile exercises. Poignantly, and as in "No Worst," the octave of "I Wake and Feel" simply absorbs these reflections on failed colloquy into the primary material of the composition of place, the speaker's definition of his isolation: colloquy itself has no status as the climax of the meditation.

Indeed, "I Wake and Feel" blocks colloquy structurally as well as psychologically. As a sonnet, the poem is complete enough; spiritually, it is incomplete, lacking its most essential part. When it is compared with St. Ignatius's Meditation on Hell and Hopkins's own contemporaneous "Meditation on Hell" (*Sermons*, pp. 241–44), the formal omission of colloquy becomes doubly striking. After some pages examining the sensory and spiritual pains of the damned, Hopkins's prose meditation can finally "*turn . . . to Christ our Lord*" in a bereft and moving prayer (Hopkins's italics). Its gasped, halting rhythms are tokens of his anguish; its incantatory repetition of pronouns, a desperate attempt to distinguish himself from the damned:

---

it seems to mean that with death there is total annihilation. . . . But while an argument might be made for such an interpretation, it does not square with what we know of Hopkins" (pp. 227–28). On the contrary, it fits exactly with Hopkins's later apocalypticism.

We have the fate of others before our eyes for our warning; our
sins are like theirs but not our fate—not hitherto: let us while we
can make ourselves safe, *make our election sure.* How? O alas Jesus
Christ our Lord, we are sinners, spare us; we have done what oth-
ers have been damned for, spare us; they died impenitent, they lie
in hell, we are on earth, there is time yet, we are sorry for our
sins, we do repent, thou spare us. Lamb of God that takest away
the sins of the world, spare us O Lord. Lamb of God that takest
away the sins of the world, graciously hear us, O Lord. Lamb of
God . . . have mercy upon us. Hail Mary. [*Sermons*, p. 264; Hop-
kins's italics and ellipsis]

The poem, however, whose composition of place (octave) and moral analysis
(sestet) correspond so exactly, point for point, with the prose meditation, in-
cludes no such colloquy; although there is a traditional "turn" between octave
and sestet, the speaker cannot make the "turn" to Christ, nor can the prayer
that Christ "graciously hear" him—in reciprocating answer—occur.

The significance of these omissions—particularly in a meditation on hell—
is manifold.[60] What must be taken, in comparison with Ignatian structure, as
Hopkins's inability to finish the exercise with a colloquy is the most drastic
index possible of his despair and self-loathing. Hell to Hopkins was an infinite
separation from God's mercy and goodness: "It is like an infinite removal of
good, the removal of good to an infinite degree, which amounts to an infinite
evil"; the sinner "is carried and swept away to an infinite distance from God;
and the stress and strain of his removal is his eternity of punishment" (*Sermons*,
pp. 133, 139).[61] The precise formal correlative of that sensation of infinite re-
moval is the omission of colloquy. In failing to represent colloquy with Christ
as the conclusion of his meditation, and in thus representing his hell as a con-
dition beyond hope of gracious reprieve, Hopkins submitted entirely to his
subject, perhaps entered so far into the agony of estrangement that he could
not finally extricate himself through faith. But whatever poetic genius one
may find in the daring honesty of this *mimesis*, whether conscious or not,
should not obscure the pain it cost him. For Hopkins's interpretation of the
Meditation on Hell, as the above citation indicates, was classically Ignatian.
The colloquy in this meditation is the point at which the exercitant compre-
hends for the first time the whole architecture of the *Spiritual Exercises*: under-

---

[60] Compare Alexander W. Allison, "Hopkins' 'I Wake and Feel the Fell of Dark'," *The Explica-
tor* 17 (1959), item 54: "It only remains for [the speaker] to make sure that his meditation has
fulfilled its traditional purpose."

[61] See also *Sermons*, p. 241.

standing both the extremity of sin and the extremity of divine mercy, he makes the choice to elect Christ and thus begins his active participation in God's redemptive design.[62] In the poem, however, no such election occurs: despite his tacit love of Christ, the speaker considers himself beyond redemption, cannot make the "turn" to Christ, and thus comes perilously close to sinning against the divine omnipotence.

Further: in the Meditation on Hell, the exercitant's ultimate model of spiritual progression should be the death, harrowing of hell, and resurrection of Christ. But Hopkins's deletion of the colloquy signifies his speaker's inability to imitate that resurrection; it underscores his profound sense that he is really one of the damned, whose pain is their "foiled action," their incapacity to express their "strain or tendency towards God" (*Sermons*, p. 137). Although in the final tercet the speaker seemingly distinguishes between himself and "the lost," he twice likens the damned to himself, in fact posits himself as the type of misery—and not vice versa. It is a common misreading of this closure to suppose that the speaker believes himself redeemed in Christ and thus calls the lot of the damned "worse" than his own; but neither the grammatical structure of the tercet nor the evidence of Hopkins's revisions supports such a conventional, and thoroughly Ignatian, view:[63]

> 12   Selfyeast of spirit a dull dough sours. I see
> (12) [Selfyeast of spirit my selfstuff sours.] I see
>
>   this   {scourge
> 13   The lost are like [it], and their {loss   to be
> (14) [Their sweating selves as I am mine, but worse.]
> 14   As I am mine, their sweating selves; but worse.

Although MacKenzie remarks that "The ambiguity of the last line was carefully corrected" in the final version,[64] the ambiguity in the reference of "worse" in fact remains—and in exacerbated form. If Hopkins ought to be distinguishing between himself and the damned, his language pulls in a different direction. First, Hopkins's introduction of the semicolon before "but worse"

---

[62] See Rahner, *Ignatius the Theologian*, pp. 91–93.

[63] See St. Ignatius Loyola, *Spiritual Exercises: "Colloquy.* Talk to Christ our Lord. Remember that some souls are in Hell because they did not believe He would come; others because, though they believed, they did not obey His commandments. . . . Remembering this, I will thank Him that He has not allowed me to die and so to fall into one of these classes. I will also thank Him for having shown me such tender mercy all my life long until now; and will close with an *Our Father*" (pp. 36–37). Compare Boyle, *Metaphor in Hopkins*, p. 155; Cotter, *Inscape*, p. 227; Gardner, *Hopkins*, 2: 340; Mariani, *Commentary*, p. 222; Wolfe, "The Paradox of Self," pp. 99–100.

[64] Norman H. MacKenzie, *Hopkins* (Edinburgh and London: Oliver and Boyd, 1968), p. 90, n. 9. The last line of "I Wake and Feel" is certainly a crux. In Hopkins's manuscript, line 12 and its revision appeared on the same line, as shown in the Textual Appendixes, p. 160.

produces in that fragmentary sentence a grammatical structure parallel to "I see . . ."—that is, "but [I am] worse." Second, instead of creating a break between "them" and "me" after "selves," he has syntactically interwoven himself and the damned in a pattern of alternation that generates a primary awareness of sameness, not of difference:

> *their* scourge to be
> as *I* am mine,
> *their* sweating selves;
> but [*I* am] worse.

If the speaker's characterization of himself as "worse" than the damned is both an egotistical hyperbole and a shocking violation of traditional theology, it nevertheless renders accurately what Eliot in *Ash Wednesday* (II) calls the "torment / Of love unsatisfied," the ghastly misery that the deprivation of colloquy induces.

The fierce irony in the speaker's self-judgment is that, experiencing a "lot" which is "worse" than that of the damned, he does not classify himself amongst them. What prevents his total identification is his adamant refusal to blaspheme against Christ; the pathos of the refusal is Job's also. Compare again the prose meditation, in which Hopkins admonished himself to hear the hideous noises of the damned, "the wailings (of despair), howls (of pain), cries (of self reproach), blasphemies against Christ our Lord and all his saints because they are in heaven and *they* lost in hell" (*Sermons*, p. 242; Hopkins's italics). But despite the speaker's silent refusal to parody colloquy by speaking *against* Christ, he cannot perform the opposite act, the election *of* Christ, nor can he justify the suffering inflicted upon him. If it is partly true that Hopkins scrupulously "was always inclined to put the final blame upon himself,"[65] the speaker of "I Wake and Feel" nevertheless fails to achieve the radical assent to God's justice that the "pious reasoning" in the prose meditation displays. There, after detailing the excruciations of the damned, Hopkins asked:

> *Can these things be?* It is terrible to me to have to speak of them, but Christ spoke of them: they must then be true. Are they just?—Yes, because God is just. But you can yourselves see they are just: if you tell your child: Let your sister alone, do not beat her, or I will beat *you* / are you unjust to threaten him? And if he disobeys you and torments her still are you unjust to carry out your threat? Are *we* not warned by God? [*Sermons*, p. 243; Hopkins's italics]

[65] Gardner, *Hopkins*, 2: 339.

"Warned by God": Hopkins's position is dogmatic. In the poem, however, he nearly rebelled against such an inflexible and legalistic view: "God's most deep decree / Bitter would have me taste" shows a far greater consciousness of divine power than of justice. Indeed, as the manuscript indicates, Hopkins initially wrote, "God's most just decree . . ."; and in cancelling that standard interpretation of divine justice—it can hardly have been the mere desire for an alliterated phrase that prompted the act—he opened his poem upon immeasurable vistas of uncertainty if not outright doubt. It is of paramount importance to "I Wake and Feel" in particular, and to the proper reading of the world of the "terrible sonnets" generally, that Hopkins finally could not bring himself to affirm, in explicit diction, that God's punishment of him was "just": the poems occur in a universe whose theological structure, quite apart from the spiritual vicissitudes endured by Hopkins's speaker, is no longer secure. What recourse to traditional conceptions of divine justice was available if, in his devotion as a priest, his "lot" was "worse" than that of the damned? This is a more extreme version of the issue broached in the revisions of "Carrion Comfort," especially in the alteration of "because" to "since" (line 10). Without quite daring to question the nature of divine justice, as in "Thou Art Indeed Just" (1889), the speaker muffles his awed confusions but stops well short of confessing a divine design behind his suffering; he accepts instead a supernatural force the significance of whose operation is indiscernible. The poem ends not with the mind's ascent to God but with the speaker's knowledge of the unreprieved horror of his own condition.

"To Seem the Stranger," the last of the "terrible sonnets" to be completed and thus in some sense Hopkins's final analysis of his torment, carries the preoccupation with failed colloquy to a bitter conclusion: the poem ends in the utter stoppage of speech and auditory receptivity. The poem's primary metaphor is linguistic: as the speaker's awareness of the ramifications of his own unwilled muteness intensifies, so too does his consciousness of God's inexplicable silence. In a remarkably clear Ignatian movement, the composition of place (lines 1–8) and "pious reasoning" (lines 9–11) develop into an obviously aborted colloquy: the last tercet, though it has the structural pattern of colloquy, does not constitute colloquy itself but rather a commentary on the sacred conversation that does not occur. At the same time, this secularized commentary contains, through an elaborate myth of Christian apocalypse, Hopkins's deepest justification of himself as a Christian man. Both the failure of colloquy with Christ and the nature of that self-justification make "To Seem the Stranger" the most profoundly Christocentric of all the "terrible sonnets." As it chronicles the devastating breakdown of all coherences in Hopkins's life, it painfully subsumes each one to the failure to realize Incarnation. Gardner, however, has argued that because the poem "deals more particularly with the poet's reaction to the social and political aspects of his exile in Dublin," it "is almost exclusively personal, and is therefore a smaller poem" than the others.[66] But Hopkins has actually utilized the materials of his personal biography in order to achieve the clarification of his transpersonal Christocentric vision. The recitation of each disaster—the divisions in family and nationality, the sexual and aesthetic failures—has as its ultimate reference the inability to achieve colloquy with Christ; and it is the mystery of the Incarnation that, even through these negative means, is thus illuminated.

The poem opens with a catalogue of severed communications whose ulti- mate meditative type is the absence of colloquy. The speaker, a "stranger" to himself as well as to others, perceives himself from a distance; he is not incar- nate in his body. He and his Anglican family do not speak the same language "in Christ," for their interpretations of the Incarnation differ: the radical jux- taposition of "strangers" with "Father and mother dear" reflects that theologi- cal schism in familial terms:

> Think not that I am come to send peace on earth; I came not to
> send peace, but a sword. For I am come to set a man at variance
> against his father, and the daughter against her mother, and the
> daughter-in-law against her mother-in-law. And a man's foes shall
> be they of his own household. [Matthew 10:34–36]

Within the family of the Catholic Church, the speaker's previous intimacy with Christ—who is now his "parting, sword and strife"—has dissolved.[67] As the allusion to the Apocalypse (Revelation 1:16, 19:15) makes plain, these discords—together with those detailed in the second quatrain—are man- ifestations of the troubled time of waiting prior to Armageddon. But while Hopkins has thus fixed the eschatological context of his poem, and thereby given to his broken relation with Christ a supercharged value, his speaker hardly experiences that time of tension with the same assured and quietly ex- pectant calm that appears to characterize the closure of "Patience." His accep- tance of isolation, if it is silent, is also uneasy and grim. As in "I Wake and Feel," the speaker intuits the ominous deafness of his audiences, both mun- dane and divine; here, however, instead of straining against his exile, he simply turns mute, desists from uttering his cries for secular or religious community:

[66] Ibid., 2: 341; see also Robert H. Goldsmith, "The Selfless Self: Hopkins' Late Sonnets," *Hopkins Quarterly* 3 (1976): 73.

[67] Compare Boyle, *Metaphor in Hopkins*, p. 118.

> England, whose honour O all my heart woos, wife
> To my creating thought, would neither hear
> Me, were I pleading, plead nor do I . . . .

This renunciation of speech involves more than the temporary triumph of the elective will over the affective will's desire for earthly solace; if it exhibits the fortitude of Christian asceticism, as well as a chaste chivalry, it also entails a virtually unwilled retreat from linguistic functioning. As the speaker slides in these lines from potential apostrophe to declarative statement, he enacts that "foiled action" of colloquy which ends in futile introversion, here marked by chiasmus; he understands that the purposelessness of speech all but necessitates his muteness. Behind this silence, which is that of the sundered human community, looms yet another failure of Incarnation, specifically linguistic in character but implicitly religious in scope: the speaker cannot create for his "heart" or "thought" any verbal incorporation that can ameliorate his self-enclosure. Inscaping the word so that others apprehend its instress, whether of passion or intellect, fails. The disconnection between conception and linguistic embodiment is directly analogous to the larger collapse of images of identity that the poems as a group reveal; seen as an emblem of the fallen condition, it is also the parody of colloquy.

As the speaker thus bluntly acknowledges the realities of his mute and deaf world, he oddly recoils to the self-distancing safety of generalized summary, self-numbing diction, deliberately mechanical parallelism and chiasmus:

> I am in Ireland now; now Í am at a thírd
> Remove.

But even this passive, flattened language cannot quell the speaker's anxiety. In the midst of the sadly rationalized self-comfort of his "pious reasoning," the very rejoinder to isolation stirs the worry that "a thírd / Remove" may but herald "all removes," greater discontinuities and estrangements:

> Not but in all removes I can
> Kind love both give and get.

The word "Remove," pointedly repeated, clarifies the poem's theological progression. Inevitably, the word recalls Hopkins's definition of hell as an "infinite . . . removal" from God (*Sermons*, p. 139). Beyond implying, biographically, the geographic, familial, and sectarian divisions evident in the poem, it suggests the beginning of an endless separation from grace and a bitterly ironic characterization of Ireland as the epitome of sin that accords wholly with the most virulent kinds of Protestant propaganda.[68] "Remove" recalls as well Herbert's use of the word in "Jordan" (I)—"Catching the sense at two removes"—to mock false poetry and thus maintain the central Platonic distinction between the ideal form and its mundane imitations. Perhaps taking a bleak delight in enduring an aesthetic bankruptcy yet worse than Herbert had described, Hopkins almost certainly intended his allusion to imply the limits and imperfections of language in expressing a presumed truth; the logocentric theory parallels in its breakdown his earlier images of failed colloquy. Furthermore, because (as in Herbert) the transition from the Platonic *nous* or Logos to the Word that is Christ is self-evident, "a thírd / Remove" encapsulates the Christocentric nature of the poem's crisis: the speaker knows his Lord but falsely and through mediation. He is parted from direct colloquy with the Incarnate Word. Thus muffled, he cannot fulfill his apostolic responsibility to incarnate the Word in his office by transmitting news of God and in particular the Word of the Apocalypse.[69] Having lost the Word, the Christian man is severed from salvation. Separated from the truth behind language, the poet cannot discover the ultimate model—the Word—for his earthly imitations. The speaker's counter-assertion that he can still "give and get" "Kind love" does nothing to alter the crisis, for the reciprocity invoked here is entirely secular and thus has no bearing on the creation of God's kingdom. Despite Hopkins's effort to conflate kindness and Christian charity in "My Own Heart," kind–ness in the "terrible sonnets" remains an unredeemed state of nature. "Kind love" has as its true opposite the supernatural love of God; and that, the speaker knows, has been withdrawn:

> Only what word
>
> Wisest my heart breeds dark heaven's baffling ban
> Bars or hell's spell thwarts. This to hoard unheard,
> Heard unheeded, leaves me a lonely began.

This is the passage that finally emerged, after much wrestling, from the terrific impulse to revise that overtook Hopkins while making a fair copy of the poem. It presents his most tortured and despondent interpretation of failed

---

[68] Compare David Anthony Downes, "Beatific Landscapes in Hopkins," 197: "The 'third remove' is an in-between state brought on by a lull in the battle between the spiritual and material consciousness." See also Bernard Bergonzi, *Gerard Manley Hopkins* (New York: Macmillan Co., 1977), who argues that the "thírd / Remove" may refer to "Hopkins's alienation from the Catholic Church itself in Ireland at that time" (p. 134).

[69] On the symbiosis between prayer and the apostolate, see, e.g., Alexandre Brou, *Ignatian Methods of Prayer*, trans. William J. Young (Milwaukee, Wis.: Bruce Publishing Co., 1949), pp. 28–29 and chap. 3 passim.

colloquy; in relation to the scheme of salvation history, it bespeaks the extent of his priestly incapacity. That the "word / Wisest" must be the Word of Christ, there can be little doubt; one may speculate that when Hopkins considered the vast discrepancy between the natural affection of human speech (a version of "Kind love") and the achievement of sacred colloquy, he was appalled and dismayed, and driven to revise the sestet in such a manner that it could offer an acceptable explanation for the impasse of prayer. It is an extraordinary aspect of the original sestet (or what remains of it) that the divine interdict against colloquy—"dark heaven's baffling ban"—initially constituted no part of that explanation:

> But what one word
> Wisest my breast holds still to bear some ban
> dumbness or death.
> Of [silence or of]

The source of the "ban" is not identified; the stress falls on the trial of the speaker's endurance; and, in writing of "dumbness or death," human frailties, Hopkins clearly took primary responsibility for his isolation and ineffectuality. The explanation, as such, is entirely conventional. What is startling in the final version is that Hopkins found that conventional explanation unacceptable: it gave insufficient credit both to his straining and to the purity of his desire; nor did it account for a conscience too neat, in this case, to assume guilt without reason.

Thus, when Hopkins changed "some ban" to "dark heaven's baffling ban," and thereby ascribed the failure of colloquy to God, he made the most radically heterodox gesture of his poetry. It is fully consonant with his theme of exile that he should have found the source for his revised imagery in Lamentations: "Thou has covered thyself with a cloud, that our prayer should not pass through" (3 : 44). Jeremiah in the desolation of Jerusalem is never, one remembers, answered by God; note, too, that Hopkins has changed Jeremiah's effort at colloquy into declarative phrasing. The manuscript revisions chronicle his inordinate trouble in gaining a phrasing that, ambiguously, both expressed his sense of divine injustice yet, dutifully, salvaged the remnants of a traditional overview of God's welcoming accessibility, despite His present withdrawal. Through ostensible problems in repetition and alliterative pattern, Hopkins sought the definition of his God: "dark heaven's dark ban," "baffling heaven's dark ban," "dark heaven's baffling ban." Hopkins could not tolerate "dark heaven's dark ban" because the repetition left little room for a punning flexibility of meaning; the phrasing imaged the celestial realm as a pervasive, nearly demonic blackness whose emanations, of the same substance as itself, were a menace. Neither could he accept "baffling heaven": a fortress of baffles (hardly the "circle-citadels" of "The Starlight Night"), by nature impervious to human supplication, much less entrance, would but mock the entire Christian vision. Nor could Hopkins confess that the "heaven-haven" of *The Wreck* (stanza 35) had become a confusion. Finally, by referring "baffling" to the "ban" rather than to heaven, and thus mollifying the impression of total darkness, he was able to preserve the minimal belief that the divine interdict against colloquy was a temporary injunction in a specific instance—perhaps even a matter of human misinterpretation—and not an eternal condition; "dark heaven"—like "God's most deep decree" in "I Wake and Feel"—could now be construed as meaning "obscure" or "secret." Thus, having alleged God to be responsible for the frustration of his ministry, Hopkins then retreated from his audacity and all but exonerated God at his own expense.

The exoneration continues, by means of another clause not in the original sestet, in Hopkins's alternative explanation for the blockage of his speaker's religious language: "or hell's spell thwarts." Here, as the inheritor of Adam's sin, the speaker seemingly accepts full responsibility for the failure, understands why the "word / Wisest" cannot pass through his unclean lips. More significant, however, is the harsh equalization of heaven and hell—both, negative powers operating to undo the speaker. As in "Carrion Comfort" and "No Worst," the speaker is torn between opposites that are nevertheless alike. The collusion of these putatively antithetical forces, and the upsetting of spiritual hierarchy implicit therein, renders the speaker a victim rather than a sinner. As in *The Wreck*, the speaker is caught between "The frown of [God's] face / Before me, the hurtle of hell / Behind . . ." (stanza 3); here, however, and against his elective will, he is prevented by both from accepting God's grace. The irony of this compelled paralysis lies in the poem's apocalyptic stationing: at the point in Christian history upon which both his own salvation and that of the world depend, the speaker chooses to make his Ignatian election of Christ in the clearest possible manner, but cannot.

Hopkins was ultimately not content to define this inability to speak the "word / Wisest" in linguistic terms alone. Because the failure involved his entire person, he translated his incapacity into a metaphor that is directly sexual and biological: after four attempts, in the final tercet, to find an adequate predicate for "breast" or "heart" ("holds," "keeps," "holds," "bears"), he decided on "breeds." The verb of sexual generation interprets Ignatian colloquy in a concretely organic way, characterizes the balked conversation with God as the stoppage of new life itself. So revolutionary was this vision that Hopkins apparently shied away from exploring its ramifications; for observe the first draft of the revised tercet:

> Only what word
>> Wisest my heart breeds dark
>> heaven's dark ban
> Bars or hell's spell thwarts. Thoughts
>> hoarded unheard

Not until later did Hopkins come to "*This* to hoard unheard." In initially writing "Thoughts," he retreated from the organic metaphor in "breeds" to a safe abstraction, severed the connection between the "word / Wisest" and the embryo, and thus made merely decorative the bodily metaphor he had just coined. When he replaced "Thoughts" with the demonstrative adjective "This," he restored his metaphor of pregnancy in its full physical force and intensified the stress on compelled behavior by altering the past participle "hoarded" to the infinitive "to hoard." In so doing, he initiated the most remarkable religious myth in his poetry; that it is fundamentally a myth of self-justification will shortly become clear.

"Breeds," most obviously, entails the feminization of the speaker: having perceived himself as husband to England, he thinks himself female in relation to God and Christ. The metaphor, which has its traditional basis in the Canticles, develops the theme of a broken heterosexual love between the speaker and "dearest him" that is implied in "I Wake and Feel." It taps the sexual mythology of religious failure which dominated Hopkins's last years;[70] that Hopkins may perhaps have used a mythology of religious sterility to embody a deep crisis in sexuality is a matter beyond the scope of this essay. Hopkins had assumed a female persona as early as "Heaven-Haven" (1864)—subtitled, "A nun takes the veil"—as he debated his own conversion. What receives emphasis in "To Seem the Stranger," however, is not the abstract chastening of worldly desire but rather a physically comprehensible, if impossible, phenomenon: the bloated straining of endless pregnancy without issue. Hopkins was perhaps remembering Isaiah 26:17–18:

> 17 Like as a woman with child, that draweth near the time of her delivery, is in pain, and crieth out in her pangs; so have we been in thy sight, O Lord. 18 We have been with child, we have been in pain, we have as it were brought forth wind; we have not wrought any deliverance in the earth. . . .

[70] See Miller, *The Disappearance of God*, pp. 355–56.

If Stephen Dedalus can glibly theorize that "in the virgin womb of the imag-
ination the word was made flesh,"[71] if Donne in "Batter My Heart" can de-
mand that God impregnate him/her by rape, Hopkins's speaker understands
the basis of the metaphor more thoroughly and, in positing the same sex-shift,
experiences only a painful deformation akin to the other images of monstrous
or animalized selfhood characteristic of the "terrible sonnets." There is little
doubt that the speaker's experience is a conscious parody of the nun's sexual
colloquy with Christ in *The Wreck* (see stanza 30): unlike the nun, the speaker
cannot bring to fruition, cannot incarnate in life, the knowledge and love of
Christ which the heart/womb is compelled to imprison. "All my undertakings
miscarry," Hopkins wrote in his 1888 Retreat Notes (*Sermons*, p. 262; italics
mine): both this verb of abortion and the image of pregnancy without term
have a particular propriety for the concerns of these poems. Not only do they
embody the general themes of impotence and frustrated achievement; they
invoke directly the death within warped self-enclosure and the futility of
solipsism.

The speaker's sex-change, perhaps the most trenchant example of disturb-
ingly fluid boundaries in the "terrible sonnets," reconstitutes the speaker of
"To Seem the Stranger," viewed whole, as an androgyne. But this is neither
the hermaphroditic Christ nor the magical androgyne, emblematizing perfec-
tion and self-completion, of hermetic tradition and popular culture. Rather, it
is the asexual, sterile androgyne, associated with spiritual isolation, demon-
ism, and decadence, who appears so frequently in *fin de siècle* literature and
art.[72] Hopkins, increasingly discomfitted by his celibate state,[73] attempted in
"To R. B." (1889) to create a positive image of the androgyne:

> The fine delight that fathers thought; the strong
> Spur, live and lancing like the blowpipe flame,
> Breathes once and, quenchèd faster than it came,
> Leaves yet the mind a mother of immortal song.

But he could not do so in "To Seem the Stranger." His speaker, in a common
confusion of androgyny with impotence, is "Time's eunuch" ("Thou Art In-
deed Just") and not one of those "which have made themselves eunuchs for the
kingdom of heaven's sake" (Matthew 19 : 12). Hopkins's reversal of Scripture is

---

[71] James Joyce, *A Portrait of the Artist as a Young Man*, ed. Chester G. Anderson (1916; rpt.
New York: Viking, 1968), p. 217.

[72] See A. J. L. Busst, "The Image of the Androgyne in the Nineteenth Century," in Ian
Fletcher, ed., *Romantic Mythologies* (London: Routledge & Kegan Paul, 1967), passim.

[73] See Hopkins, *Letters to Bridges*, p. 194.

telling: as the ironically castrated slave of the world of generation, the speaker has found the discipline of his devotion futile and the extremity of his sacrifice unacceptable to his Lord, who alone could have created spiritual honor from willed impotence. This, of course, is Hopkins's plea at the end of "Thou Art Indeed Just": "Mine, O thou lord of life, send my roots rain." The sexual pun on "roots" is patent, and the entire image is thus exactly analogous to that of stalled pregnancy in "To Seem the Stranger." In each case, the malfunctioning of the reproductive system is equated with the failure of spiritual life, whether in colloquy or in ministry; each image, moreover, implies Hopkins's sense of a great potential fertility that has been irrationally and inexplicably stanched. The further point, relevant to the development of Hopkins's self-justifying myth in "To Seem the Stranger," is not so much the profound sexism in his equation of sterile man and pregnant woman; it is rather that Hopkins, despite his debased vision of female sexuality, used precisely the image of female reproduction to achieve his defense against God. For it is primarily as a woman that his speaker appears in the last tercet of the poem.

Carrying, breeding the "word / Wisest" in her body, the speaker is not simply female. She is a type of the Virgin Mary and, ultimately, of the "woman clothed with the sun" (Revelation 12 : 1): she bears the Messiah in her womb/ heart, and not merely an imitation of the divine Logos.[74] In this most extensive of all Hopkins's parodies, the metaphor of failed colloquy is a grotesque revision of the divine gestation: the import of the inability to speak or deliver the Incarnate Word is magnified both by hagiography and eschatology, and the speaker's dysfunction becomes the primary cause for the postponement of the Apocalypse and the instituting of the New Jerusalem. Nevertheless, unlike the speaker's parody of Christ in Gethsemene ("I Wake and Feel"), this parody has a distinctly self-assertive and self-justifying cast; despite the sex-change and the surrounding suggestions of impotence, it is difficult to imagine a female emblem that Hopkins could have considered more heroic and ennobling than that of the "woman clothed with the sun." In a contemporaneous commentary on the Incarnation (26 August 1885), Hopkins described the Virgin thus:

> And this grace of the 'hypostatic order' will be that sunlight with
> which the woman, that is / she-being, not she-man, of the Apoc-
> alypse is clothed, her flesh or earthly but pre-human being is
> clothed; the incorruptible world of the angels is in attendance on
> her above, being by nature higher, as purely spiritual; and mor-

[74] Compare Boyle, *Metaphor in Hopkins*, p. 121.

tality and the world of corruption awaits her below, if she should choose, as she did, to descend onto it. [*Sermons*, pp. 170–71][75]

In assuming such a sacred persona, Hopkins asserted his conviction of his true, and now misused, worth; instead of merely acknowledging the myth of apocalyptic redemption, he appropriated it, internalized it organically, and became thereby the agency of prophecy.[76] All of Hopkins's anxious cravings for apocalypse in the earlier poems and prose have their culmination here: by becoming the Virgin, he brought, as Yeats wrote of Lionel Johnson, "A little nearer to his thought" / A measureless consummation that he dreamed"[77] and thus achieved an identicality between himself and the heavenly hierarchy. The direct internalization of the Logos, too, is an obvious counter-assertion against the sense of being at a "third / Remove" from God. In defining the woman's identity as "she-being, not she-man," Hopkins evaded his fear of a degenerate androgyny. In becoming the Virgin, he sought to ensure his own salvation and thus to allay the fear of damnation that informs the "terrible sonnets" as a whole; for, as he wrote during the Long Retreat of 1881, "the Blessed Virgin was beyond all others redeemed, because it was her more than all other creatures that Christ meant to win from nothingness and it was her that he meant to raise the highest" (*Sermons*, p. 197). And in becoming the "woman clothed with the sun," the speaker sheds the animal "fell" or pelt that symbolizes original sin in "I Wake and Feel," emerges from darkness, and is arrayed in the eternal light of saintliness for which the speaker of "My Own Heart" yearns.

The actual poem, because it buries these implications in allusion, is more negative in vision. Yet even the negativity differs substantially from that of the other "terrible sonnets," as Hopkins's manipulation of other elements in the apocalyptic myth indicates. Unlike the speaker of "My Own Heart," who accepts the organic deformity of his "blind / Eyes" as partial cause for his failure, this speaker, in assuming the roles of the Virgin and the "woman clothed with the sun," clearly denies human guilt and thus looks elsewhere to explain muted speech, blocked parturition. In a strikingly heterodox revision of Revelation, she intuits the hatred, even jealousy, that God the Father bears against the creature He has impregnated with Christ, the "word / Wisest." The hatred

[75] See also *Sermons*, pp. 197–98. Hopkins obviously had a particular interest in this component of the apocalyptic mythology of Revelation.

[76] Compare Geoffrey H. Hartman, *Beyond Formalism*: "However authentic a suffering speaks in this [a passage from *Sermons*, p. 262], it is a passive suffering. Here is where vision or prophecy or scandal might have begun. . . . Hopkins's acceptance of the rule was so absolute that it did not permit him to be more than a pawn or servant in the sacred game he intuited" (p. 246).

[77] W. B. Yeats, "In Memory of Major Robert Gregory" (stanza 3).

is not explained; the potential rivalry between Father and Son is not explored. But the ruthless suggestion of a pun in "dark heaven's baffling *ban*"—ban/ bann—clearly entails the perverse annulment of the *hieros gamos*, the mystical marriage of God and the Virgin, upon which the tercet is founded. Where Hopkins had rejoiced, in "The Blessed Virgin compared to the Air we Breathe," that "Men here may draw like breath / More Christ and baffle death," the God of this poem, in "baffling" His own Word before His birth, becomes an incomprehensible agent of death, a deicide. God's betrayal of his bride leaves her violated, sexually and spiritually abandoned; as part of Hopkins's myth of self-justification, it also nullifies His role as Father and leaves her the sole true parent of Christ. As the speaker, husband to England his wife in the octave, was greeted by her deafness and indifference, so here the speaker, God's bride, is met with silent rejection: in each case it is the speaker's spouse who abrogates the sacrament of marriage. As in "Andromeda," the true precursor of "To Seem the Stranger," she is left "With not her either beauty's equal or / Her injury's. . . ."

Hopkins's conception of a God who deliberately and rudely forestalls the fulfillment of His own apocalyptic and redemptive design is startling, and I have consciously elaborated, without qualification, the ramifications of this passage so that its total shape might be seen. Rhetorically, of course, the passage is based on an either/or construction; but when the supposedly positive and beneficent alternative is defined in such unrelentingly negative terms, the either/or construction must seem a mere face-saving formality. Nevertheless, Hopkins obviously required simultaneously a dualistic structure of argument whereby he might preserve, in more orthodox fashion, the possibility of God's innocence (or, at least, inoperant neutrality). "Hell's spell" is his brilliant epithet for the apocalyptic Antichrist of Revelation 12:3-4 who "thwarts" the coming of the Messiah, the "great red dragon" who "stood before the woman which was ready to be delivered, for to devour her child as soon as it was born." In a logical extension of "Andromeda," the speaker's child appears as "doomed dragon food." Appropriately, the Antichrist would destroy the Incarnate Word by speaking a demonic counter-language, a "spell," a desacralized enchantment whose serpentine multiplicity offers no redemptive order. That Hopkins could have associated language with rapacious murder—an amplification of the imagery in "Carrion Comfort"—shows exactly the desperate ferocity with which speech-acts are construed in the "terrible sonnets." The devouring of the Word—and by Satan, who was once among the chief of God's archangels—is the most explicit instance of the perversion of Communion in these poems; as it again emphasizes Hopkins's preoccupation with cannibalism and the threat of animal instinct, it gives final form to his central concern with blocked colloquy, for the devoured Word is of the speaker's own substance.

There can be no question that "To Seem the Stranger," despite its use of Christian myth as a hostile force, despite its virtual equation of God's "baffling ban" with "hell's spell," remains a profoundly Christian poem: its primary subject is Hopkins's all but parthenogenetic effort to give rebirth to himself as a Christian. His identification of his speaker's heart with the spotless womb that carries the second Christ is as close as he ever came, in his final years, to rebuking God for His unjust imputation of guilt, His imposition of trial by failure; it is as close as he could come to asserting both his innocence and the purity of his purpose. The stoppage of the speaker's breath is a cataclysmic event in the progression of Christian soteriology, one which unwillingly betrays the mundane world to a continuation of its own furious gnashings. "Thou Art Indeed Just" does not go so far as this: the speaker affirms only the justice of what he pleads, not the justice of his nature; God in Himself *is* just (despite the touch of qualification in the conditional "if" clause of the first line). The poem closes in submissive colloquy; it does not attempt the temerity of "To Seem the Stranger."

If Hopkins's speaker, unlike Yeats or Eliot, here senses no ironic discrepancy between his own experience and its elaboration in traditional myth, no gap between the actuality and its type or allegorical representation, it is because the stakes are too high. Without irony, however, and without any acknowledgment that a presumptuous "Selfyeast of spirit" may have been at work, the speaker finally abandons apocalyptic typology for the nearer realities of his own condition. Bereft, he castigates himself for his insularity and constricted possessiveness of the "word / Wisest":

> This to hoard unheard,
> Heard unheeded, leaves me a lonely began.

In this amplification of the second quatrain, the disillusioned recognition of powerlessness resembles, without Eliot's sardonic comedy, Prufrock's neurotic justification for maintaining silence: even if he were able to utter his prophetic knowledge of the Messiah, his message would be dismissed with blank indifference. Yet if "Heard unheeded" ostensibly refers to his failure in ministry, his inability to convert his Protestant family, much less the typically unregenerate, in the time just before the Apocalypse, the phrase also contains the most devastating charge he has yet lodged against his Lord: God, hearing, neither listens nor cares. Deaf unresponsiveness in the mundane world is but the echo of the "baffling ban" instituted by God in "dark heaven." Dependent for his public efficacy upon a visionary spiritual colloquy now abrogated by divine intention, the speaker ends with a "lonely began," uncompanioned by Christ or God. The charge in "Heard unheeded"—with all its feeling of desolate sorrow and anger, its enforced introversion and its recognition of lost Communion—is the summary of the "terrible sonnets."

IV
"THE WIDOW OF AN INSIGHT":
POETRY AND THE MINISTRY

Physician, heal thyself.

Luke 4:23

BECAUSE its speaker cannot bear or transmit Christ the Word, "To Seem the Stranger" enacts, intimately, Hopkins's failure in ministry; since the "woman clothed with the sun" is an allegorical type of the Catholic Church as well as of the Virgin, it broaches this theme from a broadly institutional, as well as personal, perspective. Yet although the poem is the only one of the "terrible sonnets" to engage this theme directly, the concern is common to them all. "Carrion Comfort" can speak *about* Hopkins's past conversion and reception into the priesthood, but it cannot actually perform a priestly function in the present. Though Hopkins may complain, in "To Seem the Stranger," that England does not hear him, he himself makes no effort to breach the silence. None of these poems postulates, as part of its rhetorical form, an individual human audience, much less a society or congregation whom the speaker serves as priest through his poetic capacity; their isolated self-enclosure is too absolute to permit those priestly and ritual gestures towards an implied audience through which he had previously fulfilled his ministry. The poems thus render the disintegration of the Christian community and, in microcosmic form, the dissolution of the visible Catholic Church. Although commentators have attended exclusively to Hopkins's relationship with God, and sometimes to its breakdown, the collapse of his connection to the religious community—no less significant than the more obvious but more private disaster—is also enacted in these poems. It is frankly a spectacle of some pathos to consider this impotence in his public institutional capacity as the concluding episode, if only in the poetry, of a man who had repudiated the Anglicanism of his family and nation, converted to Catholicism, entered the most demanding of its orders, and striven, often under adverse conditions, to serve adequately in a social role for which he was not temperamentally suited. The separation between the priest and his community that the "terrible sonnets" mirrors is the earthly correlative, within the process of daily religious life, of Hopkins's inability to sustain his communication with Christ.

Because the "terrible sonnets" lack an implied audience, they contrast in the sharpest manner possible with Hopkins's earlier poetry. This sudden cancellation of religious activity in its social dimension, however, can only be defined through its antithesis, the fullness of ministry which Hopkins had previously incorporated into his poetry; for on this matter the "terrible sonnets" provide nothing but the evidence of negation. Yet even to propose the existence of an implied audience in the bulk of Hopkins's work (to say nothing of its disappearance in the "terrible sonnets") is seemingly to disregard some known facts of his biography and to open afresh the unresolved issue of Hopkins's complicated and disquietingly ambivalent attitudes towards writing and publishing. It is essential here to make the distinction between an actual reading public exterior to the poems and the hypothesized or fictive audience Hopkins came to envisage both *for* and *in* his work; this second audience—which Hopkins later saw vanish—is the one under discussion now. But the two kinds of audience were much entwined, however unconsciously, in his mind. Indeed, the second acted as surrogate for the first; its creation was necessitated, emotionally and artistically, by Hopkins's ascetic renunciation of an earthly fame which publication before an actual reading public might have conferred.

It is well known that—with the exception of *The Wreck of the Deutschland*, "The Loss of the Eurydice," and later the three sonnets he sent to Hall Caine for an anthology[1]—Hopkins adamantly refused to attempt the publication of his own work. Bridges and Dixon of course entreated him to publish, and Dixon occasionally made surreptitious but friendly efforts to make his work known. But Hopkins obeyed with punctilious—indeed, excessive—scrupulosity the Jesuit strictures on censorship;[2] "he shrank," as Abbott says, "from asking the consent of his superiors" to publish, consistently interpreted those strictures as injunctions not to publish at all, and viewed publication as an insubordination against his order.[3] Yet Hopkins clearly distinguished be-

[1] Gerard Manley Hopkins, *The Letters of Gerard Manley Hopkins to Robert Bridges*, ed. Claude Colleer Abbott (1935; rpt. London: Oxford University Press, 1970), pp. 65, 127. Hall Caine finally did not print Hopkins's poems in his *Sonnets of Three Centuries* (London: Elliot Stock, 1882).

[2] See especially St. Ignatius Loyola, *The Constitutions of the Society of Jesus*, trans. George E. Ganss (St. Louis, Mo.: The Institute of Jesuit Sources, 1970), secs. 273, 389, 653.

[3] Hopkins, *Letters to Bridges*, p. xviii; see also *Letters to Bridges*, p. 200; and Gerard Manley Hopkins, *The Correspondence of Gerard Manley Hopkins and Richard Watson Dixon*, ed. Claude Colleer Abbott (1935; rpt. London: Oxford University Press, 1970), pp. 28, 30. In light of these attitudes it is difficult to accept the following suggestion by Alfred Thomas: "That Hopkins could have considered the possibility of the Society of Jesus' providing him with an opportunity for writing is not to be ruled out as a factor in enabling him to choose his vocation" (Alfred Thomas, "Gerard Manley Hopkins: 'Doomed to Succeed by Failure,'" *The Dublin Review* 240 [1966]: 163, n. 3). See, too, John Robinson, *In Extremity: A Study of Gerard Manley Hopkins* (Cambridge: Cambridge University Press, 1978), pp. 11, 13, who balances Hopkins's scrupulosity against the actual demands of the Jesuit order: "It was not Hopkins' commitment to the priesthood but the even more rigorous dedication to a religious order which prompted his abandonment of verse"; "It would be mistaken . . . to suggest that the Society of Jesus as such suppressed his creative impulse."

tween writing and publishing. The distinction, if it seems touched by casuist self-trickery, was also self-preservative; for Hopkins knew he needed to write. Although he burnt most of his poetry when he became a Jesuit and frequently insisted that the practice of poetry was opposed to his true vocation as a priest,[4] he was equally convinced of his religious duty not to stifle the poetic talent given him by God:

> Art and its fame do not really matter, spiritually they are nothing, virtue is the only good; but it is only by bringing in the infinite that to a just judgment they can be made to look infinitesimal or small or less than vastly great; and in this ordinary view of them I apply to them, and it is the true rule for dealing with them, what Christ our Lord said of virtue, Let your light shine before men that they may see your good works (say, of art) and glorify yr. Father in heaven (that is, acknowledge that they have an absolute excellence in them and are steps in a scale of infinite and inexhaustible excellence).[5]

When, writing to Dixon, he called Christ "the only just judge, the only just literary critic,"[6] he was implicitly characterizing Christ as the arch-poet and thus justifying both his own work and his creative role by a theory of Christian imitation. Indeed, so high a premium did he place upon his poetic activity as the satisfying of Christ's desire that, in the midst of his jaded summer of 1885, he could write with desperate fervor to Bridges, "if I could but produce work I should not mind its being buried, silenced, and going no further; but it kills me to be time's eunuch and never to beget."[7]

Thus eschewing publication as an earthly temptation to pride and disobedience, but holding the act of writing in reverence as a glorification of God, Hopkins sought to resolve this paradox by becoming the purest kind of writer, the one who cares only for the writing and nothing for its public success. Though he would doubtless have been pained to recognize it, Hopkins exemplified—strangely, and in an extreme Catholic form—early tendencies in the "aesthetic" movement that, under Pater's tutelage, was later to have such influence. Had he lived free from the moral fastidiousness of the Jesuit order and his own conscience, such an attitude towards writing would have been

---

[4] See Hopkins, *Letters to Bridges*, pp. 42–43, 61; *Correspondence of Hopkins and Dixon*, pp. 14–15. Hopkins also felt that the study of music ran counter to his priestly vocation (*Letters to Bridges*, p. 126).

[5] Hopkins, *Letters to Bridges*, p. 231.

[6] Hopkins, *Correspondence of Hopkins and Dixon*, p. 8.

[7] Hopkins, *Letters to Bridges*, p. 222.

difficult enough to maintain. As it was, it is hardly surprising that Hopkins, caught between two absolutist positions, was forced to make compromises. Although he could barely acknowledge the fact openly, Hopkins discovered that he could not survive, as a poet, without a tangible earthly audience for his work; nor could he sustain his initial rationalization of writing solely to satisfy Christ and thus maintaining the purity of his own endeavor. He was trapped in the uncomfortable choice between sullying his labor by risking a human audience and not writing at all. He tried to deny his dilemma. To Bridges he claimed, with a flair borrowed from Whitman, that "a poet is a public in himself"; and to Dixon he dismissed the deleterious consequences of writing without an audience: "The life I lead is liable to many mortifications but the want of fame as a poet is the least of them."[8] But to strike a compromise he gradually began thinking, in hesitant and veiled terms, of posthumous publication as a way of serving God without accruing personal benefit, yet securing that sense of an actual reading public which he required to prevent his fear of oblivion from burgeoning: "All therefore that I think of doing is to keep my verses together in one place—at present I have not even correct copies—, that, if anyone shd. like, they might be published after my death."[9] But the concept of a future audience, though it eased some of the pressure, also proved itself insufficient; the consciousness of an immediate present that informs the poetry also infused Hopkins's real demand for an actual audience.[10] It is here, in his efforts to create for himself a present audience, that the strains between the poet and the priest are most evident.

Hopkins turned first to Bridges, then to Dixon and Patmore, his family, and a few fellow Jesuits.[11] He cautioned Dixon, "You are welcome to shew my poems to anyone you like so long as nothing gets into print."[12] The coupling here of a blanket permission and a strict taboo is characteristic of the tension Hopkins endured for the sake of his scrupulous obedience. And he feared personal contamination: "It would be easy to explain it [publication of a poem] to the Provincial," Hopkins wrote, making light of obstacles he had previously seen, "but not so easy to guard myself against what others might say."[13]

[8] Ibid., p. 59; Hopkins, *Correspondence of Hopkins and Dixon*, p. 28.

[9] Hopkins, *Letters to Bridges*, p. 66; see also Hopkins, *Correspondence of Hopkins and Dixon*: "You see then what is against me, but since, as Solomon says, there is a time for everything, there is nothing that does not some day come to be, it may be that the time will come for my verses" (p. 95).

[10] See Alison G. Sulloway, *Gerard Manley Hopkins and the Victorian Temper* (London: Routledge & Kegan Paul, 1972), pp. 101–2, n., for a helpful commentary on this matter. Sulloway believes, however, that Hopkins had only a future audience in mind.

[11] See Hopkins, *Letters to Bridges*, p. 196.

[12] Hopkins, *Correspondence of Hopkins and Dixon*, p. 31.

[13] Ibid., p. 29.

Hopkins's desire to be liberated from the twistings and responsibilities these moral considerations imposed is manifest in his statement to Dixon: "I could wish, I allow, that my pieces could at some time become known but in some spontaneous way, so to speak, and without my forcing." [14]

But it is in Hopkins's comment to Bridges that his strenuous effort to maintain an utter rectitude in allowing others to read his work emerges most clearly: "I do not write for the public. You are my public and I hope to convert you." [15] More than his confession of devout friendship, this is the germ of Hopkins's major attempt to reconcile the ends of poetry with those of his faith—to conceive his art, in the most profound way, as *utile* as well as *dulce*. He would later write to Dixon that the Society of Jesus "values, as you say, and has contributed to literature, to culture; but only as a means to an end. Its history and its experience shew that literature proper, as poetry, has seldom been found to be to that end a very serviceable means." [16] In Bridges, Hopkins found the opportunity to resolve the duality between means and ends. For was not Bridges the poet most likely to be aided spiritually if he were approached —not merely most serviceably, but most appropriately—through poetry? By claiming that the conversion of Bridges was his foremost poetic goal, Hopkins could argue that through his poetry he was serving God in his priestly capacity, that he was concerned not with his own fame but with the salvation of souls and thus with the coming of the New Jerusalem. His formulation of this ulterior rhetorical and ministerial purpose was obviously crucial. Although he could not address Bridges directly as an individual until the very last poem Bridges received from him ("To R.B." [1889]), Bridges gave him an immediate and constant audience through whom he could dispel the terror of writing *in vacuo*; and he provided Hopkins with a situation by which he could allay his anxious fear that the writing of poetry was a selfish waste of talent.

While granting the signal importance of Hopkins's conscious creation of Bridges as his primary human audience, however, one may question whether the poems themselves substantiate his formulation or whether they imply an audience other than Bridges. Hopkins seems to have used the notion of Bridges as audience in a synecdochic manner—as the concrete situation and occasion from which to devise imaginatively a larger audience than Bridges himself. For unless one assumes Hopkins so tactless as to seek Bridges's conversion by main force or by sheer immersion in Catholic doctrine and imagery, the poems hardly seem written for an audience as unsympathetic to Catholic thought and as unfamiliar with Christian theology as Hopkins actually consid-

[14] Ibid., p. 28.
[15] Hopkins, *Letters to Bridges*, p. 46.
[16] Hopkins, *Correspondence of Hopkins and Dixon*, p. 93.

ered Bridges to be. The intricate vision of Christian history in "God's Gran-
deur" or the reliance upon Catholic iconography in "Spring"—to take exam-
ples at random—do not appear conceived to convert a man as hostile to
orthodoxy as Bridges. Nor do the poems possess those elements of argument
and persuasion one would expect of works addressed to the uninitiate; Ignatian
logic and methods of progression have efficacy, as rhetorical modes, only for
those who have some acquaintance with the general outlines of meditative
tradition.

Rather, the poems posit an audience who participates in the same world and
shares roughly the same beliefs as Hopkins himself: he writes to his own kind,
not to an antagonist. In directing his work to an imagined community of the
faithful, implied within the poems, his purpose was obviously not to convert
but to deepen and enrich the religious understanding of those who already
accepted Catholic teaching; he thus spared himself from being attacked on ac-
count of his own conversion to Rome. Instead of pretending to speak to an
individual, he could now speak both *to* and *for* a congregation; he could thus
fulfill that part of his priestly role which required that he typify or embody his
audience. He could write of the sacraments, and of the sacrament in nature,
without profaning them before an unclean public. He could invoke the Incar-
nation and administer Communion without fearing that the mysteries might
be misunderstood or disregarded. He could act as if, in taking responsibility
for the spiritual welfare of his fictive congregation, he was working for the
salvation of the entire Christian community and thus abetting the prosecution
of God's design. Hopkins's envisaging of a Catholic audience for his poems,
however amorphous and vaguely defined, enabled him—far more than with
Bridges as audience—to suppose that the writing of a poem was comparable to
the performing of his daily sacerdotal functions or the celebrating of the Mass;
it enabled him to minimize the fundamental discrepancy between his poetry
and his vocation that still obtained when he wrote to Bridges the irreligious. It
was only with such a hypothesized audience, quasi-idealized and strangely ex-
trapolated from the factual audience of Bridges alone, that Hopkins could
truly fulfill his priestly role; and that is why his unconscious formulation of
such a communal audience was so vital. If Hopkins's job of creating an audi-
ence was less practically difficult than Yeats's and Lady Gregory's at the Abbey
Theatre, it was no less necessary. Precisely because the delicate compromise
that such an audience represented in reconciling conflicting claims in
Hopkins's life was attained with such precarious feats of balancing, its disap-
pearance in the "terrible sonnets" becomes—like the loss of images from na-
ture and the failure of colloquy—a radical gauge of his psychic state.

Hopkins's fictive audience, although not characteristic of every poem preceding the "terrible sonnets," is yet unmistakably present. His most common means of creating that audience is his recurrent use of the first-person plural pronoun, in either nominative or possessive form. Merging the personality of his speaker with communal emotion, need, or religious condition, he then issues forth as the spokesperson for the group through whom the experience of renewal becomes possible. In thus subsuming his own individuality, he sheds that element of personal interest in a situation or moral crisis which, even in an expression of loss, can conduce to pride; the method of public incorporation in the fictive audience, though it appears as modesty, derives from the stark ascetic strain in Hopkins's character and intimates his continued suspicion of the Romantic sublime. Thus, in "Nondum," linked in mode to the earlier "Barnfloor and Winepress" (1865), he articulates the bereft anxiety of the Christian community confronted by God's silence and absence:

> We guess; we clothe Thee, unseen King,
> With attributes we deem are meet;
> Each in his own imagining
> Sets up a shadow in Thy seat;
> Yet know not how our gifts to bring,
> Where seek Thee with unsandalled feet.
>
> [stanza 3]

The first-person singular pronoun in the last two stanzas represents less the speaker's separation from his community than his example to them of the resurgence in private faith that ought to result from public supplication. In "The Leaden Echo and the Golden Echo," the communal "we"—carrying the sense of renewed security and hope—is a distinguishing aspect of the "Golden Echo" portion. Similarly, in "Spelt from Sibyl's Leaves," it expresses the sharing of a common doom (e.g., "Óur évening is over us; óur night' whélms, whélms, ánd will end us"); but Hopkins's purpose here is not to gain a personal easement of grief through the generalized diffusion of the emotion but to embody dramatically the theological truth of the Apocalypse as a cataclysm for human society. "The Soldier" shows yet another kind of intention behind the plural pronoun: the casting of a poem as homily or sermon. By acting as if his own curiosity were that of his public, Hopkins's speaker can create a unity of understanding. This method, in turn, allows him to lead his audience from earthly analogue and daily situation to Christ; it is the social version of Hopkins's use of images from nature:

> Yes. Whý do we áll, seeing of a soldier, bless him? bless
> Our redcoats, our tars? Both these being, the greater part,

But frail clay, nay but foul clay. Here it is: the heart,
Since, proud, it calls the calling manly, gives a guess
That, hopes that, makesbelieve, the men must be no less;
. . . .
Mark Christ our King. He knows war, served this soldiering through;
He of all can reeve a rope best. There he bides in bliss
Now, and séeing somewhére some mán do all that man can do,
For love he leans forth . . . .

Note that the "Yes" of assent, the phrase "Here it is," and the inclusion of the
audience in the act of blessing all contribute rhetorically to the involving of
the congregation. With "Hurrahing in Harvest," Hopkins attempts a differ-
ent mode of sermon, one which exploits a rhetorical vacillation between pri-
vate and public experience in order to demonstrate, through his own example
to others, the possible richness that may be discovered in unexpected areas.
The phrase "*our* Saviour" (line 6) taps the world of mutually accepted belief:
the speaker's individual experience as a communicant of Christ in nature is
then one that is potentially accessible to all Christians; the deliberately imper-
sonal naming of himself as "the beholder"—in "These things, these things
were here and but the beholder / Wanting"—makes that accessibility of Com-
munion evident.

The Wreck of the Deutschland illustrates the same alternation from private to
public modes in its seminal and most elaborate form; indeed, it is instructive
to remember that Hopkins began the poem with the relatively public narra-
tive of Part the Second, not with the impassioned, lyric, and private invoca-
tions of Part the First.[17] For all the introverted intensity of the speaker's private
relation with the nun and with Christ, a passion that almost overtakes the
narrative movement of Part the Second, his ultimate effort is to wrest clear of
individual vision in order to articulate communal value, the world of mundane
experience upon which religious heroism acts. His shift of focus from the nun
to the other shipwrecked passengers (stanza 31) thus marks a central develop-
ment in the poem's evolution:

Well, she has thee [Christ] for the pain, for the
Patience; but pity of the rest of them!
Heart, go and bleed at a bitterer vein for the
Comfortless unconfessed of them—

With his first use of the first-person plural pronoun (stanza 33),

[17] See Hopkins, *Letters to Bridges*, p. 44.

> Our passion-plungèd giant risen,
> The Christ of the Father compassionate, fetched in the storm
> of his strides[,]

he utters his understanding that Christ and the mystery of the Resurrection operate perpetually in history, and not merely in his own conversion; in so doing, he transcends the private prayers and meditations of Part the First. The poem can then close with the speaker, as priest, issuing a public prayer to the nun on behalf of the English Catholic community for the conversion of the entire nation:

> Dame, at our door
> Drowned, and among our shoals,
>
> . . . .
>
> Let him [Christ] easter in us, be a dayspring to the dimness
> of us, be a crimson-cresseted east,
> More brightening her, rare-dear Britain, as his reign rolls,
> Pride, rose, prince, hero of us, high-priest,
> Our hearts' charity's hearth's fire, our thoughts' chivalry's
> throng's Lord.

In this clear enactment of sacerdotal function, springing from his acceptance of the priesthood in Part the First, the speaker focusses the religious import of the wreck within the cosmic perspective of Christian history; the final language of jubilation has behind it the emotive desire of the entire "throng."

Hopkins, in the poems before the "terrible sonnets," was as much concerned to address his fictive audience directly as he was to articulate its feelings. When he described to Bridges what he called "bidding"—"a nameless quality which is of the first importance both in oratory and drama"—he was also defining the rhetorical aim of his own poetry:

> I mean the art or virtue of saying everything right *to* or *at* the hearer, interesting him, holding him in the attitude of correspondent or addressed or at least concerned, making it everywhere an act of intercourse—and of discarding everything that does not bid, does not tell. I think one may gain much of this by practice.[18]

"Bidding" involved not only the regulation of rhythm and vocabulary but the proper adjustment in form and tone of address; thus inscaping a public, as he did also the phenomena of nature, he created the audience by which he justi-

[18] Ibid., p. 160; Hopkins's italics.

fied his poetry. It is a comprehensible paradox that the poet who so rigorously denied himself an actual audience should so assiduously have adumbrated methods for luring the attention of a hypothetical audience within his poems; and it is paradoxically strange that when Hopkins was too distraught to care at all for a fictive audience—in the "terrible sonnets"—his poems became most directly accessible to the actual audience he never dared court. The poetry which resulted from the "bidding" of an audience is not strictly dramatic; it is, as Hopkins himself knew, "oratorical," [19] a poetry tending more towards declamation than towards personal interaction with an audience individuated within the poem. Although this poetry obviously pays debt to developments in nineteenth-century poetics, it is only by stretching the term to the point of uselessness that the poems can be called "dramatic monologues"; and certainly Hopkins had not the interest of Tennyson and Browning, even Arnold, in experimenting with the genre. [20] The element of gentle exhortation in the word "bidding," with its touch of Ignatian chivalry, suggests both the tone and the degree of forcefulness Hopkins sought to achieve in his address. His speaker, though he constantly desires to instruct and improve his audience, never does so with condescension; he seeks instead to become—most properly for a priest —a human type of the Paraclete, one who encourages by coaxing and example rather than by precept. In "The Starlight Night," for instance,

> Look at the stars! look, look up at the skies!
> O look at all the fire-folk sitting in the air!
> The bright boroughs, the circle-citadels there!

the exclamatory style conveys not so much a note of command as an excited urgency of desire that others perceive the spiritual emblems he loves. In the sestet he invents in them the eager curiosity he would have them possess, and then answers their implied query with, "These are *indeed* the barn; withindoors house / The shocks" (italics mine). The conversational quality in this encouragement to comprehend divine symbol occurs again in "The Blessed Virgin"; here, the speaker is so earnest with Ruskinian fervor to train the untutored eye to see the sacrament in nature that he not only gestures towards the heavens but helps to position his audience physically:

---

[19] Ibid., p. 46. Todd K. Bender, *Gerard Manley Hopkins: The Classical Background and Critical Reception of his Work* (Baltimore, Md.: Johns Hopkins University Press, 1966), p. 158, who applies the term "bidding" to Hopkins's mode of self-address, seems to misunderstand the concept.

[20] For a useful study of dramatic monologue in Hopkins's pre-conversion poetry, see Florence K. Riddle, "Hopkins' Dramatic Monologues," *Hopkins Quarterly* 2 (1975): 51–66; Hopkins later abandoned the form.

> Again, look overhead
> How air is azurèd;
> Oh how! Nay do but stand
> Where you can lift your hand
> Skywards: rich, rich it laps
> Round the four fingergaps.
>
> [lines 73–78]

This is a more intimate advice than that of the hymnal "Easter" (1866?), in which the speaker virtually chants his instructions for the proper reception of the Eucharist to the potentially "happy throng" that may crowd God's church; but the mood of passionate exhortation and the concern for adequate spiritual apprehension in his community are the same. Even when Hopkins seems most to be engrossed in a private and reflective lyric, he does not forget the "bidding" of his audience—as in the sestet of "The Caged Skylark":

> Not that the sweet-fowl, song-fowl, needs no rest—
> Why, hear him, hear him babble and drop down to his nest,
>   But his own nest, wild nest, no prison.

With this urging, too anxious to be imperative, the poem assumes the rhetorical status of a sermon; the function of the initial analogy, beyond the poet's imitation of God in the making of analogy itself, lies in the educative assistance it provides in clarifying for his audience the definition of original sin and its consequences. But it is "Pied Beauty" that most perfectly fuses the lyric and homiletic tendencies. The resounding announcement of the natural, not Biblical, text for exposition—"Glory be to God for dappled things"—moves swiftly and easily into a catalogue of illustrations whose tone of delivery is one of fresh delight in perceptions newly gained in private rather than one of old knowledge repeated in public. The witty Herbertian parenthesis—"(who knows how?)"—cajoles the audience into a comfortable awe, and the poem then closes with the most unmistakable of all Hopkins's public exhortations: "Praise him." Yet the grace in this closure is that the injunction is also a self-address filled with a profound sense of personal duty; that duty, in turn, derives from the speaker's priestly responsibility to be worthy of his congregation. Hopkins asks of his audience no more than of himself; to such a modest art does his "bidding" aspire.

Both by acting as spokesperson, priestly intercessor for his community, and by "bidding" his audience directly to a greater religious consciousness, Hopkins aimed at reconciling his vocation with his art. He achieved that recon-

ciliation most explicitly, however (if only occasionally) through the poetic de-
lineation of ritual. For in ritual he simultaneously satisfied his need to speak
both *for* and *to* his audience; by engaging in ritual or sacramental acts, his
speaker can unite individuals in the *ecclesia* and sanctify members of the earthly
community in the sight of God. Thus enabled to cast his speaker in an entirely
priestly role, Hopkins was concerned not simply with incorporating thematic
references to ritual into the poetry (as in *The Wreck*, stanza 30, with the allu-
sion to the Feast of the Immaculate Conception) but with the dramatic enact-
ment of his ecclesiastical office. The attempt to have the action of the poetry
duplicate his behavior as priest, if it reflects his fear of fissure between them,
attests as well to his devout involvement in the redemptive mission of the
Church. It is hardly accidental, moreover, that so many of Hopkins's poems of
ritual deal with the Eucharist; for it was primarily his commitment to the
Doctrine of the Real Presence of Christ within the wafer and the wine substan-
tially that led Hopkins first to the Anglicanism of Newman, Pusey, and
Keble, and then to Catholicism. Thus, in "Easter Communion" (1865), as he
experimented even before his conversion with taking orders, he summoned his
imagined congregation to the eucharistic service:

> Pure fasted faces draw unto this feast:
> God comes all sweetness to your Lenten lips.

In "The Bugler's First Communion" (1879), he discusses with fictive members
of his parish the Communion he has just administered; notable here is the
speaker's priestly pleasure in having been specifically requested to do so. "At the
Wedding March" (1879) portrays the priest as he celebrates the sacrament of
marriage and invokes the divine type from which the sacrament derives. Simul-
taneously, he affirms his own commitment to his vocation and thus demon-
strates the efficacy of ceremony for the celebrant as well as for its participants.

The most suggestive of the poems of ritual, however, partly because it
makes an unconscious transition to the "terrible sonnets," is "Felix Randal"
(1880). The poem is Hopkins's richest evocation of his feeling for ministry and
for the administering of the sacraments. In the octave, as he converses with
others about the death of Felix, he refers to two rituals he has performed for
him in the past (Communion, line 7; extreme unction, line 6) and gives him
his benediction in the present. These rituals, plainly, are not only the priest's
fulfillment of his responsibilities and his consolation of the farrier; they mark
his own participation in the eternity of Christian time and a moving experi-
ence of Christian fellowship far more engaging than Wordsworth's use of the
Cumberland beggar:

This seeing the sick endears them to us, us too it endears.
My tongue had taught thee comfort, touch had quenched thy tears,
Thy tears that touched my heart, child, Felix, poor Felix Randal[.]

But the poem has another note, announced at the very outset; as Mariani has shown,[21] the poem finally transcends it:

Felix Randal the farrier, O is he dead then? my duty all ended,
Who have watched his mould of man, big-boned and hardy-handsome
Pining, pining . . . .

It is the note not simply of disappointment and sorrow but of a radical frustration and broken reciprocity. It is the not quite self-centered feeling that Felix's death has cancelled—generally, and not merely in this specific case—the priest's function and identity: ". . . my duty all ended" is an emphatically absolute phrase. Indeed, the poem ironically shows the priest deprived of enacting the final ritual of death, the pronouncing of the benediction at the deathbed; for all the months that the priest has labored, the farrier has cheated the priest by dying in his absence. If the farrier has looked to the priest for comfort, the priest depends, still, upon Felix as the vehicle whereby he may maintain his vocation. Even though the administering of extreme unction *to* the farrier is the priest's formal mode of possessing *for* the Church the natural experience of death by asserting its religious character, death for *this* priest nullifies his power to say, in effect, *"What I do is me: for that I came"* ("As Kingfishers Catch Fire"). It makes the future administering of the sacraments impossible and thus renders him impotent; for there is not in this poem the theological consciousness that the sacraments, as manifestations of the ahistorical *ecclesia*, have an existence independent of their specific application. Here, then, in this hint that with Felix's death the Christian system suffers grave disorder, is the beginning of the hypersensitivity to anticipated fragmentation that in the "terrible sonnets" reveals itself, in part, as a neurotic predilection for obsessive and anti-synecdochic thinking: as the burnt finger in Hopkins's 1880 Retreat Notes absorbs and engulfs the entire person, so the death of Felix is construed to have a disproportionately negative effect upon the Church and its priest. Here, too, in the priest's exclusion from ritual enactment, is the beginning of that larger sense of apostolic impotence in the face of imminent apocalypse that has issue in "The Times Are Nightfall" (early 1885?)[22] as well as in "To Seem the Stranger":

[21] Paul L. Mariani, *A Commentary on the Complete Poems of Gerard Manley Hopkins* (Ithaca, N.Y.: Cornell University Press, 1970), pp. 166–73.

[22] The dating of this poem is problematical. See Gerard Manley Hopkins, *The Poems of Gerard*

> The times are nightfall, look, their light grows less;
> The times are winter, watch, a world undone:
> They waste, they wither worse; they as they run
> Or bring more or more blazon man's distress.
> And I not help.

It is thus neither sufficient nor accurate to speak in merely general terms of the vacuum of silence in which the "terrible sonnets" occur. Their emptiness —considered as a social phenomenon, the concomitant of the silence of God— is of a very specific kind. Hopkins's fictive audience dissolves; the fragmentation of the religious community parallels the breach in reciprocity between himself and the Incarnation in nature. Only "Patience"—in the tercet beginning "We hear our hearts grate on themselves"—approaches the earlier mode of public speech; but even here the subject is not communal experience so much as self-division and the body's private communication with itself. When Hopkins's imagined audience is not presumed to be deaf or indifferent ("To Seem the Stranger"), or when it is not metamorphosed, parodically, into a monstrous world of echoes ("No Worst"), it disappears absolutely. Phrased differently, the "terrible sonnets"—with their incoiled opening lines and recurrent recourse to self-address, self-debate—embody Hopkins's raw and lonely recognition that, despite his assiduous cultivation of a surrogate fictive audience, he had for years been writing to no actual audience at all. Whether that recognition preceded the summer of 1885 and thus contributed materially to the impervious self-enclosure of the "terrible sonnets" is a matter for speculation. But it is clear that the disappearance of that fictive audience meant the end of Hopkins's delicately constructed balancing of the conflicting claims his art entailed. The resulting solipsism of the poems is implicitly a confession of his despair and his failure. Whereas Browning consciously created, in the dramatic monologue, a form that intentionally severed the connection between speaker and external reader, Hopkins suffered the discontinuity of his imagined society as a trauma only slightly less disastrous than his inability to sustain a coherent vision of the natural world.

From a religious perspective, the absence of the fictive human audience corresponds exactly with Hopkins's failure to achieve colloquy with God in the immediate present: the languages of prayer and of ministry are stopped simultaneously. The priest cannot serve his community: he cannot articulate their

---

Manley Hopkins, 4th ed., revised and enlarged, ed. W. H. Gardner and N. H. MacKenzie (London: Oxford University Press, 1967), p. 314. Robinson, *In Extremity*, misses the allusion to Rev. 12:14 and thus argues that " 'the times' are here what they would be anywhere else, political and social" (p. 155).

prayers, cannot give them counsel or encouragement, cannot bid them to participate in the supernatural life of the Church and the Ruskinian vision of nature's sanctity. So little can he administer the sacraments that he can only portray himself, in "I Wake and Feel," as a parody of the Eucharist. Hopkins later acknowledged this failure in "To R.B.":

> I want the one rapture of an inspiration.
> O then if in my lagging lines you miss
>
> The roll, the rise, the carol, the creation,
> My winter world, that scarcely breathes that bliss
> Now, yields you, with some sighs, our explanation.

The confessed loss of "the carol," communal song, touches by its plangent intimacy. Despite his attempts in "Carrion Comfort" and "To Seem the Stranger" to reclaim his weakened priestly identity, in the "terrible sonnets" his speaker is largely represented as a man divested of his ecclesiastical office. If the spectacle of that denuding endows the poems with some of their tragic power, it must be remembered that the deprivation of those functions for which he cared so deeply, even in the poetry, was for Hopkins a grievous torment unmitigated by any belief in heroic dignity gained from suffering. What mattered most to Hopkins, in the simultaneous dissolution of his priestly conversations with God and with the fictive community he served, was not the personal tribulation he endured; it was instead his anguished awareness of contributing to the fragmentation of the Church. Beyond his intuition that God may have withdrawn Himself from the world or that England would be deaf to his entreaties loomed his understanding that the primary elements in the *ecclesia*—God and Christ, Their priest, and his community—had become, like nature itself, atomized and disjunct. It is hardly to be questioned that Hopkins took responsibility for the disjunction, despite his believing in the Apocalypse as part of God's design, and that he conceived the central failure of his ministry to be his inability to mediate between humankind and divinity.

A priest without a congregation, a Jesuit blocked from colloquy with God, Hopkins was left with an exhibitionism he must have despised: poems whose motive seemed not the praise of God but the personal catharsis of private anguish, an incoherent and sometimes animalized agony which he thought so little the model of Christian humiliation and so much the venial travesty of Christ's suffering that he could but represent his pain as parody. If he could see that "my asking to be raised to a higher degree of grace was asking also to be lifted on a higher cross" (*Sermons*, p. 254), Hopkins could observe with equal clarity the contemptible puniness of his misery and could utter a self-mocking prayer addressed, significantly, to no one: "tame / My tempests there, my fire and fever fussy" ("The Shepherd's Brow"). His earlier capacity for amplifying his own experience so that it became an aspect of the public Christian consciousness had vanished. When he ordered the "terrible sonnets" as he did in fair copy, he exerted his last effort to make his suffering instructive. With the failure of that effort in the unexpected revisions of "To Seem the Stranger," his earnest desire to communicate acceptable Christian truth to the only audience now left him—Bridges—was thwarted also. The poems were indeed written, as Hopkins insisted in language rife with an exact religious knowledge of his degree of failure, "against my will."

TEXTUAL APPENDIXES

A

THE MANUSCRIPTS IN FACSIMILE AND THE TEXTS OF THE "TERRIBLE SONNETS"

The following pages present Hopkins's manuscripts of the "terrible sonnets" in facsimile (Bodl. MS. Eng. poet. d.150, ff. 29, 31, 33, 35) with facing transcriptions of the drafts. Poems other than the "terrible sonnets" also appear on the facsimile pages; although I have noted their presence, I have not transcribed them. Line numbers have been supplied; a line number in parentheses— e.g., (9)—indicates that the line does not read as in the final version. Hopkins's spacing of punctuation marks has been normalized. For a complete table of textual readings and a comparison of those readings with the fourth edition of Hopkins's *Poems*, see Appendix B.

Sigla

[ ]   word or passage deleted
[?]   illegible material deleted
~~done~~   word or passage crossed through in deleted unit
( )   editorial indication of poem

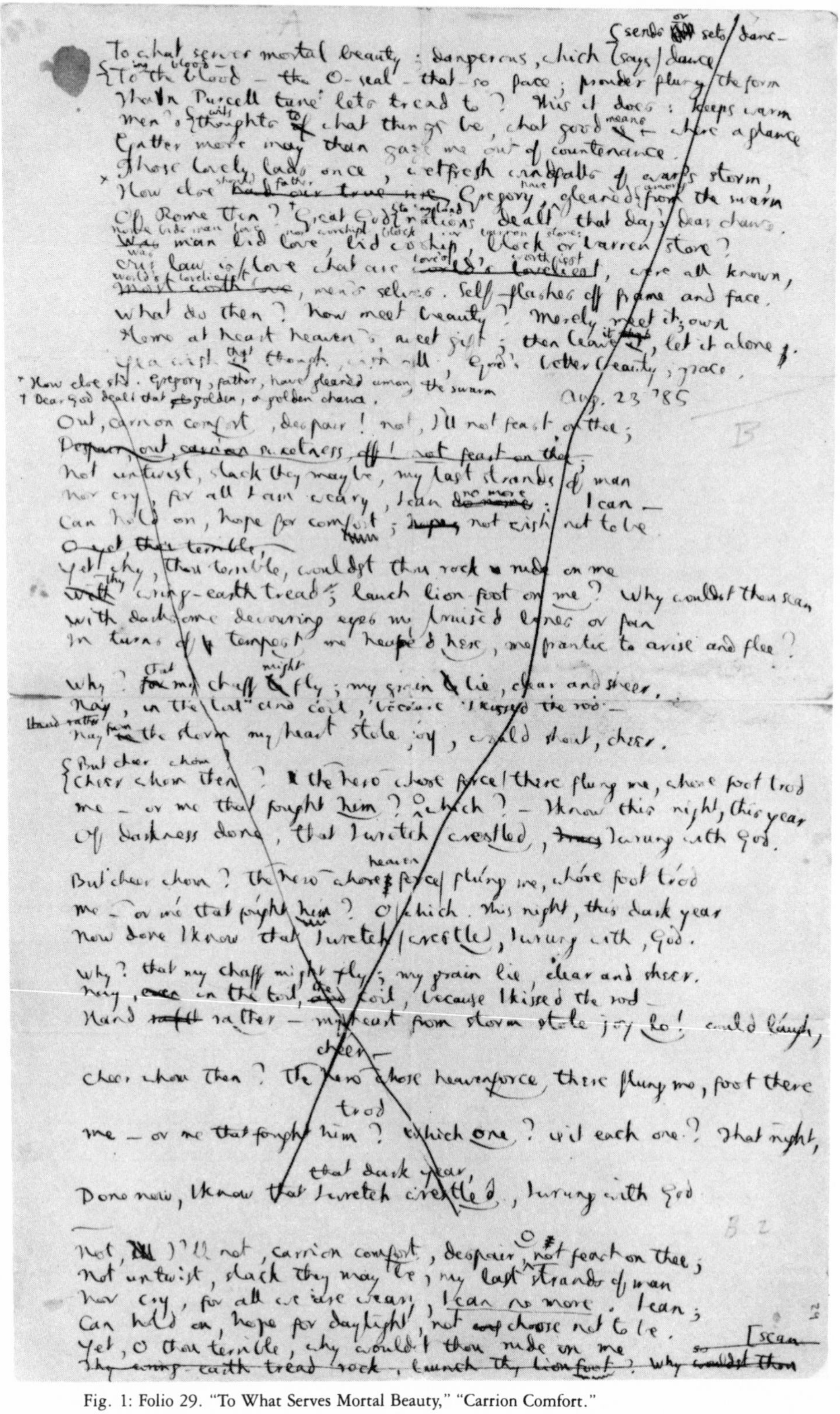
A

{sends or sets / dance—
To what serves mortal beauty—dangerous; which [says/] dance
{To the blood—the O-seal-that-so face; prouder flung the form
Than Purcell tune lets tread to? This it does: keeps warm
Men's {thoughts / wits to the things that are, what good means—where a glance
Gather more may than gaze me out of countenance.
Those lovely lads once, wet-fresh windfalls of war's storm,
How else should father Gregory have gleaned from the swarm
Of Rome then? Great God's nations dealt that day's dear chance.
Was man bid love, bid worship, block or barren stone?
Our law is love what are love's worthiest, were all known,
World's loveliest—men's selves. Self flashes off frame and face.
What do then? how meet beauty? Merely meet it; own
Home at heart heaven's sweet gift; then leave, let it alone.
Yea, wish that though, wish all, God's better beauty, grace.
* How else should Gregory, father, have gleaned among the swarm
† Dear God dealt that golden, or golden chance.
Aug. 23 '85

B

Out, carrion comfort, despair! not, I'll not feast on thee;
~~Despair, out, carrion sweetness, off! not feast on thee~~;
Not untwist, slack they may be, my last strands of man
Nor cry, for all I am weary, I can no more. I can—
Can hold on, hope for comfort; not wish not to be.
~~O yet, thou terrible,~~
Yet why, thou terrible, wouldst thou rock rude on me
Thy wring-earth tread; launch lion-foot on me? Why wouldst thou scan
With darksome devouring eyes my bruised bones or fan
In turns of tempest me heaped here, me frantic to arise and flee?
Why? That my chaff might fly; my grain lie, clear and sheer.
Nay, in the toil and coil, because I kissed the rod—
Hand rather—Nay, in the storm my heart stole joy, could shout, cheer.
{But cheer whom
{Cheer whom then? the hero whose force there flung me, whose foot trod
me—or me that fought him? O which?—I know this night, this year
Of darkness done, that I wretch wrestled, wrung with God.
But cheer whom? The hero whose heaven-force flung me, whose foot trod
me—or me that fought him? O which. This night, this dark year
Now done I know that I wretch wrestle, wrung with God.
Why? that my chaff might fly; my grain lie, clear and sheer.
Nay, in the toil, coil, because I kissed the rod—
Hand rather—my heart from storm stole joy, lo! could laugh, cheer—
Cheer whom then? The hero whose heaven-force there flung me, foot there trod
me—or me that fought him? Which one? is it each one? That night, that dark year,
Done now, I know that I wretch wrestled, wrung with God

B 2

Not, I'll not, carrion comfort, despair, not feast on thee;
Not untwist, slack they may be, my last strands of man
Nor cry, for all we are weary, I can no more. I can;
Can hold on, hope for daylight, not choose not to be.
Yet, O thou terrible, why wouldst thou rude on me
~~Thy wring-earth tread rock, launch thy lion-foot?~~ Why so [scan

Fig. 1: Folio 29. "To What Serves Mortal Beauty," "Carrion Comfort."

FOLIO 29

("To What Serves Mortal Beauty")

("Carrion Comfort")

(1) Out, carrion comfort, despair! not, I'll not feast on thee;

(1) [Despair, out, carrion sweetness. off! not feast on thee;]

(2) Not untwist, slack they may be, my last strands of man

$\qquad\qquad\qquad\qquad$ no more
(3) Nor cry, for all I am weary, I can [do no mo]: I can—

(4) Can hold on, hope for comfort; [hope;] not wish not to be.

(5) [O yet, thou terrible,]

(5) Yet why, thou terrible, wouldst thou rock [?] rude on me

$\qquad\qquad$ thy
(6) [With] wring-earth tread; launch lion-foot on me? Why wouldst thou scan

(7) With darksome devouring eyes my bruisèd bones or fan

(8) In turns of [a] tempest me heaped here, me frantic to arise and flee?

$\qquad\qquad$ that $\qquad$ might
(9) Why? [for] my chaff [to] fly; my grain [to] lie, clear and sheer.

(10) Nay, in the toil and coil, because I kissed the rod—

[Hand rather] [from]
(11) Nay [to] the storm my heart stole joy, would shout, cheer.

$\qquad$ ⎧ But cheer whom?
(12) ⎩ Cheer whom then? [?] the hero whose force │ there flung me, whose foot trod

(13) Me—or me that fought him? O which?—I know this night, this year

(14) Of darkness done, that I wretch wrestled, [I ?] I wrung with God.

$\qquad\qquad\qquad$ heaven
(12) But cheer whom? the hero whose‡force │ flúng me, whóse foot tród

(13) Me—or mé that fóught him? O │ which. This night, this dark year

(14) Now done I know that I wretch │ wrestled, I wrung with, God.

(9) Why? that my chaff might fly; my grain lie, clear and sheer.

$\qquad\qquad\qquad$ the
(10) Nay, [even] in the toil, [and] coil, because I kissed the rod—

(11) Hand [?] rather—my heart from storm stole joy Lo! could láugh,

$\qquad\qquad\qquad$ chéer—
(12) Cheer whom then? the hero whose heavenforce there flung me, foot there

$\qquad\qquad\qquad$ trod
(13) Me—or me that fought him? Which one? is it each one? That night,

$\qquad\qquad$ that dark year,
(14) Done now, I know that I wretch wrestled, I wrung with God.

$\overline{\qquad}$

$\qquad\qquad\qquad\qquad\qquad$ [ɪ]
(1) Not, [I'll] I'll not, carrion comfort, despair, O not feast on thee,

(2) Not untwist, slack they may be, my last strands of man

(3) Nor cry, for all we are weary, I can no more. I can;

(4) Can hold on, hope for daylight, not [wis] choose not to be.

(5) Yet, O thou terrible, why wouldst thou rude on me

$\qquad\qquad\qquad\qquad\qquad$ [so] $\qquad$ scan
(6) [Thy wring-earth tread rock, launch thy lion foot? Why wouldst thou]

149

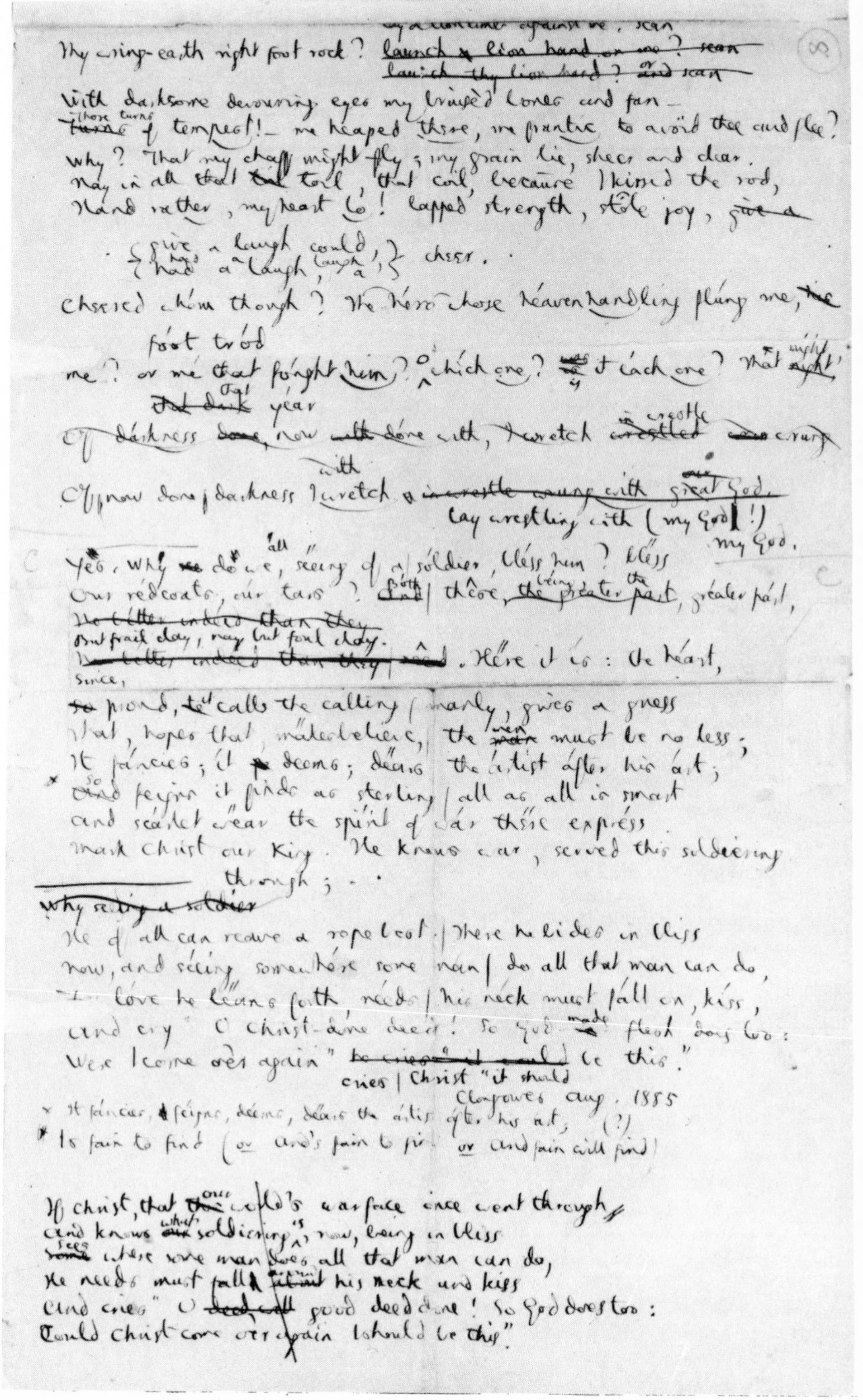

Fig. 2: Folio 29v. "Carrion Comfort," "The Soldier."

FOLIO 29v

("Carrion Comfort")

lay a lion limb against me, scan

(6) Thy wring-earth right foot rock? [launch a lion hand on me? scan]

or

[launch thy lion hand? and scan]

7   With darksome devouring eyes my bruisèd bones and fan—

Those turns
(8) [Turns] of tempest!—me heaped there, me frantic to avoïd thee and flee?

9   Why? That my chaff might fly; my grain lie, sheer and clear.

(10) Nay in all that [toil] toil, that coil, because I kissed the rod,

(11) Hand rather, my heart lo! lapped strength, stôle joy, [give a]

$$\left\{ \begin{array}{l} \text{give a laugh could,} \\ \text{had a} \quad \text{laugh} \\ \text{had a laugh, a} \end{array} \right\} \text{cheer,}$$

(12) Cheered whóm though? The héro whose héaven handling flúng me, [his]

fóot tród

[was]   [/] níght,

(13) Me? or mé that fóught him? O which one? [is] it éach one? That [night,]

is

that
[that dark] yéar

in wrestle

(14) [Of dárkness done, now with dóne with, I wretch wrestled wrun wrung

our

14 Of [,] now done [,] darkness I wretch [in wrestle wrung with great God.]

lay wrestling with (my God [!]!)

my God.

("The Soldier")

151

Nand rather, my heart lo! lapped strength, stole joy, wou
laugh,   cheer.

(early g Tom)

the garlanded with squat and surly steel,
the fallow bootėd navvy has piled his pick   (A
And rips out rockfire homeforth—sturdy Dick;
Tom Heart-at-ease, that's all now for his meal
Sure, 's bedſſ. Be his lot low, handily he swings it—
that néėr need hunger, should be seldom sick, [thi
seldomer heartsore : thát treads through, prickproo
thousands of thorns, thoughts. And, in commonweal
I little reck lacklevel if all had tread:
Country if honour is all us
cheer whon though? the hero whose heaven-handling flúng me
                    felt tród

                    (Pitched past pitch of grief

no worst, there is none : ¿grief past pitch of grief,
More pangs at fore pangs schooled will wilder wri
At fore pangs more pangs schooled will wilder wing

                            O there   topy, grief
Worst! No worst; no there is none. Grief past grief
And more pangs, schooled at fore pangs, wilder wring.

no worst, there is none. Pitched past pitch of grief,
more pangs will, schooled at forepangs, wilder wring.
Comforter, where, where is the you comforting?
Mary, mother of us, where is your relief?
                leave
My cries case herds-long ; huddle in a main, a chief.
Woe, world-sorrow ; on an áge-old ánvil wince and sing—
then lull, then leave off. Fury had shrieked "No ling

Fig. 3: Folio 31. "Carrion Comfort," "Tom's Garland," "Carrion Comfort," "No Worst."

FOLIO 31

("Carrion Comfort")

11 Hand rather, my heart lo! lapped strength, stôle joy, would
                 laugh,   cheer.

("Tom's Garland," lines 1–10)

("Carrion Comfort")

12 Cheer whóm though? The héro whose héaven-hand|ling flúng me,
                 fóot tród

("No Worst")

                    { Pitched past pitch of grief
(1) No worst, there is none: { grief past pitch of grief,
             fore
(2) More pangs at [pan] pangs schooled will wilder wring
(2) At fore pangs more pangs schooled will wilder wring

               O there   tops grief
(1) Worst! No worst [, no there] is none. Grief past grief
(2) And more pangs, schooled at forepangs, wilder wring.

1 No worst, there is none. Pitched past pitch of grief,
2 More pangs will, schooled at forepangs, wilder wring.
3 Comforter, where, where is [thy] your comforting?
4 Mary, mother of us, where is your relief?
       heave
5 My cries [come] herds-long; huddle in a main, a chief-
6 Wóe, wórld-sorrow; on an áge-old ánvil wínce and síng—
7 Then lull, then leave off. Fury had shrieked "No ling-

ering! Let me be fell: force I must be brief."
O the mind, mind has mountains; cliffs of fall
Frightful, sheer, down, not fathomed. Hold them cheap
may who ne'er hung there. Nor does long our small
Durance deal with that steep or deep. Here! creep,
wretch, under a comfort serves at scarce-while : all
Life death does end and each day dies with sleep.

Wretch, under a comfort serves in a whirlwind : all

┐ Frightful, sheer, not man's fathoming . Hold them cheap
└   no-man - fathomed .   —   —   —   —

not, I'll not, ⟶ carrion comfort, , Despair, not feast on thee
not untwist — slack they may be — these last strands of m
In me ór, most weary, cry I can no more . I can ;
Can something, hold, hope daylight
                    hope, with day come, not choose not to be

But ah, but, O thou terrible, why wouldst thou rude on m
Thy wring-world
     wring-earth ⟩ right foot rock ? Lay a lion limb again
                    me ? scan
with darksome devouring my eyes my bruisèd bones ? and fa
in turns of tempest, me heaped there ; me frantic t
                    avoid thee and flee ?
why? That my chaff might fly ; my grain lie, sheer and clea
Nay in all that toil, that coil, since (seems) I kissed the ro

Fig. 4: Folio 31v. "No Worst," "Carrion Comfort."

FOLIO 31v

("No Worst")

8   Ering! Let me be fêll: force I must be brief."

9   O the mind, mind has mountains; cliffs of fall

(10) Frightful, sheer [,] down, not fathomed. Hold them cheap

11   May who ne'er hung there. Nor does long our small

12   Durance deal with that steep or deep. Here! creep,

(13) Wretch, under a comfort serves at worst whiles: all

14   Life death does end and each day dies with sleep.

13   Wretch, under a comfort serves in a whirlwind: all

(10) ⎰ Frightful, sheer, not man's fathoming. Hold them cheap
     ⎱   [,]
     —— —— no-man-fathomed. —— —— ——

("Carrion Comfort")

D

1   Not, I'll not, [ca] carrion comfort, [d]espair, not feast on thee;

2   Not untwist—slack they may be—these last strands of man

3   In me ór, most weary, cry I can no more. I can [;];

4   Can something, [hold, hope daylight]
                  hope, wish day come, not choose not to be

5   But ah, but [,] O thou terrible, why wouldst thou rude on me

6   Thy wring-world⎰ right foot rock? lay a lion limb against
         wring-earth⎱   me? scan

7   With darksome devouring eyes my bruisèd bones? and fan,

8   O in turns of tempest, me heaped there; me frantic to
               avoïd thee and [fle] flee?

9   Why? that my chaff might fly; my grain lie, sheer and clear.

10   Nay in all that toil, that coil, since (seems) I kissed the rod,

155

's not ining, see you ; unconscious or rather — of skies
Betweeen the mountains —

"Not of all my eyes / see, wandering along on the world,
Is anything a milk to the mind so, so sighs deep
Poetry to it, as a tree chose boughs break in the sky.
Say it is 'ashboughs : whether on a December day and furled
Fast or they in clammyish lashtender combs creep
Apart wide and new-nestle at heaven most high.
They touch heaven, tabour on it ; how their talons sweep
The smouldering enormous winter welkin ! Spa May
Mells blue and snowwhite through them, a fringe and fray
Of greenery : it is old earth's groping towards the steep
                           May
             Heaven she childs us by.

                    they   or hovering on it
They touch, ————, talons on it, hovering ; here, there hurled,
                                       with
                                        talons sweep

The smouldering enormous winter welkin. Eye,
             with   But more cheer able   when May
Mells blue and snowwhite through their fringe and fray
Of greenery and old earth gropes for, prays at the steep
             Heaven whom she childs us by,
             Heaven with it whom she childs
                                    things by

FOLIO 33

("My Own Heart")

13   'S not wrung, see you; unforeseentimes rather—as skies
14   Betweenpie mountains—

("Ash-Boughs")

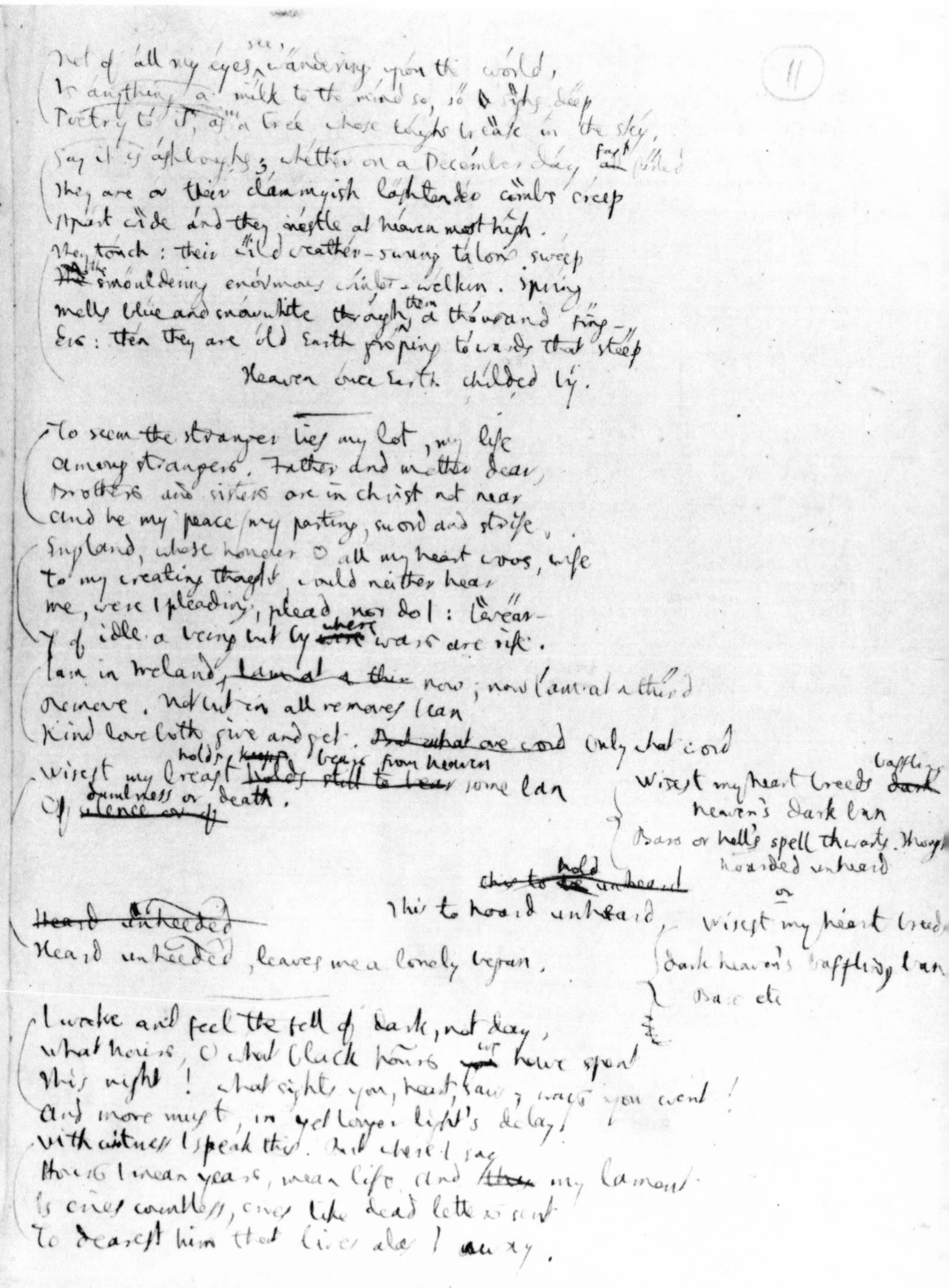

Not of all my eyes see, wandering on the world,
Is anything a milk to the mind so, so sighs deep
Poetry to it, as a tree whose boughs break in the sky.
Say it is ashboughs: whether on a December day fast furled
They are or their clammyish lashtender combs creep
Apart wide and they nestle at heaven most high.
They touch: their wild weather-swung talons sweep
The smouldering enormous winter-welkin. Spring
Mells blue and snowwhite through them a thousand thing —
Eye: then they are old Earth groping towards that steep
Heaven once Earth childed by.

To seem the stranger lies my lot, my life
Among strangers. Father and mother dear,
Brothers and sisters are in Christ not near
And he my peace/my parting, sword and strife.
England, whose honour O all my heart woos, wife
To my creating thought, would neither hear
Me, were I pleading, plead nor do I: I wear-
y of idle a being but by where wars are rife.
I am in Ireland now; now I am at a third
Remove. Not but in all removes I can
Kind love both give and get. Only what word
Wisest my breast holds, bears from heaven some ban
Of dumbness or death.
This to hoard unheard,
Heard unheeded, leaves me a lonely began.

Wisest my heart breeds baffling
heaven's dark ban
Bars or hell's spell thwarts. This
hoarded unheard
or
Wisest my heart breeds
dark heaven's baffling ban
Bars etc

I wake and feel the fell of dark, not day.
What hours, O what black hours we have spent
This night! what sights you, heart, saw; ways you went!
And more must, in yet longer light's delay.
With witness I speak this. But where I say
Hours I mean years, mean life. And my lament
Is cries countless, cries like dead letters sent
To dearest him that lives alas! away.

Fig. 6: Folio 35. "Ash-Boughs," "To Seem the Stranger," "I Wake and Feel."

FOLIO 35

("Ash-Boughs")

("To Seem the Stranger")

1 To seem the stranger lies my lot, my life
2 Among strangers. Father and mother dear,
3 Brothers and sisters are in Christ not near
4 And he my peace / my parting, sword and strife.
5 England, whose honour O all my heart woos, wife
6 To my creating thought, would neither hear
7 Me, were I pleading, plead nor do I: I wear-
        where
8 Y of idle a being but by [were] wars are rife.
9 I am in Ireland [, I am at a thir] now; now I am at a third
10 Remove. Not but in all removes I can
11 Kind love both give and get. [But what one word] Only what word

              holds [keeps] bears from heaven   baffling
(12) Wisest my breast [holds still to bear] some ban   (12) Wisest my heart breeds [dark]
        dumbness or death.   heaven's dark ban
(13) Of [silence or of]   13   Bars or hell's spell thwarts. Thoughts
                                                              hoarded unheard

                              hold   or
                    [this to be unheard]
              13 This to hoard unheard,   12 Wisest my heart breeds
     [Heard unheeded]   dark heaven's baffling ban
14   Heard unheeded, leaves me a lonely began.   Bars etc

("I Wake and Feel")

1 I wake and feel the fell of dark, not day.
              we
2 What hours, O what black hours [you] have spent
3 This night! what sights you, heart, saw; ways you went!
4 And more must, in yet longer light's delay.
5 With witness I speak this. And where I say
6 Hours I mean years, mean life. And [this] my lament
7 Is cries countless, cries like dead letters sent
8 To dearest him that lives alas! away.

159

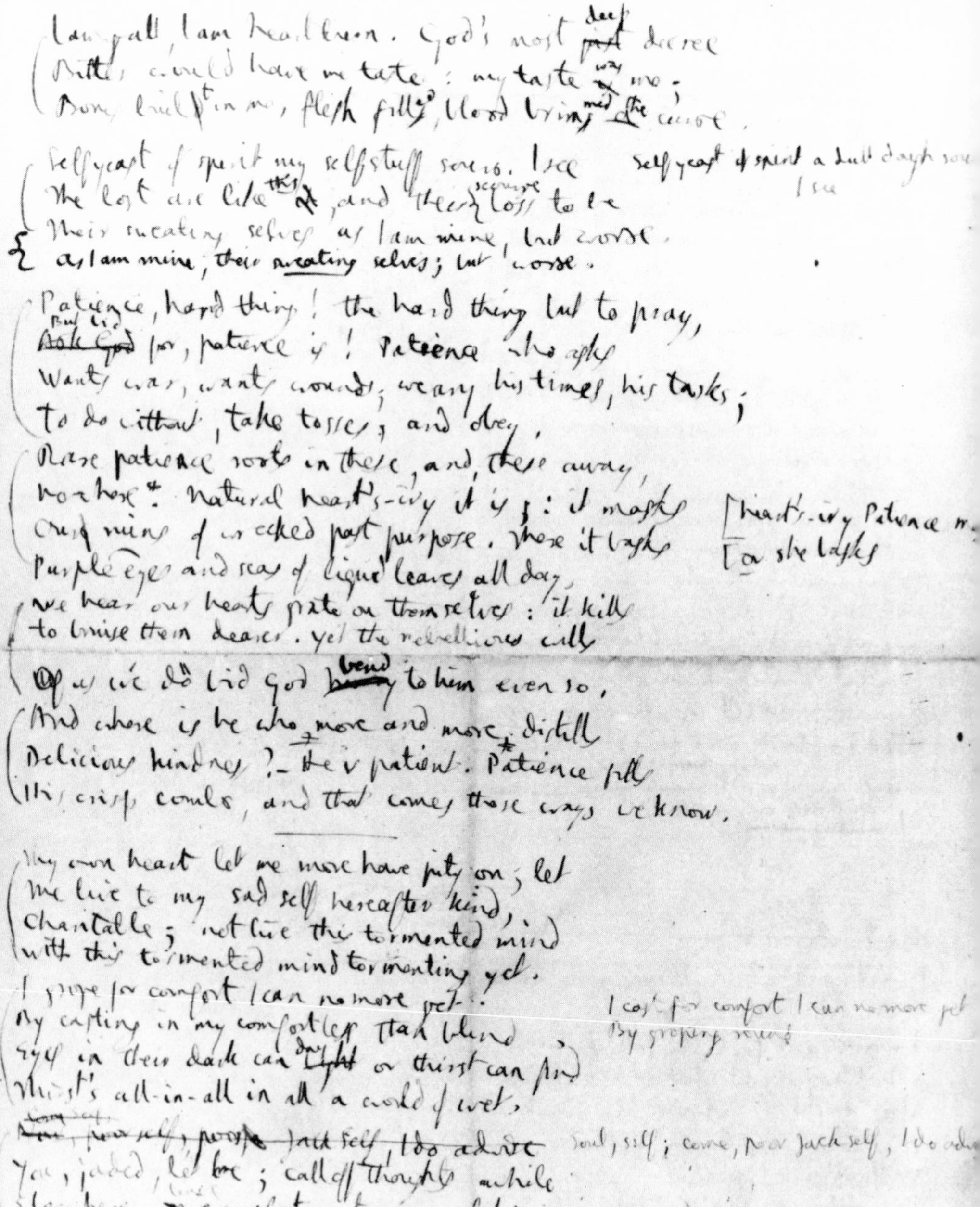

I am gall, I am heartburn. God's most deep ~~past~~ decree
Bitter would have me taste: my taste was ~~of~~ me;
Bones built in me, flesh filled, blood brimmed the curse.

Selfyeast of spirit my selfstuff sours. I see
The lost are like this ~~of~~, and their scourge loss to be
Their sweating selves as I am mine, but worse.
As I am mine, their sweating selves; but worse.

Selfyeast of spirit a dull dough sours. I see

Patience, hard thing! the hard thing but to pray,
But bid ~~Ask God~~ for, patience is! Patience who asks
Wants war, wants wounds; weary his times, his tasks;
To do without, take tosses, and obey.
Rare patience roots in these, and, these away,
Nowhere. Natural heart's-ivy is : it masks
Our ruins of wrecked past purpose. There it basks
Purple eyes and seas of liquid leaves all day.

[heart's-ivy Patience m.
[a she basks

We hear our hearts grate on themselves: it kills
To bruise them dearer. Yet the rebellious wills
Of us we do bid God bend ~~bring~~ to him even so.
And where is he who more and more distills
Delicious kindness? – He is patient. Patience fills
His crisp combs, and that comes those ways we know.

My own heart let me more have pity on; let
Me live to my sad self hereafter kind,
Charitable; not live this tormented mind
With this tormented mind tormenting yet.
I grope for comfort I can no more get
By casting in my comfortless than blind
Eyes in their dark can day ~~light~~ or thirst can find
Thirst's all-in-all in all a world of wet.

I cast for comfort I can no more get
By groping round

~~Soul, poor self, poor Jackself, I do advise~~
You, jaded, let be; call off thoughts awhile
Elsewhere; leave ~~the~~ comfort root-room; let joy size
At God knows when to God knows what; whose smile
's not wrung, see you; unforeseen times rather, as skies
Betweenpie mountains, lights a lovely mile.

Soul, self; come, poor Jackself, I do advise

Fig. 7: Folio 35v. "I Wake and Feel," "Patience," "My Own Heart."

FOLIO 35v

("I Wake and Feel")

$$\text{deep}$$
9   ⟨I am gall, I am heartburn. God's most [just] decree

                      was
10   ⎜Bitter would have me taste: my taste [is] me;

         t   ed   med the
11   ⎝Bones buil[d] in me, flesh fill[s], blood brim[s] [a] curse.

(12) ⎛Selfyeast of spirit my selfstuff sours. I see   12 Selfyeast of spirit a dull dough sours.

                  this   ⎧scourge   I see
13   ⎝The lost are like [it], and their ⎩loss to be

(14) ⎧Their sweating selves as I am mine, but worse.
14   ⎩As I am mine, their sweating selves; but worse.

("Patience")

1   ⟨Patience, hard thing! the hard thing but to pray,

    ⎛But bid
2   ⎜[Ask God] for, patience is! Patience who asks
3   ⎜Wants war, wants wounds; weary his times, his tasks;
4   ⎝To do without, take tosses, and obey.

5   ⎛Rare patience roots in these, and, these away,
6   ⎜Nowhere. [?] Natural heart's ivy it is [;]: it masks   heart's-ivy Patience masks
7   ⎜Our[?] ruins of wrecked past purpose. There it basks or she basks
8   ⎝Purple eyes and seas of liquid leaves all day.

9   ⎛We hear our hearts grate on themselves: it kills
10   ⎜To bruise them dearer. Yet the rebellious wills

    ⎜Of   bend
11   ⎝[We] us wé dö bid God [bring] to him even so.

12   ⎛And where is he who [,] more and more [,] distills
13   ⎜Delicious kindness?—He is patient. Patience fills
14   ⎝His crisp combs, and that comes those ways we know.

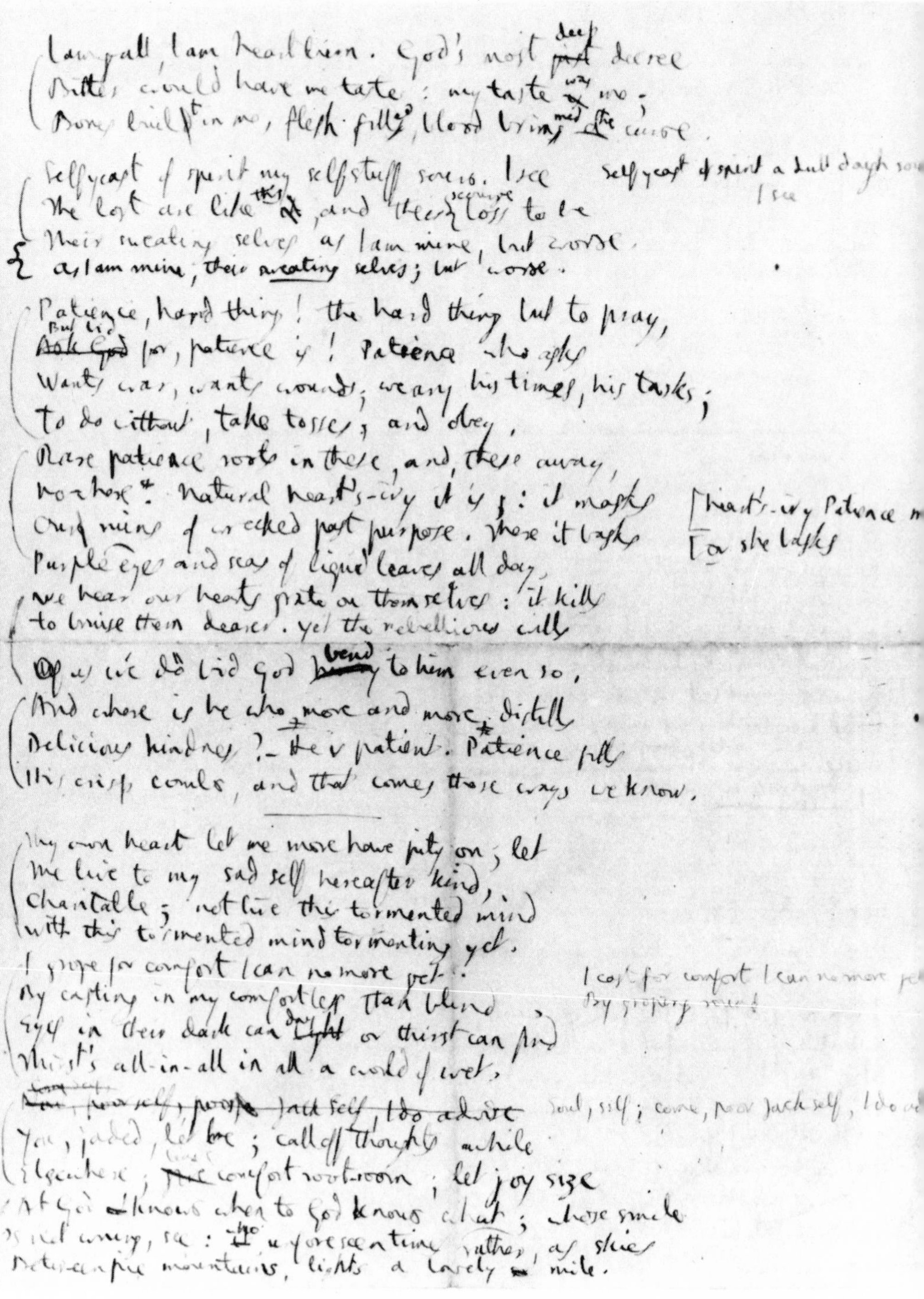

Fig. 7: Folio 35v. "I Wake and Feel," "Patience," "My Own Heart."

FOLIO 35v

("My Own Heart")

1   /My own heart let me more have pity on; let

2   (Me live to my sad self hereafter kind,

3   (Charitable; not live this tormented mind

4   \With this tormented mind tormenting yet.

(5)   ,I grope for comfort I can no more get   5 I cast for comfort I can no more get

(6)   / By casting in my comfortless than blind   6 By groping round

                    day

7   (Eyes in their dark can [light] or thirst can find

8   \Thirst's all-in-all in a world of wet.

      [Come self,]

(9)   ,[Now, poor self, poorJa Jack Self, I do advise]   9 Soul, self; come, poor Jack self, I do advise

               b

10   You, jaded, lét [m]e; call off thoughts awhile

             leave

11   \Elsewhere; [give] comfort root-room; let joy size

12   /At God [?] knows when to God knows what; whose smile

               who

(13)   ('S not wrung, see: [it] unforeseen times rather, as skies

(14)   \Betweenpie mountains, lights a lovely [?] mile.

13   'S not wrúng, see you; unforeseentimes rather—as skies   (from folio 33)

14   Betweenpie mountains—   (from folio 33)

B
TABLE OF TEXTUAL READINGS

The following table compares my readings of Hopkins's final manuscripts of the "terrible sonnets" with those given in *The Poems of Gerard Manley Hopkins*, 4th ed., revised and enlarged, ed. W. H. Gardner and N. H. MacKenzie (London: Oxford University Press, 1967), rightly considered to be more authoritative than the previous editions by Bridges (1918), Charles Williams (1930), and Gardner alone (1948).

Where Gardner and MacKenzie have adopted an emendation made by Bridges upon which Bridges commented in his notes to the first edition and upon which Gardner and MacKenzie also remark, I have thus indicated: G&M (Bridges). In many cases, particularly with Hopkins's use of musical signs, Gardner and MacKenzie have given an accurate reading of the manuscripts in their notes but have not incorporated those readings into the printed text itself; here, the reading in the printed text is listed as a variant from the manuscripts, but an asterisk (G&M*) indicates their inclusion of the manuscript reading in their notes.

The comparison proceeds according to poem and line, in the order found in folios 31 and 35 of the manuscripts of the "terrible sonnets."

"No Worst, There Is None"

6 Woe,]   woe, G&M*

6 wórld-] world- G&M*

6 sorrow; on an] sorrow on an G&M*

6 áge-] age- G&M*

6 ánvil] anvil G&M*

6 wĭnce] wince G&M

6 wĭnce] wínce G&M (thus in notes)

6 śing—] sing— G&M*

7 "No] 'No G&M

8 Ering! ering! G&M

8 fêll:] fell: G&M*

8 brief."] brief'. G&M

"Carrion Comfort"

1 comfort,] comfort, G&M

4 be] be. G&M

5 terrible,] terrible, G&M*

7 devouring] devouring G&M

8 O in] O in G&M

8 tempest] tempest G&M*

8 there;] there; G&M*

8 frantic] frantic G&M*

8 avoïd] avoid G&M*

9 that] That G&M

11 rather] rather G&M*

11 lo!] lo! G&M*

11 stôle] stole G&M*

11 cheer.] chéer. G&M

12 whóm] whom G&M

12 The héro whose] The hero whose G&M

12 héaven-hand|ling flúng me] heaven-handling flung me G&M

12 héaven-hand|ling flúng me] héaven-handling flung me G&M

                                               (thus in notes)

13 or me that fóught him?]   or me that fought him?   G&M*
13 which one?]   which one?   G&M*
13 éach one?]   each one?   G&M
13 yéar]   year   G&M
14 wretch]   wretch   G&M*

"To Seem the Stranger"

7   I wéar-]   I wear-   G&M
8   Y]   y   G&M
9   Í am at a thírd]   I am at a thírd   G&M*
14 unheeded,]   unheeded,   G&M

"I Wake and Feel"

2   hoūrs]   hours   G&M*

"Patience"

2   patience is!]   Patience is!   G&M (Bridges)
6   heart's-]   heart's   G&M
6   ivy]   ivy,   G&M (Bridges)
8   Purplé eyes]   Purple eyes   G&M
11 wé dò]   we do   G&M

"My Own Heart"

6   comfortless]   comfortless,   G&M (Bridges)
9   Jack self,]   Jackself,   G&M
13 'S]   's   G&M
13 wrúng,]   wrung,   G&M
13 you; unforeseentimes]   you; unforeseen times   G&M
13 rather]   rather   G&M

INDEX

All works are indexed by author.

Abbott, Claude Colleer, 130

Abrams, M. H., 4

à Kempis, St. Thomas. *See* Thomas à Kempis, St.

Analogical imagination. *See* Hopkins, Gerard Manley, "Terrible sonnets"

Apocalypse, the, 20, 25, 90, 122; and Hopkins's changed perceptions of, 22, 36–38, 56, 57; and Hopkins's poetics, 35, 39, 42; and Hopkins's sense of ministry, 116, 121–22, 137, 141, 143; and Hopkins's situation in Ireland, 36; and Hopkins's view of Christian history, 35–36, 37–39, 92–93; and the Incarnation, 35–39

Arnold, Matthew: and dramatic monologue, 138; "The Buried Life," 77; *Empedocles on Etna*, 3; "The Forsaken Merman," 54; "Resignation," 77

Auden, W. H.: *Horae Canonicae*, 10

Bailey, Benjamin, 31, 68n85

Barthes, Roland, 85, 86

Baskin, Leonard, 55n65

Baxter, Richard, 5n3

Beattie, James, 33n

Bender, Todd K., 80

Blair, Hugh, 33n

Blake, William, 27; "The Divine Image," 55

Bonaventura, St., 40n40, 85n24

Boyle, Robert, 44, 60

Bridges, Robert, 131, 132; attitude toward Hopkins, 10–11; attitude toward Hopkins's poems, 11; dislike of Catholicism, 10–11, 133–34; editor of Hopkins's *Poems* (1918), 7, 11; as Hopkins's audience, 10–11, 132–33; Hopkins's desire to convert, 11, 133; as Hopkins's link to a hypothesized Catholic audience, 133–34; Hopkins's literary executor, 7; influence on subsequent editors, 7–8; urged Hopkins to publish, 130. *See also* Hopkins, Gerard Manley, Life *and* "Terrible sonnets," Characteristics

Brooke-Rose, Christine, 44

Browning, Robert: and dramatic monologue, 138, 142; and metamorphic imagery, 54; and pathetic fallacy, 33; "Childe Roland to the Dark Tower Came," 54; "Porphyria's Lover," 33

Burke, Edmund, 25

Caine, Hall, 130

Calvinism, 79

Catholicism: England's conversion to, 36, 36n35; in Ireland, 36; modes of purgation and illumination in, 8, 12–14; and Romanticism, 5, 31, 34; and suicide, 97n45; teleology of suffering in, 14, 93–94, 101, 106–107, 113, 117. *See also* Apocalypse, the; *Imitatio Christi*; Incarnation, the

Clough, Arthur Hugh: "Dipsychus," 77

Coleridge, Samuel Taylor, 5n2, 27, 41; and pathetic fallacy, 32–34; and reciprocity, 30–31; *Biographia Literaria*, 33n; "conversation poems," 57; "Dejection: An Ode," 30, 31n28; "Frost at Midnight," 3, 25, 33, 41; "The Nightingale," 32–34; "On Poesy or Art," 33n; "This Lime-Tree Bower my Prison," 5, 30–31

Colloquy. *See* Hopkins, Gerard Manley, "Terrible sonnets," Characteristics; Loyola, St. Ignatius

Cotter, James Finn, 13, 39–40, 98–99

Crashaw, Richard, 68

Dante, 98n

Darwin, Charles, 55

Descartes, René, 54

Devlin, Christopher, 23

Dixon, Richard Watson, Canon, 131, 133; as Hopkins's audience, 132; urged Hopkins to publish, 130

Dramatic monologue, 57, 138, 142

Donne, John, 5n3, 82n14; "Batter My Heart," 45, 120

Downes, David Anthony, 12–13, 22, 80

Eliot, T. S.: *Ash-Wednesday*, 51, 112; "Gerontion," 77; "The Love Song of J. Alfred Prufrock," 45, 124; "Preludes," 68; *The Waste Land*, 105

Evolution, 55

Gardner, W. H., 51, 113–14

Gregory, Isabella Augusta Persse, Lady, 134

Hallgarth, Susan A., 22

Herbert, George, 5n3, 37, 139; "The Collar," 59; "Jordan" (I), 104, 116; "The Pulley," 59; "The Size," 65; "Virtue," 43

Higher Criticism, the, 4, 55

Designer: Randall Goodall
Compositor: G & S Typesetters, Inc.
Printer: Thomson-Shore, Inc.
Binder: John H. Dekker & Sons, Inc.
Text: Garamond 10/13
Display: Garamond